Scientific Co-edition
Instituto de Investigaciones Estéticas
UNAM

A. ARELLANO HERNÁNDEZ, M. AYALA FALCÓN, B. DE LA FUENTE,
M. DE LA GARZA, L. STAINES CICERO, B. OLMEDO VERA

# THE MAYAS OF THE CLASSICAL PERIOD

Jaca Book

ANTIQUE COLLECTORS' CLUB

Editorial Advisor
Davide Domenici

Translation
Kim López Mills
Sergio Negrete

Color Maps and Drawing of Uaxactún
Stefano Martinelli, Luino

Cover
Detail of a sculpture in Copán,
Honduras (photo M. Vautier)

This volume was made with
the support of
MUSEO NACIONAL DE ANTROPOLOGIA, Mexico

Color Photograph Credits:

M. de la Garza, Mexico: 73, 115.
Dirección General de Publicaciones del CONACULTA, Mexico: 87, 88, 97,
100, 104, 106, 107, 108, 109, 110, 111, 112, 113, 114, 118, 131.
D. Domenici, Milan: 9, 11, 35, 36, 37, 68, 86.
V. Domenici, Milan: 1, 2, 39, 40, 46, 48, 49, 50, 51, 91, 92, 95.
Instituto de Investigaciones Estéticas,
Universidad Nacional Autónoma de México (UNAM), Mexico: 116, 117.
Justin Kerr, New York: 89, 98, 99, 101, 102, 103, 119, 120,
121, 122, 123, 124, 125, 126, 127, 128, 129, 130, 132, 133.
A. Maffeis, Milan: 19.
M. Vautier, Paris: 4, 7, 12, 13, 14, 16, 18, 20, 21, 22, 24, 26, 27, 28, 29,
30, 31, 33, 34, 42, 43, 44, 53, 54, 55, 56, 58, 59, 60, 61, 63, 64, 66,
67, 69, 70, 71, 74, 76, 77, 78, 80, 81, 83, 84, 85, 90, 93, 96, 105.

ISBN 88-16-69002-X

Printed and bound in Italy

Antique Collectors' Club:
5 Church Street, Woodbridge, Suffolk IP12 1DS, England
Tel. 01394 385501 - Fax 01394 384434
and
Market Street Industrial Park
Wappingers' Falls, NY 12590, USA
Tel. 914 297 0003 - Fax 914 297 0068

Editoriale Jaca Book:
Via Gioberti 7, 20123 Milano, Italy
Tel. 39 2 48561520/29 - Fax 39 2 48193361

# Index

# Foreword

One of the main reasons for the creation of the pre-Columbian Corpus was to further knowledge among a vast range of readers about the various cultures in Middle America and other regions in the continent. To this day, nine volumes have been published and more are on their way. The acceptance that these books have had among readers has been such that those in charge of this task have felt the need of continuing on with it and widening the knowledge on other ancient American cultures.

Today we are presenting the Mayan civilization, one of the most amazing pre-Columbian cultures. It was located in a large portion of Mexico's southern territory, as well as in Guatemala, Belize, El Salvador, and Honduras. During a period of more than one thousand years the Mayas let their influence be felt, leaving a deep imprint in history through their art, including the hieroglyphs engraved on multiple steles and monuments, all of which are a tremendous source of information to researchers. It is no surprise that 18th century Palenque would become so attractive to visitors who began to uncover an immense jungle that for centuries had hidden the remains of cities, tombs and men.

This volume is dedicated to the Classic period of the Mayas. Four distinguished women researchers have put together their knowledge and experience to speak to us about them. Doctor Beatriz de la Fuente and her collaborators wrote about the creative power of the Mayas as seen in their architecture, painting, ceramics and sculpture. Doctor Mercedes de la Garza refers to the religion of the ancient Mayas, and Bertina Olmedo gives us a view into the archaeological history of the region –chronology, settlement patterns, as well as the economic, political and social structure of this civilization. Maricela Ayala delves into the intricate paths of the Maya writing system, considered one of the most significant guides for the study and understanding of this people.

In the following pages we will encounter a unique culture. The authors, who are researchers from Mexico's National Autonomous University and the National Institute of Anthropology and History, have made this introduction possible, and we applaud and thank them for their outstanding work. The reader can rest assured that he or she is going to set off on a centuries-old voyage into one of the most amazing peoples in the world. Let us then begin our voyage into the heart of the Mayan people.

*Eduardo Matos Moctezuma*

# The Mayas of the Classic Period

*Bertina Olmedo Vera*

*Introduction*

The first accounts regarding the Mayas reached Europe during the 16th century by way of Spanish soldiers and priests who had participated in the conquest of the New World and the conversion of its people to Christianity.

They wrote extensive descriptions of the ruins they discovered in the conquered lands. Spanish priests began to write the history of the region by compiling interesting testimonies on the lives and customs of the inhabitants. This knowledge was intended to be used also to subject and convert them.[1]

The manuscripts arrived in Spain but were put aside in files and ignored. As for the ruins, they were no longer visited, due largely to their distant location and difficult access. For many years most of these ruins remained hidden beneath the dense vegetation of the jungles in southeast Mexico and northern Central America.

Until the second half of the 18th century, reports on the discovery of a magnificent city in the tropical jungles of Chiapas reached king Charles III of Spain. The findings aroused such curiosity that the king had the area thoroughly explored. Thus began the era of travelers and explorers who sent back to the Old World fascinating accounts of a rare and extraordinary civilization. As the news of this culture spread throughout Europe, scholars attempted to explain its origins, most always comparing it with the Egyptian, Greek, Roman, and Chaldaic. Very few dared to admit that this was a unique and original indigenous culture.

Among the first explorers were two Spanish military officers, Antonio del Río and Guillermo Dupaix –now referred to as the precursors of Mayan archaeology– who were sent by the Spanish Crown to explore the reported ruins in the town of Palenque, Chiapas.

Captain Antonio del Río was the first sent on official mission, and in 1787 he explored the ruins and wrote a detailed report to Spanish authorities. Since this was the first description of a Mayan site the manuscript was later printed and sent abroad. Under extreme and adverse conditions, and by order of Spanish authorities, he removed weeds and vegetation from the buildings and unearthed burial offerings and

1. Drawing by J. L. Castañeda of a tablet removed by G. Dupaix from the Palace of Palenque (from *The Art of Maya Hieroglyphic Writing*).

objects. In the meantime, his draftsman, Ricardo Almendáriz, was sketching a graphic record on 25 plates.

The unearthed objects, the manuscripts, as well as the sketches, were sent to Spain but for many years remained ignored. However, in 1822 a British librarian and publisher saved them from extinction when he purchased a copy of the manuscript and the illustrated plates in London, where they had arrived under mysterious circumstances. The manuscript was published in English under the title: *Description of the Ruins of an Ancient City, Discovered near Palenque... from the Original Manuscript Report of Captain Don Antonio del Río: Followed by Teatro Critico Americano... by Doctor Paul Felix Cabrera.*

The volume included 16 plates by Almendáriz, engraved by the artist Jean Frédéric Waldeck (figure 3). As for the archaeological pieces, they were presumably sent on display to the Royal Museum of Natural History in Madrid. In 1804, almost two decades after Del Río's expedition, king Charles IV of Spain ordered retired military officer Guillermo Dupaix to continue research on Palenque's pre-Hispanic remains.

Dupaix was so overjoyed with the mission –due to his tremendous interest in the region– that he carefully planned a four year-long expedition. On his way to Palenque he visited and described places such as Chalco, Xochimilco, Mitla, and Monte Albán, among others.

Lord Kingsborough included a copy of Dupaix's report and the drawings of a Mexican artist named José Luciano Castañeda (figures 1, 2) in one of the volumes of his masterpiece: *Antiquities of Mexico*, published in London between 1821 and 1848.

Dupaix's manuscripts reflect his deep interest in pre-Hispanic cultures and his fascination for their scientific discoveries. He was especially impressed with the aesthetic perfection of the monuments in what he called «the celebrated city of Palenque».

Regarding the inaccuracies in some of Castañeda's drawings, it is thought that he may have «embellished» them according to his own aesthetic conceptions. However, there are reasons to believe that these were only copies made by European artists and published in Europe, while the original and more accurate drawings were later found by researcher José Alcina Franch (1970).

Among the adventure chronicles of the explorers two major ideas stand out regarding Mayan civilization. However, these were mere speculation due to the fact that the explorers were under constant pressure by their employers in Spain who demanded information on the identity of these people.

In the first place, Del Río believed that the hieroglyphs were a form of writing. Dupaix understood they had no resemblance to those in Egypt, nor to those in Central Mexico, and that this was what gave a unique character to this civilization.

Secondly, both Del Río and Dupaix supposed that Palenque's ancient inhabitants depicted the members of their governing body in the stucco engravings, and that the hieroglyphs narrated the city's history.

This idea was a good lead for future research, but it was rejected, and for many years researchers worked with a hypothesis that deviated from the reality of the Mayan people, as we shall see later.

It is also important to mention that the conclusions of both explorers were refuted in light of new discoveries. Both Del Río and Dupaix erroneously concluded that the inhabitants of Palenque lived in a peaceful social and political environment.

The first reports led many amateur explorers to visit the region –many of them with intentions of becoming famous– in search of pre-Hispanic ruins, focusing primarily on temples and palaces, as well as on the carved stone monuments. Their contributions were quite varied: they ranged from picturesque descriptions and long dissertations about the origins, duration and disintegration of this culture, to amazing drawings and engravings of the ruins, and maps of the settlements. They even made molds of the figures decorating the buildings. Unfortunately, this was followed by constant looting of the sites, and original pieces were sent abroad.

The journals and reports show the difficulties they encountered in their expeditions, such as illnesses, lack of indigenous manual labor and economic resources, and political problems. But they also evince the great sense of wonder they experimented before the new discoveries and their deep interest in any manifestation of this culture.

Among the explorers and travelers of the 19th century, several became famous as forerunners of Mayan archaeology: Juan Galindo, Jean Frédéric Waldeck, the abbot Charles Étienne Brasseur de Bourgbourg, Augustus Le Plongeon, Désiré Charnay, John Lloyd Stephens, and Frederick Catherwood.

Stephens and Catherwood have a special place in the history of Mayan archaeology.

2. Drawing by J. L. Castañeda of a stucco from the Palace of Palenque (from *Palenque. Esplendor...*).

3. Stucco relief at Palenque in an engraving by J. F. Waldeck (from *Palenque. Esplendor...*).

4. John Lloyd Stephens (from *The Art of Maya Hieroglyphic Writing*).

Stephens (figure 4), an American attorney who wrote for money about his travels, was convinced that readers would be greatly attracted to the news about undiscovered lands. When Stephens came upon Antonio del Río's manuscript and Waldeck's engravings he realized that a travel book on the ruins of this exotic and unknown civilization would prompt even greater interest.

Stephens was able to convince the United States government to send him on a diplomatic mission to Central America where he began his adventure. Between 1839 and 1842 he explored a vast expanse of territory, describing more than forty Mayan sites. He wrote two books that had immediate success and were splendidly illustrated by British architect Frederick Catherwood, who accompanied him on his voyages (figure 5).[2]

Stephens' research opened a new phase in Mayan studies when he clearly stated that the ruins they had explored were not built by Celts, Vikings or Egyptians but rather by an indigenous people, born and raised in the area. In one of his visits to Uxmal he said:

«The people here are skilled in architecture, sculpture, drawing –and without any doubt possess great culture and refinement. They emerged here, just like its fruit and plants, without models or teachers, unique and independent, and untouched by the Old World.»[3]

Through his observations he concluded that the inhabitants he encountered in those lands were direct descendants of an ancient civilization who were capable of producing magnificent works of art, and thus could not be considered savages. Today this type of reasoning seems commonsensical and is generally accepted. However, at the time it meant a breakthrough in the prevailing line of thought.

Stephens' books were written in an easy style and were accompanied by Catherwood's extraordinary drawings which gave readers a clearer image of the Mayan world. Stephens is known as the «founder of the Mayan culture» because through his

5. Chichén Itzá's Quadrangle of the Nuns, drawing by F. Catherwood (from *Colha e i maya dei bassipiani*)

research and opinions, guided by his acute common sense, the study of this civilization acquired great importance.

Toward the end of the 19th century, the investigative work of British archaeologist Alfred Percival Maudslay (figure 6) was outstanding. Now he is considered by many as the first Mayan archaeologist. He believed that the only way to really know about this lost civilization was to study the surviving material vestiges and to do so he perfected his recording techniques. Percival's book *Archaeology: Biologia Centrali-Americana*, published in London between 1889 and 1902, is a superb document on his explorations: excavation reports, site maps, photographs (figure 7), as well as drawings of the monuments and hieroglyphs.

With Percival, the era of independent voyagers and explorers drawn mainly by personal interests came to an end, and was followed by one of institutional archaeological projects.

Toward the end of the 19th century, scientific institutions –mainly North American museums, universities and societies– began funding different projects as interest in Mayan studies increased tremendously.

6. Alfred Percival Maudslay in a well-known photograph taken inside one of the buildings at Chichén Itzá (from Graham, 1987).

One of the most important projects were the large-scale excavations began in Copán in 1890 and in Holmul in 1912, both funded by Harvard's Peabody Museum. The excavations focused primarily on cleaning and mapping the ceremonial sites of the Classic period.

The Carnegie Institution of Washington financed very important expeditions and projects in the Mayan region; among these, the ruins at Chichén Itzá. Between 1923 and 1940, this project did archaeological research and began the reconstruction of the ruins. Around the time between 1926 and 1937, the Carnegie Institution of Washington supported the Uaxactún project, which established the first chronological sequence of the Lowlands based on the study of hieroglyphs, ceramics and the architectural development of the site. In 1932 and 1940 it funded the expeditions to Calakmul which resulted in the mapping of 106 monuments in the center of the site, as well as a detailed study of the monuments and their inscriptions.

An expedition in 1925, funded by Tulane University and directed by Frans Blom, focused on linguistic and ethnological aspects, and carried out important research on the preservation of the Mayan archaeological monuments known at the time.

Starting in 1949, archaeologist Alberto Ruz Lhullier directed an outstanding project by the National Institute of Anthropology and History, thank to which he discovered a magnificent pre-Hispanic tomb within the Temple of the Inscriptions, at Palenque.

But after fifty years of large-scale explorations, the excavations into the monuments had revealed very little about their original inhabitants. The mapping of the monument sites hardly produced any information about the entire surface area they covered, their age, or time of occupation.

The archaeologists never spoke about the functions of the buildings and knew very little about the origins of the ceramic, jade or bone objects they discovered. However, the information gathered during this period would prove to be of great value for future research. The archaeologists photographed or made drawings of hundreds of stone monuments and objects. They also made excellent maps and registered thousands of glyphs and carved and painted images.

During this time the major representatives were: Sylvanus G. Morley, a North American archaeologist who carried out numerous expeditions to the Southern Lowlands and was later chosen by the Carnegie Institution of Washington to direct an archaeological project (between 1924 and 1940) to reconstruct the Chichén-Itzá ruins; and sir J. Eric S. Thompson, a renowned British archaeologist and epigrapher who began his career working for Morley in Chichén-Itzá, and who believed in combining archaeology with history and ethnography to get a more complete picture of ancient cultures.[4] These two brilliant researchers successfully synthesized contemporary versions regarding the development of the ancient Maya.

The ideas set forth by both scientists are the basis of what has been currently described by some authors as «the traditional model of Mayan civilization.»[5]

A major problem regarding this model was that many of the theories expounded by it were based on false or mistaken assumptions. In recent decades it has given rise to harsh debate and has been outgrown in more than one aspect.

As a result of this model the Mayan world had developed the romantic aura of a peaceful region inhabited by gods and anonymous priests who possessed the secrets to cosmic order and time —and the idea prevailed until only recently. According to this theory an elite class of priests instructed the Mayan people on how to execute magnificent works of art and architecture, and to burn great extensions of jungle to promote agriculture and self-sufficiency.

*Following page:*
7. The Temple of the Sun at Palenque before the dig in a picture taken by Maudsley at the end of the 19th century (from Graham, 1987).

According to this version, the people lived in the country –not in the cities– and had established perfect harmony with their environment. The ceremonial centers remained empty except on special occasions, such as religious ceremonies and market days. The model stated that Mayan culture was superior, did not practice human sacrifice, and did not believe in war like other cultures in Mesoamerica. Proofs of this theory, they said, could be gathered from the inscriptions on monuments, steles, lintels, wall paintings and ceramic objects. The artwork depicted the Mayas' obsession with time, as well as the images of the priests and gods that they worshipped.

According to Morley and Thompson the Mayas of the Classic period remained isolated from the political and economic activities of the rest of Mesoamerica, especially from Teotihuacan, in Central Mexico, and Monte Albán, in Oaxaca. They believed that because of the dense tropical jungle and their isolation from other important cultural centers, the Mayas maintained a homogenous culture, different from other Mesoamerican civilizations.

Therefore, according to this traditional model the Classic period, though brief, was the most important one, during which this civilization reached its zenith. What occurred before the years 300 and 900 A.D. was irrelevant because the rural villages during the Pre-Classic period seemed to have been extremely modest and humble, and the remains of the Post-Classic period evinced an era of decadence and the closing of the Mayan civilization.

But there was a reason for this romantic vision. The early explorers and archaeologists focused their research on the impressive monuments of the Classic period. Their major interest concentrated on the cultural undertakings of the affluent classes, such as the construction of magnificent pyramid temples and splendid palaces, the carved decoration on monuments, and the use of luxury items of great beauty and value. Because many of the archaeologists themselves belonged to an affluent society, it is quite probable that they directed their interests to their counterparts in Mayan society.

Very little was known at the time about hieroglyphic writing, and it is no wonder that its interpretation could have been speculated upon to support the model of a peaceful civilization and a governing class mainly interested in supernatural and religious issues.

This picture began to change about thirty years ago. Progress in deciphering Mayan writing has shown that the content of the inscriptions is not religious, astronomic, or esoteric, but rather of a more historical and mundane nature.[6]

Recent techniques and approaches in modern archaeology have revealed how the Mayas reacted to economic and ecological pressures, as well as their relations with other cities in the Mayan territory and with the rest of Mesoamerica. The Mayan world may have lost a great deal of its mystique under this new perspective. However, much has been gained in the understanding of its development.

The new model used in interpreting Mayan civilization is based on the work of epigraphers and on varied projects which have multiplied during the second half of the 20th century. In some cases, old theories have been revised.[7] In others, progress has been lineal, with new interpretations of old problems.

However, the general focus has changed. Current projects are more inclined to study the periods that preceded the Classic in order to understand the origin and evolution of the Mayan civilization. They also explore a realm of subjects that range from demography, eating habits, housing, craftsmanship, and the way of life of the common folk.

Current archaeological research does not concentrate on the great structures of

Classic period ceremonial centers. Nevertheless, conservation of these buildings prevails, as well as excavations within them to determine the function of each element and to decode information on hieroglyphs that have already been deciphered over the last decades.

The predominant focus of current projects is on the areas surrounding the ceremonial centers in search of information on normal everyday living.

The prime goal is to establish the relationship between these areas and the ceremonial centers in order to understand how cities like Palenque, Copán and Yaxchilán functioned. Archaeologists attempt to give equal importance to the research of vestiges pertaining to all the levels of Mayan society, from peasants and artisans, to rulers. Regional studies focus on the neighboring areas of large settlements, the relationship between important centers, the extent of each area's influence, etc. New techniques on recollection, digging and analysis are applied in these projects.

The greatest efforts now are in integrating the rapidly increasing amount of evidence gathered by archaeologists, topographers, ethnic historians, epigraphic experts, physical anthropologists, paleobotanists, paleozoologists, as well as experts in ceramics, stones, dating techniques, etc.

In the following lines we shall mention only some of the many projects which have been carried out in the area over the last decades. We will give a general idea of the subjects that are currently being studied in Mayan archaeology and which form the basis of a new explanatory model.

Outstanding among these is the project on settlement patterns undertaken by archaeologist Gordon R. Willey, from Harvard University, in a site called Barton Ramie, located in Valle del Río, Belize. Willey started the project in the fifties, marking a new era in archaeological research in America. For the first time emphasis was placed on domestic buildings, which were mapped and excavated, and which rendered valuable information on the daily lives of common people and their dynamic relationship with the environment. After Willey few have been the projects which do not take into consideration these settlement patterns, a tool which has proved fundamental in establishing the urban character of the main centers of the Mayan region.

Another outstanding project, carried out in Tikal between 1956 and 1970, was sponsored by the Pennsylvania University Museum and initially directed by Edwin Shook, and later by William R. Coe. The project opened up different perspectives on Mayan civilization thanks to new approaches and more advanced archaeological methods –including a detailed account on settlement patterns based on Willey's studies–, and slowly but forcefully replaced the traditional research model.

The Copán project was started in 1975 by the government of Honduras and has been directed by brilliant archaeologists like Gordon Willey, Claude Baudez, William T. Sanders, David Webster, as well as William Fash and Ricardo Agurcia, who are currently working in the Acropolis of Copán. This is a multidisciplinary project that has been sponsored by North American and Honduran institutions and whose major objectives have focused on the restoration and conservation of the ceremonial center, as well as on research on the development of the old city and its relation with the surrounding areas. The project has produced a vast amount of information as a result of the joint efforts of epigraphers and archaeologists. The members of the project have also published the results of their research, thus allowing a greater understanding of the most important aspects of Mayan civilization.

In 1979, Ray T. Matheny began research at El Mirador, the first and largest Mayan city in the Petén jungle in northern Guatemala. This site is the greatest concentration of civilian and religious buildings in the Mayan area, and is believed to have been inhabited by tens of thousands of individuals. The project was sponsored by the New World Archaeological Foundation at Brigham Young University and by the National Geographic Society. Results of the excavations have greatly increased the knowledge about the late Pre-Classic period since this site flourished between 100 B.C. and 150 A.D.

Between 1980 and 1983, the Belize Archaic Archaeological Reconnaissance project was directed by Richard S. MacNeish from the R.S. Peabody Foundation. It is the first project whose goal was to do research on the most ancient prehistoric periods of the Mayan zone: the Paleo-Indian and the Archaic (10000-2000 B.C.). MacNeish's studies permitted a greater insight into the question of human occupation in the region, casting aside the traditional theory that the Lowlands did not become populated until the Pre-Classic period.

Arthur A. Demarest has led the Petexbatún Regional Archaeological Project in the tropical jungle of northern Guatemala since 1989. The region comprises the rugged areas overlooking the Petexbatún Lake, south of Río de la Pasión (Dos Pilas, Tamarindito, Arroyo de Piedra, Aguateca, and Punta de Chimino). The project is outstanding because its researchers tell us the history about the place: the birth of a dynasty and the wars that followed before the area was abandoned in the 9th century.

In 1988, Jeremy A. Sabloff, sponsored by the National Science Foundation, finished the fieldwork for his project in Sayil, in the Puuc region of the Northern Lowlands. One of his objectives was to study the time of prosperity in the region after the collapse of the Southern Lowlands registered in the 9th century. The area was practically unexplored so he did intensive research on the settlement patterns in different moments of its history.

Towards the end of 1992, Mexico's National Institute of Anthropology and History and the Consejo Nacional para la Cultura y las Artes (National Council for Culture and the Arts) began an important government program aimed at protecting, preserving and publishing the results of research on archaeological sites in Mexico. The program known as *Special Archaeological Projects* included various sites in the Mayan region: Palenque and Toniná in Chiapas, Calakmul in southern Campeche, Chichén Itzá and Dzibilchaltún in Yucatán, and Kinichná and Kohunlich in southern Quintana Roo. The projects include archaeological exploration and large-scale restoration and preservation. Some areas have museums. We will briefly summarize the principal objectives of each of the projects in the program.[8]

The Palenque Special Project was first directed by Arnoldo González Cruz and later by Rosalba Nieto. It has focused mainly on archaeological exploration and research of the buildings and structures in the central area, as well as in architectural compounds on the outskirts. The idea is to gain better insight into the internal functioning of Palenque, the chronology of ceramic objects, the sequence followed in the construction of buildings, the location and characteristics of the dwelling-places and their relation with neighboring areas.

On 1 June 1994 the members of this project discovered the tomb of a woman of great hierarchy located within a building near the Temple of the Inscriptions (Temple XIII). On the other hand, in the tour of the fifty kilometer area surrounding Palenque 49 pre-Hispanic settlements were mapped and some explored with test pits to recover archaeological material that would allow to relate them to the city's nucleus. A new museum was recently inaugurated to display the findings of this project.

Archaeologist Ramón Carrasco directed the Special Project of Calakmul in the jungle of Petén, Campeche, sponsored by the state government, the Secretaría de Turismo (Ministry of Tourism), the Secretaría de Desarrollo Social (Ministry of Social Deve-

*Following page:*
8. Stele 11 at Yaxchilán in a picture taken by Teobert Maler in the 19th century (from Graham, 1987).

18

lopment) and the Instituto Nacional Indigenista (National Institute for Indian Affairs). The project entails archaeological research and conservation of the site located in one of Mexico's largest ecological reserves. It is said that this site was one of the most important cities in the Mayan Classic period. The main objectives of the project are to determine the role of Calakmul in the regional policy of Petén and to determine if it had functioned as the capital of the region, according to the theoretical model proposed by several contemporary authors.

Archaeologist Enrique Nalda, head of the Quintana Roo Special Archaeological Project, selected the sites known as Dzibanché, Kinichná and Kohunlich because, as he expressed: «From an archaeological standpoint they are located in a transition area between two centers of cultural development –central Petén (Early Classic and Middle) and Yucatán (Late Classic and Post-Classic). They are essential in order to understand the shifting of these cultures and the formation of new political centers during the phase of evacuation from the central area.»[9]

Dzibanché and Kinichná are relatively unknown sites. Their exploration is thus focused on the history of their occupation, settlement patterns and livelihood; their chronology and architecture, as well as the roles they played in the region. On the other hand, in more explored areas like Kohunlich, the project focuses on the liberation and consolidation of structures in the ceremonial center, as well as on excavation of housing complexes, in accordance with the work done by the Southeast Regional Center between 1971 and 1981.

The Special Chichén Itzá Project is directed by archaeologist Peter Schmidt. His team of researchers has been doing restoration and conservation work, as well as archaeological exploration and digging in the most powerful and important centers of the Northern Lowlands during the Terminal Classic and Early Post-Classic periods.

The main questions that this project has dealt with have been to determine the entire extension of the site, and reconstruct its internal organization throughout time, its water supply system for urban and agricultural consumption, cronological refinement, and preservation of the site. Intensive work is being done primarily in mapping out the area to mark digging zones. Outstanding work has been undertaken in superimposed buildings, and streets and structures have been uncovered and restored.

Before the arrival of the Spaniards Dzibilchaltún was one of the largest urban centers that flourished in Yucatán. Since the start of the Special Project, directed by archaeologist Rubén Maldonado, major work has been done in research, excavation and reconstruction of the city, including a pre-Hispanic road or sacbé and a nearby housing complex. But the central part of this project was the construction of the Museum of the Mayan People, an ecological museum within the archaeological site of Dzibilchaltún.

Another museum is currently under construction in the ancient city of Toniná, in the valley of Ocosingo, Chiapas, and is part of the Special Archaeological Project directed by Juan Yadéun.

To date, a lot of reconstruction has been done in this pre-Hispanic city's Sacred Space. It consists of a pyramidal structure with seven platforms on which palaces and temples form the largest Acropolis in the Mayan region. Many objects have been uncovered and will be on display in the museum to show the cultural sequence of Toniná and its relation with other powerful centers in the region.

The Mayan civilization emerged in a vast extension of territory in southeast Mexico and northern Central America and reached its greatest splendor during what is known as the Classic period. Characteristic of this civilization are a series of cultural traits distributed in a uniform fashion throughout this region. According to scholars of Mayan culture, these traits include monumental architecture in ceremonial centers with false arch vaults and ridges that increase the height of the buildings, the development of hieroglyphic writing and a complex calendar, a long count dating system (which was amazingly refined and absolute), the presence of stele-altar sculpture structures, polychrome ceramics of great quality, as well as a highly artistic and sophisticated style of bas reliefs and mural paintings.

## Environment

The vast territory of the Mayan civilization included part of what are now the Mexican states of Chiapas and Tabasco and the entire Yucatán peninsula, Guatemala, Belize, and part of Honduras and El Salvador. This territory measures approximately 400000 square kilometers and is in a cultural area known as the Mesoamerican Southeast. Modern-day inhabitants of this territory use dialects related to the Mayan linguistic group.

The pre-Hispanic Mayan culture developed in an environment that has been divided into three diffcrent geographic and cultural zones (figure 9).

SOUTH ZONE: The Highlands in southern Guatemala, and from southeast Chiapas to western El Salvador. It is a volcanic region of lava, ash and obsidian, with mountains rich in minerals like jade, serpentine, cinnabar, and hematite; warm valleys, pine forests, lakes and large plateaus.

Great rivers such as the Usumacinta, the Grijalva and the Motagua are born in the highest part of this region, which is also the birthplace of the famous quetzal bird. Kaminaljuyú, in Guatemala, is one of the most well known sites in this area.

The altitude along the Pacific region descends abruptly forming a coastline where some Mayan groups settled and used to their advantage the rich volcanic soil. Agriculture flourished due to constant rains.

From a cultural viewpoint this zone is quite unusual. In fact, some authors do not include it within the area where Classic Mayan culture developed. This is because, on the one hand, the sites from this era show an influence from Central Mexico; on the other hand, no evidence has been found of the most important features that distinguish Mayan culture. However, this territory forms part of the geographic setting of the pre-Hispanic and contemporary Mayas. As we shall see, the study of this area is necessary to understand the beginnings of Mayan civilization.

CENTRAL ZONE: It is a vast territory located between the Gulf of Mexico and the Caribbean and represents the heart of the Mayan civilization. The region includes what is known as the Southern Lowlands, part of Honduras, Belize, Guatemala, Chiapas, and Tabasco. The area is marked by its rainforest, exuberant with palm, mahogany, *sapodilla*, ceiba, *chicozapote*, and silk-cotton trees. It was once an area densely inhabited by jaguars, alligators, venomous serpents, deer, rabbits, armadillos, eagles, and turkeys. Drainage is abundant since the area consists of extensive shoals (large swamp depressions) and some lakes, including flowing rivers such as the Usumacinta, on whose banks cities like Yaxchilán and Piedras Negras were erected. Along the mid course of the Motagua River, apple-green jade –the most precious jewel in Mesoamerica– was deposited in the form of pebbles and large rocks. The center of the region is Petén, where most of the Mayan Classic period sites have been uncovered.

NORTH ZONE: This region is known as the Northern Lowlands, which includes the coast line and swamplands of Quintana Roo and Campeche, and the limestone platforms on the Yucatán peninsula, where rain is scarce and low forest and thorn like vegetation predominate. Except for some lakes in the east, the area lacks superficial water layers. However, in some parts there are natural water reservoirs, known as *cenotes*, formed by collapsed underground caves. In the areas where natural reservoirs did not exist the ancient Mayas built huge bottle-shaped water tanks or wells known as *chultunes*. The only elevations throughout the North Zone are the Puuc hills which form a chain of low mountains that crosses the north of Campeche and southeast Yucatán. Predominant fauna in the region includes deer and wild boar, as well as marine fauna on the coast. Salt extraction was intensely exploited in this area during the pre-Hispanic era. The Mayan culture flourished in this area during the Post-Classic period.

*Chronology*

While most research projects continue to focus on the Classic period, recent ones are more interested in earlier periods and the cultural sequence of the Mayan territory. MacNeish's research into the swamplands of Belize has uncovered one of the most ancient sites in the Mayan area and has shown that there was native population in the region long before the Pre-Classic period.

We can more or less estimate that a cultural sequence began more than 10000 years ago. At that time the Mayan territory was inhabited by hunting and gathering groups who later became semi-nomadic and lived in temporary camping settlements. Evidence shows that the earliest agricultural practices with corn began around the year 2500 B.C. In the places where they settled for longer periods they began to experiment with different plants, and according to pollen analysis, large extensions of land were burned before planting the seeds. During these periods, the population in the region had become semi-nomadic, combining hunting and harvesting activities.

Toward the year 1800 B.C., more permanent farming villages began to form in the South Zone, near the fertile soils on the coastal plains. Profound changes occurred in technology and in the society during this period. Archeological findings evince new agricultural tools and the invention of ceramics in the form of figurines and small vases. Social stratification was also detected in the burial sites. It seems that this style of life did not occur at the same time in other areas of the Mayan region because the earliest farming villages began to appear in the North and Central zones toward the year 800 B.C.

In the beginning of our era the population in the Lowlands had begun to build the foundations of a complex civilization that flourished during the Classic period, considered the golden period of Mayan culture, primarily in the Central Zone. The Classic period presumably began in the year 292 A.D. The date corresponds to the long count date inscribed on Stele 29 in Tikal. According to the date inscribed it is the oldest known Mayan stone monument (figures 10-11).

This period ends toward the year 910 A.D. with the downfall of the great cities of the Central Zone (the date is inscribed on Stele 6 of Itzimté). The Classic period has been defined as one in which the Mayas of the Southern Lowlands built stone monuments dated in long count.[10] This period has been divided into Early Classic (250-

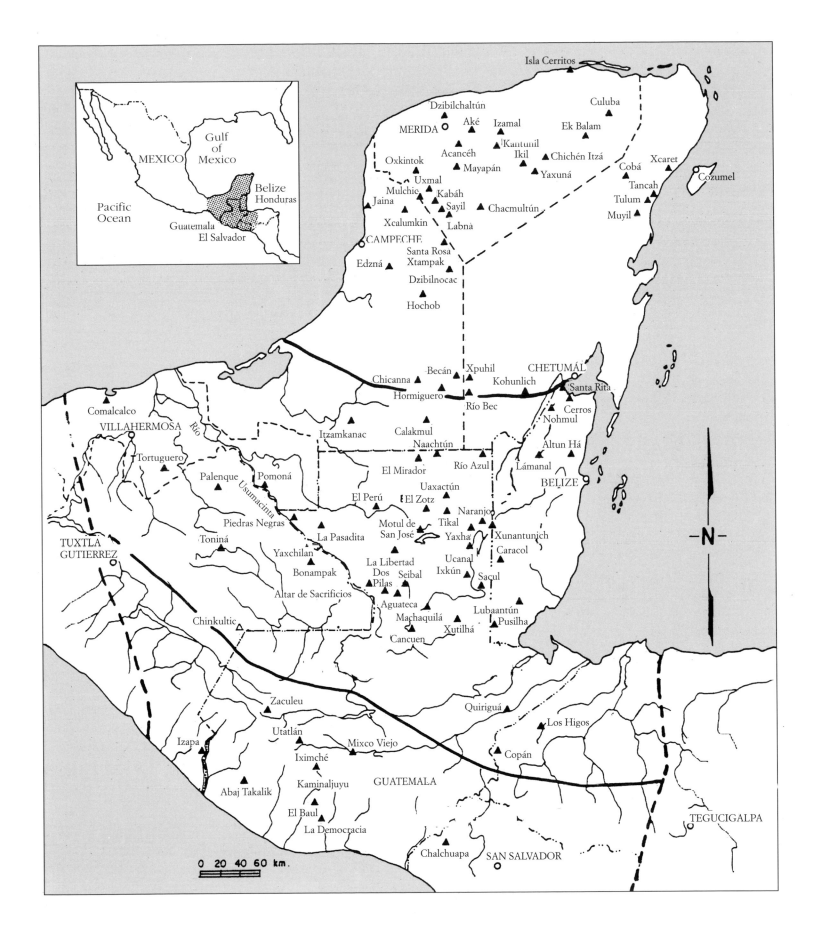

9. Map of the Mayan area showing the three main geographical-cultural zones as well as the major archaeological sites (drawing by A. Reséndiz).

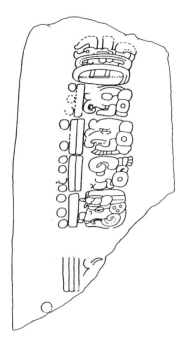

600 A.D.) and Late Classic (600-900 A.D.) due to the profound cultural changes that took place.[11]

The Early Classic period is characterized by the powerful influence of the Teotihuacan culture. For reasons that are yet unclear, this influence ceased around the 7th century, giving way to the era of maximum Mayan cultural and economic development (corresponding to the Late Classic period).

Some authors consider that there was yet another stage in this period, known as Terminal Classic, which presumably occurred between the years 800 and 1000 A.D. This phase is characterized by two major events. On the one hand, the decadence and flight from the great cities in the Southern Lowlands as a result of an alleged phenomenon known as «the downfall of the Mayan civilization». A second event was the rise of powerful city-states in the Northern Lowlands, a region that reached its splendor during the Post-Classic period.

During this last phase Mayan influence spread to distant areas within Mesoamerica, leaving traces in sites like Cacaxtla, El Tajín, and Xochicalco.

10. Rear side of Stele 29 at Tikal where the earliest date in Long Count ever found in the Mayan Lowlands (8.12.14.8.15, 13 Men) is recorded, which corresponds to July 8, 292 A.D. (drawing by W.R.Coe, from Miller, 1986).

*Beginnings of a Civilization*
*The Pre-Classic Period (1800 B.C.-250 A.D.)*

The origin of the Mayan civilization continues to be one of the major unresolved questions in modern archaeology. New discoveries have defied the traditional concept that placed the origin of the civilization during the Classic period, and according to which the Pre-Classic was a period in which people lived in primitive villages, while the Post-Classic was one of cultural decline. It is now believed that the ancient Mayas were more advanced and sophisticated.

Recent investigations have continued to bring forth questions regarding the birth of this great Mesoamerican civilization, but we will attempt to find answers to some. For example, how and where did this civilization arise? How did it change throughout time, and why? Were the achievements of the Classic period a result of the people's own inner development, or were they due to invasions of more advanced neighbors?

Fortunately, archaeology has shown tremendous progress over the last few years in research on Mayan culture before its era of splendor in the Classic period.[12]

Archaeologists used to believe this complex society was born in the Lowlands just before the year 300 A.D. The traditional belief was that the difference between the modest villages that characterized the Pre-Classic period and the impressive buildings of the Classic lay in that people from other areas began to migrate to the Mayan region and introduced these changes. However, recent excavations have proven this theory to be untrue. Although the roots as well as the progress and accomplishments of the Mayas were not the product foreign intrusion, they were not an isolated people and were indeed influenced by other Mesoamerican cultures.

The beginning of the Pre-Classic period is marked by the permanent settlement in farming villages as a way of life in all of Mesoamerica. This begins to occur in a Mayan area around 1800 B.C., specifically on the plains along the Pacific coast, in the Mexican state of Chiapas, Guatemala and El Salvador. For reasons yet unknown and despite recent searches, sites from the Pre-Classic period have not been found in the Highlands, nor in the North and Central zones.[13]

The first villages were formed by small groups of palm-roof adobe huts always built near a source of water. The inhabitants of these villages created very fine and sophisticated ceramic work –known to be one of the most ancient in Mesoamerica–

11. Front side of the above stele, with the representation of a ruler of Tikal (drawing by W.R. Coe, from Miller, 1986).

and were the creators of burnt clay human figurines which became very popular during that period (figure 13).

With time, the villages regrouped into larger political entities under the rule of a larger town of approximately 1000 inhabitants, that acted as the capital. Social stratification begins within these capitals: some houses are larger than others, some burial grounds have more modest offerings than others, etc.

Before the year 1000 B.C. this area began to receive a strong influence from the Olmecs, whose culture was gathering momentum all along the Mexican Gulf coast, and it would reach its greatest splendor during the Middle Pre-Classic period.

It was precisely during this phase (1000-300 B.C.) when the rest of the Mayan area began to change with the appearances farming villages in the Highlands and Lowlands. It is hard to describe the cultural development in this region during the Pre-Classic phase on account of the practical difficulties involved in the digging process. Most of the material vestiges lie deeply buried under the structures that were later built in overlapping levels, as was customary to do in Mesoamerica. Thus, the ethnic

| DATES | PERIODS | NORTHERN HIGHLANDS | SOUTHERN LOWLANDS | HIGHLANDS AND THE PACIFIC COAST |
|---|---|---|---|---|
| 1530 | Colonial | 1528: F. de Montejo conquers Yucatán | 1697: Conquest of Tayasal, last independent Mayan city | 1523: P. de Alvarado conquers the Highlands |
| 1200 | Late Post-Classic | Mayapán | Tayasal (Itzá) | Quiché and Cakchiquel states |
| 1000 | Early Post-Classic | Toltec influence on Chichén Itzá | Itzá | |
| 900 | Terminal | | 910: Itzimté Stele | |
| 600 | Late Classic | Puuc Chenes Río Bec | Mayan cities boom | Cotzumalhuapa |
| 250 | Early Classic | | 534-593: Hiatus inscriptions 292: Stele 29 at Tikal | Teotihuacan influence in Kaminaljuyú |
| 100 | Proto-Classic | | | Chiapa de Corzo |
| <None> 300 | Late Pre-Classic | First monumental structures | Uaxactún: E VII sub | Kaminaljuyú (Miraflores phase) El Baúl Abaj Takalik |
| 800 | Middle Pre-Classic | | | Izapa |
| | Early Pre-Classic | | | Ocós |
| 2000 | | | First occupation in Cuello (Belize) | |

12. Chronological table of the Mayan area.

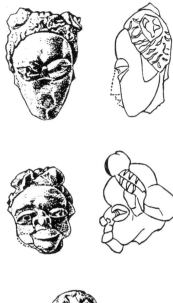

13. Ceramic figurines from the Ocós phase, Early Pre-Classic (from M. Coe, 1987).

origin of the first sedentary inhabitants is yet uncertain. Some remains that have been uncovered reveal that they already made elaborate ceramic objects but did not have a writing system and their development was poor regarding the arts and architecture. These groups of farmers settled in small villages and mainly harvested corn and engaged in a primitive barter system.

One of the places that began to be colonized during this period was Kaminaljuyú, located in a vast fertile valley west of Guatemala City, in the Highlands. The earliest villages in the Lowlands have been found in the valley of Copán in Honduras, the Altar of Sacrifices and the Seibal in Guatemalan Petén (materials here indicate some Olmec influence), and Cuello, in northern Belize.

Towards the middle Middle Pre-Classic the population of the Central zone was marked by a tremendous growth and there are first traces of public monumental architecture. Small villages had begun to transform into cities. Such was the case of Nakbé, in the northern Guatemalan Petén, where discoveries have been made of large buildings and platforms that date from 750 B.C. Although quite modest, they are proof of the transformation from a simple to a more complex way of life. The first traces of a cultural and social transformation appear at this time, but it would yet take centuries before the main traits of Mayan culture would become appearant, something which occurred during the last phase of the Pre-Classic.

In order to have a better understanding of the origins of Mayan civilization several archaeological projects have focused on exploring the cultural vestiges immediately preceding the Classic period. Results have shown that there were complex urban centers in all the Mayan area that date back at least to 300 B.C. This year marks the beginning of the Late Pre-Classic, also known as Proto-Classic. It is now known that during this time class differences were already firmly established and that a political system of dynastic succession (which would later characterize the Mayan era of splendor) was beginning to take form.

Numeration, writing and calendarical systems begin to appear and large-scale architectural projects arise, transforming sites like Tikal, Cerros, Lamanai (figure 14; plates 46-48), Cuello, and Dzibilchaltún into more complex centers. A more uniform artistic style begins to disseminate in places like Uaxactún, Cerros, Tikal, El Mirador, Lamanai and Nakbé, where pyramidal platforms were adorned with spectacular plaster masks representing their deities (figures 15, 16; plates 7, 8, 48). More complex icon symbols begin to appear in many sites, such as the one representing Venus, which seems to have been related to war.

At a regional level the Mayan centers during the Late Pre-Classic were always in

14. Structure N10-43 at Lamanai, Belize, an example of the big pyramids typical of the Late Pre-Classic (from M. Coe, 1987).

contact thanks to their participation in trade activities. The flourishing of Lamanai, a port in northern Belize, is a clear example of this. Here raw materials were exchanged for manufactured goods between the Highlands and the Lowlands. The regions that stood out most during this phase were Izapa and Kaminaljuyú, in the South Zone, and El Mirador, Uaxactún (plates 4-8) and Tikal, in the heart of the Central Zone. Prototypes of deities of the Classic Mayan pantheon, as well as the first traces of calendaric and writing systems, have been found in the first two. The Central Zone is a key area to understand the birth of the complex societies that characterized the next period. As for the North Zone, the Late Pre-Classic is represented in sites such as Edzná, in Campeche, where its inhabitants built a complex hydraulic system.

The Culture of Izapa in the South Zone is believed to have been the result of a fusion of Olmecs with the local cultures that had begun to develop in places like Abaj Takalik, El Baúl, Kaminaljuyú, as well as in Izapa.

The Olmec culture was a determining influence on the course of Mayan history because it may have been responsible for introducing the calendar and writing in the region. In fact, the oldest monuments in which the long count is used have been found in sites where the Olmec culture flourished: Stele C, found in Tres Zapotes, Veracruz, is marked with a date that corresponds to the year 31 B.C. (figure 17); a stele in Chiapa de Corzo, in the heart of Chiapas, is dated 36 B.C. (figure 190), and Stele 1 in La Mojarra, south of Veracruz, is marked by dates that correspond to the years 143 and 156 A.D. (figure 19). In the Mayan area long count and writing begin to be used in the South Zone where the Culture of Izapa flourished and later spread to the Lowlands.

Izapa was founded near the Pacific coast, on the southeastern hills of Chiapas. Whether this site belonged or not to the Mayan area is still under debate. Research has found that from a geographical standpoint it is exactly on the southeastern boundary. Culturally, its inhabitants spoke a dialect related to Mixe-Zoque, a linguistic family that included the Olmec culture, according to some researchers.

Thus, Izapa is considered a midpoint in time and space between the Olmecs of the Middle Pre-Classic and the Mayas of the Early Classic periods. Although this area was inhabited from the beginnings of the Pre-Classic, the splendor of the Culture of Izapa took place in the late phase of this period, when the direct antecedents of Mayan culture are established. It is at this time that we see the first steles and altars carved in bas-relief with mythic and historical scenes (figures 18, 58, 59, 60, 132, 166; plates 87, 88), as well as representations of ancestral figures or prototypes of the gods that would later make up the Mayan pantheon, and the introduction of iconographic

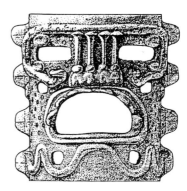

15. Samples of Pre-Classic large masks. Above: large mask from structure E VII sub at Uaxactún (from Covarrubias, 1957). Center: Representation of the Sun God in the first temple at Cerros, Belize). Below: Clay censer found at the Cerros town (from Schele and Freidel, 1990).

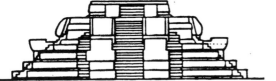

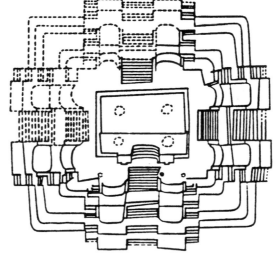

16. Ground plan and side views of structure E-VIIsub at Uaxactún, Guatemala (from Kubler, 1984).

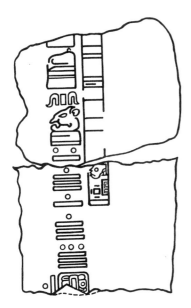

17. Rear side of Stele C at Tres Zapotes, Veracruz, displaying the date (7.16.6.16.18 [6 Etznab]) which corresponds to September 3, year 31 B.C.(from Marcus, 1992).

motifs that would later be present in the art of the Central Zone during the Classic period. Here we have found no evidence of the use of writing or the calendar. But in Abaj Takalik, a nearby site that shows evidence of Olmec intrusion, inscriptions dated in long count begin to appear, as in Stele 2, considered an example of the Izapa style in its purest form. Further southeast is El Baúl, a site where Stele 1 dated in long count corresponds to the year 37 A.D. (figure 21).

In the Highlands, the Izapa style flourished in Kaminaljuyú during the phase known as Miraflores (Late Pre-Classic). Most of the mounds at this site belong to this era and it is believed that Izapa ruled over most of the region, as well as over the Southern Lowlands. Pyramids are used here for the first time as funeral monuments with luxurious tombs that have been found built inside monumental pyramidal plat-forms. The tombs contain opulent offerings and the remains of sacrificed victims. Ka-minaljuyú abounds with stone sculptures in the Izapa style, as the enormous granite steles with Izapan gods reveal (figure 20). One of the steles is engraved with a text that has not yet been deciphered, although it is similar to Mayan writing of the Classic period.

By the time of the closing of the Late Pre-Classic, Kaminaljuyú had already been abandoned and was in ruins. However, a short time later it recovered its splendor after the invasions from Central Mexico.

Research in El Mirador has helped to clear false hypotheses advanced by tradi-tional archaeology. This site is a good example of the high levels of development reached by the Mayas as far back as the Pre-Classic. In fact, before Ray T. Matheny initiated his archaeological project in 1979, this site had been catalogued as repre-sentative of the Classic period on account of its size and the magnificence of its constructions. Now we know that this site flourished many years before, during the Late Pre-Classic, when it was inhabited by tens of thousands of individuals.

If we consider the enormous extension of the surface area of El Mirador (approxi-mately 16 square kilometers), with its impressive architectural complexes, such as El Tigre or Danta, built by the Maya towards 150 B.C.; with its squares adorned with steles and plain altars; with its paved avenues and rainwater deposits, we are forced to conclude that this was with all certainty one of the first capital cities of Mayan

18. Stele 23 (left) and Stele 7 (right) at Izapa, Chiapas (from G.W. Lowe, T.A. Lee and E. Martínez Espinosa, 1982).

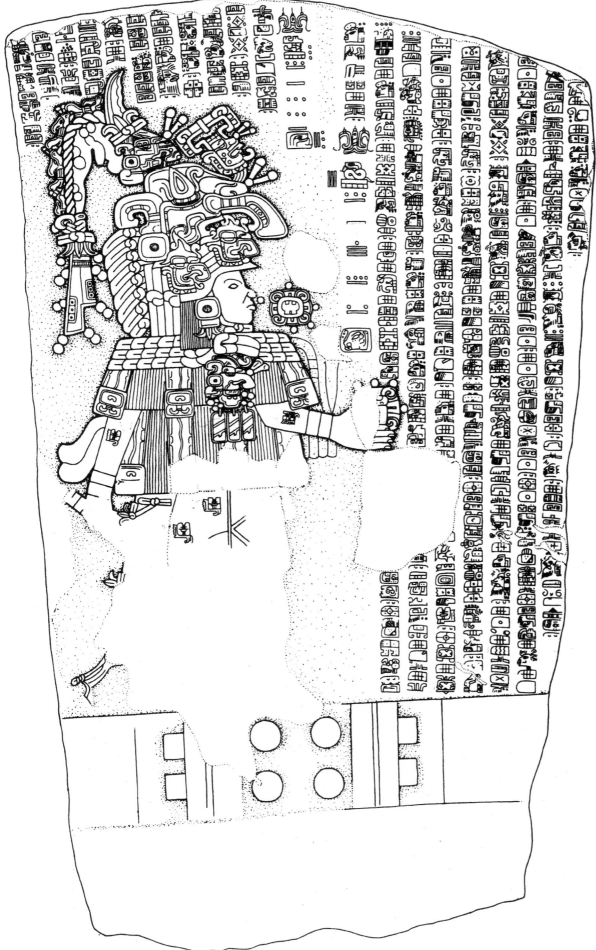

19. Stele 1 at La Mojarra,
Veracruz (from Justeson and
Kaufman, 1993).

civilization. Indepth research at this site has proved of great value in shedding light on important aspects of Mayan history. Thanks to archaeological evidence, and considering the work involved in mantaining a city this size, it is possible to infer the great complexity that Mayan society had reached long before the Classic.

The strategic position of El Mirador, located between the Yucatán peninsula and the southern Mayan region, as well as the road network connecting the city with other Pre-Classic centers, indicates that it may have been a place in charge of controlling trade in the region. Despite its short-lived splendor —of approximately 300 years— it was abandoned around the year 150 A.D. probably due to struggles among the major power centers of that time.

El Mirador was again occupied many years later, during the Classic. The new settlers built their homes on top of the old ones and resumed activities in the enormous temples and public buildings that remained from the Pre-Classic city.

Most of the structures in Uaxactún belong to the Late Pre-Classic period. Researchers have found that at that time they were already using the false arch domes. During this era, Izapa style mural paintings were found in the temples and tombs of Tikal.

It is evident that cultural development during this period was extraordinary and that Mayan civilization undoubtedly had its roots in this region. The Mayas of the Classic inherited a splendid culture that would later be developed to maximum levels. However, they also inherited many social problems, such as an increasing population, and competition and power struggles among major centers. These conflicts forced them to find new forms of economic and political organization.

The writing system and the long count calendar introduced in the Southern Lowlands as political propaganda beacons of the changes that were about to occur. The oldest date in long count inscribed on a monument from the Central Zone marks the beginning of the period of greatest splendor.

20. Stele 11 at Kaminaljuyú (from *Palenque, Esplendor...*).

21. Stele 2 at Abaj Takalik, Guatemala (from Bernal, 1969) and Stele 1 at El Baúl, Guatemala, dated in the year 37 A.D. (from M. Coe, 1987).

*The Mayan Area in the Classic Period*
*(250-900 A.D.)*

General Considerations

22. Burial 166 at Tikal, example of funerary customs among Pre-Classic Mayas (from W. R. Coe, 1977).

We have observed that during the Pre-Classic period Mayan culture was first influenced by Izapa and Teotihuacan and later developed a more independent character. During the Classic period, cultural traits became more uniform throughout the Mayan region. Great cities with monumental masonry buildings began to spread all over the territory.

The squares in many ceremonial centers were adorned with steles and altars, with pictures of their rulers and inscriptions dated in long count. Many of the temples surrounding the squares were crowned by ridges and reached impressive heights. Some of the rooms in the buildings had domes with false arches. The sophisticated Mayan artistic style is evident in painting –as seen in small scale polychrome ceramics or in extraordinary murals– and in sculpture –as shown by the steles, lintels, and splendid panels with bas-relief engravings that adorn the squares, palaces and temples. During this time population increased tremendously, commerce and agriculture activities intensified and wars became constant.

As we mentioned before, this period has been divided into two phases based on the differences in archaeological remains. This difference undoubtedly responds to profound social disorder reflected by a temporary interruption (534-593 A.D.) in the building of inscribed monuments.

During the first phase –the Early Classic– the ruins show a marked Teotihuacan influence as shown in the Mayan imitations of tripod bowls from Central Mexico, as well as in imported objects with green obsidian from mines in the central state of Hidalgo, then ruled by Teotihuacan. Sloping wall-vertical panel architecture is present in some sites.

During the second phase –the Late Classic– foreign influence ceases and Mayan culture develops its own character and leads the region to its era of greatest splendor.

Just as in the previous period, the South Zone was still susceptible to foreign influence. During the first phase of the Classic period Teotihuacan culture traits appeared in the Highlands, where the Izapa culture had once flourished. We must remember that Kaminaljuyú was abandoned towards the end of the Pre-Classic, but that it again became populated and achieved great importance around 400 A.D., when Teotihuacan influence was most evident, particularly in the architectural style of the ceremonial center (figures 24, 25). Unfortunately we know very little about the relationship between these two centers. Perhaps Kaminaljuyú was reinstated during this period as a port for important trade activities thanks to a strategic position which gave it control over the resources of a great variety of ecosystems. Or maybe some of its wealthy inhabitants, in order to gain more prestige, imported objects from Teotihuacan (figure 26) and copied its architectural style, in vogue then throughout most of Mesoamerica.

Others believe that Kaminaljuyú was conquered by Teotihuacan and converted into an enclave from where they could control production and distribution towards Central Mexico of important products like obsidian from El Chayal (figure 23); jade from Motagua and cocoa from the Pacific coast. The fact is that Teotihuacan influence prevailed during this era in the South Zone, and although there are some Mayan traits, some important elements are missing, such as Long Count inscriptions, monumental sculptures like steles or altars, or false-arch domes.

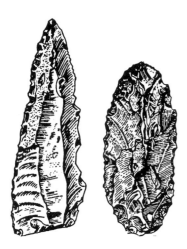

23. Obsidian tools from the finding at El Chayal, Guatemala (from M. Coe, 1987).

Whereas in the Central Zone Mayan culture flourished with all of its characteristic traits. A dynastic political system was established and wars for conquest and succession take place and began to shape the region's political history. In places such as Tikal, Uaxactún, and Yaxhá, Teotihuacan presence is also as evident as not altogether clear. It is believed that Teotihuacan colonies may have settled there and that there was a firmly established trade relationship, especially between the Petén area and Central Mexico as is seen through imported materials from both areas.

Supposedly Teotihuacan exerted certain political influence in some sites as is evident in a Tikal stele which shows Mayan rulers dressed in Teotihuacan military uniform (figure 27; plate 89). This could mean that their royal lineage originated in the most important capital of Central Mexico through Kaminaljuyú or that the rulers used Teotihuacan military symbols and clothing because they considered them prestigious and were clearly intended to legitimize their status. Whatever the nature of this relationship, archaeological remains have proven that the strongest contacts between the Mayan Central Zone and Teotihuacan occurred between the 4th and 5th centuries of the present era.

Very little is known about the early phase of the Classic period in the North Zone. The style of the vestiges is similar to that of the Central Zone, especially of the Petén region. Teotihuacan influence also reached the most remote areas, as is apparent in some of the architectural styles found in sites of the Yucatán peninsula, such as Acanceh, Dzibilchaltún, and Becán.

The beginning of the 7th century was witness to the political and economic downfall of Kaminaljuyú and to the severe crisis shook the very core of the Central Zone. Between the years 534 and 593 A.D., and for reasons that are yet unclear, its inhabitants stopped creating steles and brutally mutilated the public monuments of their ceremonial centers. However, they did not abandon the sites. They regained stability years later, and as Teotihuacan influence ceased, the era of great prosperity and splendor known as the Late Classic began.

Meanwhile, towards the east, in El Caracol[14] and Copán, the transition between the two phases of the Classic period was different. Monuments were built with hieroglyph inscriptions during the referred interval of crisis. In Caracol, inscriptions show the ruling dynasty's political power at the time. Copán, however, did not suffer violent incidents like Petén, perhaps due to its isolation. Its dynasty was founded in the early 5th century and continued uninterrupted as far as the year 820 A.D.

24. Detail of the decoration on a Mayan vessel from Tikal where a building in Teotihuacan style is shown (from Freidel, Schele and Parker, 1993).

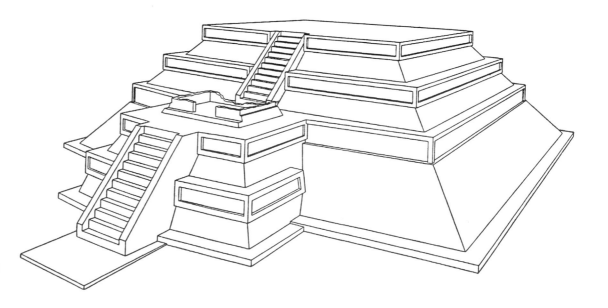

25. Teotihuacan style building at Kaminaljuyú, Guatemala (from Willey, 1966).

While the Late Classic period is considered the golden age of Mayan culture, not all Mayan zones faired equally. Development in the South Zone Highlands declined gradually. On the other hand, the Nahua culture of the *pipiles* appeared in the area close to the Pacific coast, known as Cotzumalhuapa in the fertile lands of the Piemonte zone (figure 28).

There were two outstanding traditions or cultural spheres in the North Zone: one in Cobá, east of Yucatán, and another in Uxmal and Kabah, on the western side of the peninsula. The first one is characterized by its clear Petén influence, and the second by the development of an individual artistic style, known as *Puuc*. The Central Zone had an incredible rebirth after its period of political instability. Cities stand out for their increasing population and architecture and the arts reach the height of their splendor in places like Tikal, Copán, Toniná, Palenque, Bonampak, and Yaxchilán.

## Settlement Patterns and Political Organization

Early explorers at the turn of the century archaeologists never doubted that the Mayan ruins of the Classic period were the remnants of magnificent cities inhabited by thousands of people who lived in huts surrounding the monumental areas. However, around the Thirties Thompson and other archaeologists began to spread a completely opposite idea: that there were never any real cities in the Mayan area; that the ceremonial centers remained virtually «empty» and that people in nearby rural communities only visited them on market days or holidays. The ceremonial centers pro-

26. Teotihuacan tripod vessel from Kaminaljuyú (from Willey, 1966).

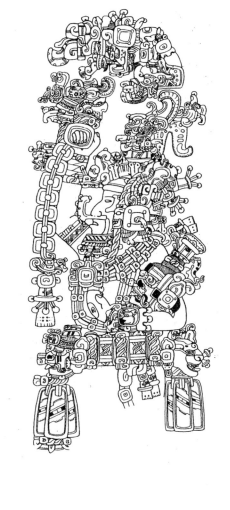

27. Stele 31 at Tikal, dated in the 445 A.D. Ruler Stormy Sky is flanked by two characters in Teotihuacan attire and carrying Teotihuacan objects (from Schobinger, 1994).

28. Stele 3 at Bilbao, Santa Lucía Cotzumalhuapa (from Willey, 1966).

vided services to a vast territory, and in exchange its inhabitants participated in the building and maintenance of the public buildings.

Modern archaeology has in this case recovered old hypothesis supported by stronger foundations supplied by the application of detailed studies on settlement patterns. Pioneering these studies in Mesoamerica was Gordon R. Willey, who defined this concept as the manner in which man organizes his housing and other important community buildings in a dynamic relationship with his natural environment. According to Willey, the study of different settlement patterns offers important clues about technology and public institutions. For this reason, it is important to record not only the monumental buildings in an urban site but also the lower platforms where farmers built their modest homes, nearby water sources, topography, and the different types of soil. Maps with this kind of information are analyzed in search for patterns and to determine the possible function of the structures and the relationship of the settlement with the environment. Thanks to these studies we now know that Tikal was a city in its own right and not only a splendid ceremonial center. The careful recording and mapping of the area revealed a dense population, with thousands of housing knolls over a vast area of land (figure 29; plate 10). At least 40000 people lived in Tikal toward the year 600 A.D. in a 63 square kilometer area surrounding the monumental nucleus. Much of this population was dedicated to farming and agriculture, while others took part in artistic, religious, military, management and trade activities, in a true urban community.

The magnificent Mayan cities were not as well planned as in the case of Teotihuacan.[15] Their growth seems more anarchic, with the addition of temples, palaces and other buildings, and it is difficult to establish boundaries.[16] A typical Mayan city had a ceremonial and administrative center surrounded by residential complexes distributed in an irregular manner over a vast land area.

Temples, royal palaces, public buildings and squares were distributed within the ceremonial centers. This is where the ruling class lived, where the administrative and religious activities were carried out, and where city dwellers got together for specific activities.

These centers were veritable cosmological models as shown by the shape, order, and adornments on the facades. In some cases a predominant architectural style is recognizable in the temples. This style is known as the «pattern of three» –a major temple in the middle and two more facing each other forming a central square. This may be related to the triad of gods that recurrently appear in Mayan mythology. On the other hand, the squares and pyramids symbolically reproduced the sacred landscape created by the gods –the steles stuck in the squares resemble cosmic trees that connect the netherworld with the heavens. The altars, almost always placed in front of the steles, would represent the earth, from where men and plants are born. The pyramidal temples were built to resemble the sacred mountains or *uitz*. The main doors or gates are adorned with the open fauces of the earth monster, symbolizing the entrance to the cave leading to the heart of the earth or the entrails of a mountain; a supernatural world inhabited by gods and ancestors. Some of the funeral monuments of the Mayan area consist of nine-bodied pyramidal foundations that could be related to the concept of nine levels that the dead had to cross to reach the netherworld or Xibalbá. The recreation of a sacred geography in ceremonial centers allowed the Mayan people to communicate with their gods or ancestors through complicated rituals carried out by the supreme ruler, who was allegedly the only person who had the power to establish such communication.

Domestic units for extended families were distributed around these centers or monumental nuclei. These units were built over stone platforms to avoid floods during the rainy season. The units were basically composed of rooms separated according to their function (sleeping, cooking, or storing) and distributed around a square patio (figure 30). The elite domestic units were generally grouped in elegant residential complexes near the ceremonial centers, and the best lands. The common people had to settle each time a little farther away from the more privileged areas.

In some cases the cities communicated with each other through straight limestone roads, or *sacbeoob* (plate 73), whose function is still a matter of controversy –Was it political, commercial or religious?

The determining factors for the foundation of the cities were the nearby sources of water and fertile soils. But the growth pattern is explained by other sociopolitical and economic factors. Among these we can mention the control over strategic natural resources. As we shall see later, this situation created hierarchical relationships between the sites, in which those located in privileged areas dominated over the others.

At a regional level, the settlement patterns in the Mayan area were complicated and varied with time. It seems that during the first phase of the Classic period the territory was inhabited by autonomous political units –known as provinces by some authors– which were composed of several villages. Some of these provinces maintained their unity because they were governed by members of the same lineage, and others because they depended on a major city such as Tikal and Uaxactún. During the Late Classic, the Mayan golden era, these political units reached a higher level of organization –by their own will, through coercion, or due to alliances– when some

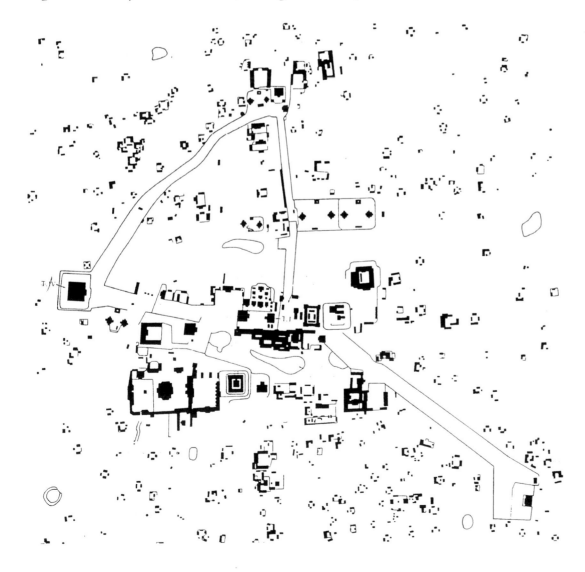

29. Map of Tikal where housing units are shown around the ceremonial center in the absence of any urban planning (adapted from Kubler, 1984).

of the capitals managed to stand out as powerful regional centers whose structure is reflected in the hierarchical settlement pattern. Their importance is revealed through the texts found in monuments, as well as by the size of the settlements, their number, and the quality of the public buildings. There were capital cities or major centers, cities or secondary centers, towns, villages, and hamlets.

The major centers served as capital cities of specific regions or city-states and generally had a particular architectural and artistic style. Through military supremacy and strategic marital alliances among the elite the capital cities managed to establish complete dominion over towns, villages and hamlets. This system of dominance of a handful of powerful centers over weaker ones prevailed throughout much of Mesoamerica.

It is difficult to establish the number of capitals existing in the Mayan area during this time. Hierarchical positions tended to vary in time from one site to the next and a capital could fall in favor of another. However, the most important were: Copán (plates 51-55), in the Central Zone, which functioned as the capital of the southeast region; Tikal[17] (plates 9-14), and its great rival Calakmul (plate 15) were the most powerful centers of central Petén.

Yaxchilán (plates 35-38) dominated the regions of the Usumacinta river and Palenque (plates 19-30) and was the capital of the northwestern region. In the North Zone the situation was different because although Cobá (plates 42-45), Dzibilchaltún, Becán, and toward the end of the period, a group of sites in the Puuc region (plates 64-80) were important, none of them consolidated a real regional state during this period. This occurred until the Post-Classic, around the year 950 A.D., when Chichén Itzá (plates 81-84) consolidated its central power over the Yucatán peninsula.

Progress in the interpretation of texts inscribed on the Mayan monuments of the Classic period has allowed us to begin to understand the political relations between the sites. A clear example is the identification made by Mayan researcher Heinrich Berlin (1958) of some glyphs in many sites in the Central Zone. These consisted in a main sign followed by two smaller elements. Berlin noticed that the latter were relatively constant and that the main sign changed from site to site. From this he suggested that it was the name of the city or of its royal lineage. Now we know that these signs identified the territory controlled by the ruler whose title appeared next to the main sign. Berlin called them «emblem glyphs» (figures 31, 179, 187). Later studies

30. A housing complex at the Colha site, Belize (from *Colha e i maya...*).

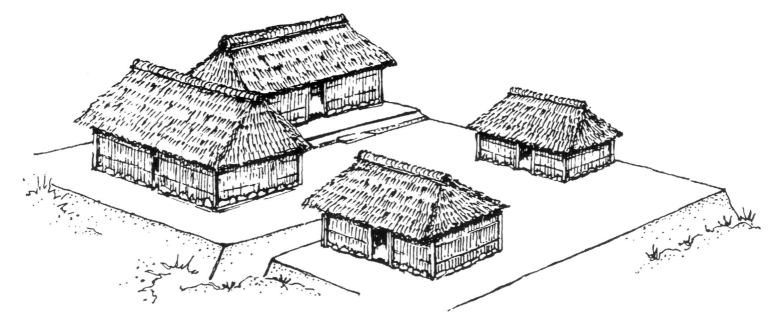

about these glyphs (Martin and Grube, 1995) along with recent iconographic and archaeological research have shown there was indeed a hierarchy of major centers dominating over dependent or weaker centers. For instance:

- At a first glance, emblem glyphs seem to be alike in structure; however, a possessive prefix (*y*) has been discovered in some together with the title of the ruler, which expresses the dominant-subordinate relation among rulers of the different sites. The word *ahau*, «lord or governor», designates the highest rank, and *y-ahau*, «the man who belongs to», was the vassal.
- The texts having to do with enthronements sometimes include a sentence formed by an introductory clause which means the ruler arose to the throne «by mandate» or «under the sponsorship» of a foreign *ahau*, whose emblem glyph and name complete the rest of the phrase. This could imply there were rulers subordinate to more powerful figures, something that had never before been seen (figure 34).
- The great capitals used the glyph «Took the Seat» (figure 32) to indicate that the ruler had been enthroned, in contrast with other glyphs in the subordinate centers, such as the glyph known as «Tooth Ache» (figure 33).
- The Classic iconography sometimes represented the *ahau* of a certain place as the conqueror of other lords or of entire regions.
- There are records of marriages that took place between a royal woman of a capital and the local ruler of a less important center (figures 35, 36); this strengthened ties between dependent centers and the state capital, although sometimes it reverted when the son rebelled to establish his own autonomy. Other documented diplomatic exchanges reveal that some sites controlled weaker ones, acting as intermediaries in their internal affairs. Such is the case of royal visits for funeral or for the enthronement of a local ruler, aimed at assuring political power over the successor (figure 37).

The political situation was always quite unstable. Secondary or dependent centers rebelled frequently. In the Puuc regions of northern Yucatán there was a time when a confederation of villages was constituted in the region of Río de la Pasión, in the central Petén. These villages were intimately related because they were governed by members of the same lineage. Recent research has revealed that those villages depended on the great regional state dominated by Tikal, and that later they were organized into the Petexbatún Confederation formed by Aguateca, Tamarindito, Dos

PALENQUE

CALAKMUL?

YAXCHILÁN

COPÁN

TIKAL

31. Some Emblem Glyphs of the major Mayan cities (drawing by R. Pérez Enríquez).

32. Two examples of the glyph «He Seated Himself» indicating the enthronement of a ruler in an important center (from Marcus, 1992).

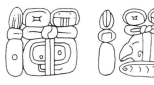

33. The glyph «Toothache» showed the enthronement of a ruler in a secondary center (from Marcus, 1992).

34. The glyph u-kahiy, «made by him», indicates the intervention of a ruler of a major center in the enthronement of a lord in a secondary center (from Martin and Grube, 1995).

Pilas, La Amelia, and Seibal. Together they later obtained their independence from Tikal, but power struggles weakened them and Seibal took over, establishing itself as the capital at the end of the Classic period. States would disintegrate and later reconsolidate.

It is very possible that most of the wars of the Classic period (figure 39) were fought among subservient centers or against the regional capital. There is little evidence of wars between state capitals except for the documented wars between Tikal and Calakmul (if the identification of this city with the emblem glyph «serpent-head» is correct), who fought for centuries. Calakmul once defeated Tikal, a much celebrated event, as the monuments of the victorious city show. Wars allowed dependent centers to reach higher levels of political influence. Seibal, for instance, became one of the most powerful centers in the Lowlands.

As we mentioned before, it is very difficult to determine the number of regional states during the second phase of the Classic period[18] (figure 41). According to the information on a stele in Copán from the year 731 A.D., the four major capitals of the Mayan world at the time were: Copán, Tikal, Calakmul (?) and Palenque. Martin and Grube referred to them as «superstates». This four-way organization, in which each capital corresponded to a direction of the universe, was due fundamentally to their world-view: each of the four capitals represented the most powerful city on each of the quadrants of the Mayan world according to the vision of the ruler of Copán, who ordered the erection of this stele. Some researchers believe there were five regional states in the Late Classic because they include Yaxchilán as a regional capital in the Central Zone. Based on the distribution of particular architectural styles, some researchers believe there were 15 to 17 regions or city-states in the Low Lands, each with a large urban center or capital.

To this day the limits of power for each regional state have not been clearly defined and therefore the original hierarchy of the sites cannot be determined.[19]

## Social and Economic Organization

The basic unit of Mayan society was an extended family whose members lived in housing compounds, as mentioned earlier, where they shared daily activities. The housing complexes formed groups of families that were related to each other because they belonged to a same lineage and venerated a common ancestor.

Daily activities were divided among the domestic group by gender and age. So, for example, women were in charge of weaving the family clothes, preparing the nixtamal (corn meal for *tortillas*); they ground the corn, cooked and made the kitchen ceramic pieces. The women and children took care of the animals —turkeys, dogs, pidgeons— mostly used as food. Others were used to satisfy other needs; bees for honey and wax, and cochineal wood louse for its deep red pigment.

Men were in charge of agricultural and farming activities, hunting, fishing and gathering. They also made their own work tools and instruments. Some researchers like Sanders believe that the housing compounds were practically self-sufficient,[20] and although there may have been specialized artisans (lapidaries, potters, etc.), they did not work full-time.

Evidence of small orchards, cared of by the women and children, was found in many sites near the housing areas. They produced vegetables, fruits, flowers, medicinal plants, and spices. However, with time these orchards proved to be insufficient to feed a growing population. To satisfy the increasing demand for food they created sophisticated agricultural systems. They cultivated vast extensions of jungle using a «knock over and burn» system (extensive agriculture); they benefited by the swamps near rivers by building raised fields, much like the *chinampas* in Central Mexico. They also built stonewalled terraces to avoid landslides that could damage their crops (intensive agriculture).[21]

The construction and maintenance of dams, canals, and other irrigation systems for intensive farming implied massive and complicated work that was directed and managed by the state. Undoubtedly, the control over water gave the ruling elite enormous power.

Through these agricultural systems the inhabitants of the Mayan area had access to a great variety of foods that the paleobotanists have identified through analysis of the soil's organic content. Their studies indicate that besides the Mesoamerican basic crops, such as maize (*Zea mays*), beans (*Phaseolus vulgaris*), chile (*Capiscum spp.*), squash (*Cucurbita sp.*), and tomato (*Physalis sp.*), the Mayas ate cacao beans (*Theobroma cacao*) (figure 42), *achiote* (*Bixia orellana*), amaranth (*Amaranthus spp.*) and browse (*Brosimum alicastrum*); roots such as cassava (*Manihot esculenta*), *jícama* (*Pachyrrhizus erosus*), and sweet potato (*Ipomea batatas*); and fruits, including vanilla (*Vainilla fragrans*), *chayote* (*Sechium edule*), avocado (*Persea orellana*), sapodilla (*Maniklara zapota*), anonas (*Anona reticulata*), soursop (*Anona muricata*), cherimoy (*Anona cherimola*), plum (*Spondias sp.*), guava (*Psidium guajava*), mammee (*Pouteria zapota*), prickly-pear (*Opuntia sp.*), papaya (*Carica papaya*), and pineapple

35. These two steles at El Perú, Guatemala represent the lord of the city (left) and his wife (right), a Lady from Calakmul, Campeche. She was probably the sister of «Jaguar's Claw», ruler of Mexico's powerful center. 692 A.D. Late Classic (from Marcus, 1992).

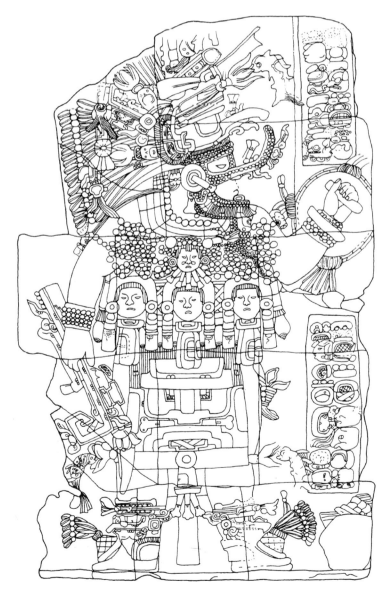

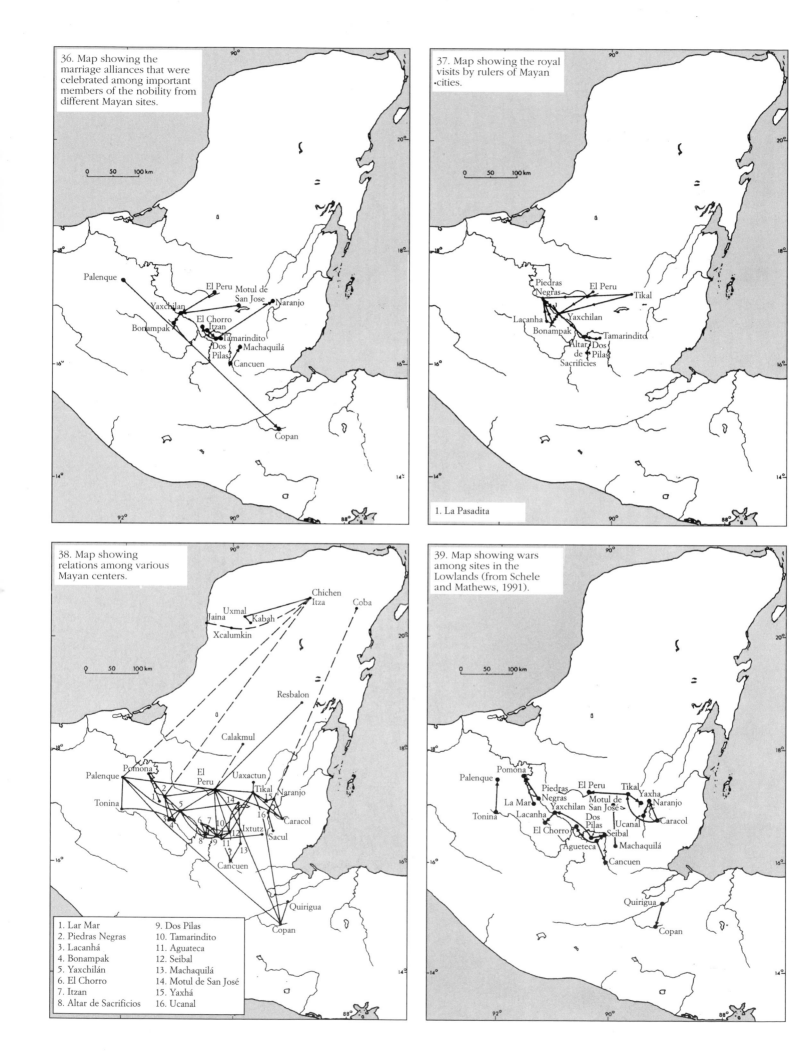

36. Map showing the marriage alliances that were celebrated among important members of the nobility from different Mayan sites.

Palenque
El Peru
Motul de San Jose
Yaxchilan
Naranjo
El Chorro
Itzan
Bonampak
Tamarindito
Dos Pilas
Machaquilá
Cancuen
Copan

0  50  100 km

37. Map showing the royal visits by rulers of Mayan cities.

Piedras Negras
El Peru
Tikal
Lacanha
Yaxchilan
Bonampak
Tamarindito
Altar de Sacrificies
Dos Pilas

0  50  100 km

1. La Pasadita

38. Map showing relations among various Mayan centers.

Chichen Itza
Coba
Uxmal
Jaina
Kabah
Xcalumkin
Resbalon
Calakmul
Pomona
El Peru
Uaxactun
Palenque
Tikal
Naranjo
Tonina
Caracol
Ixtutz
Sacul
Cancuen
Quirigua
Copan

0  50  100 km

1. Lar Mar
2. Piedras Negras
3. Lacanhá
4. Bonampak
5. Yaxchilán
6. El Chorro
7. Itzan
8. Altar de Sacrificios
9. Dos Pilas
10. Tamarindito
11. Aguateca
12. Seibal
13. Machaquilá
14. Motul de San José
15. Yaxhá
16. Ucanal

39. Map showing wars among sites in the Lowlands (from Schele and Mathews, 1991).

Palenque
Pomona
Piedras Negras
El Peru
Tikal
Yaxha
La Mar
Motul de San José
Naranjo
Tonina
Lacanha
Yaxchilan
Ucanal
Dos Pilas
Caracol
El Chorro
Seibal
Agueteca
Machaquilá
Cancuen
Quirigua
Copan

0  50  100 km

1. Cerros site, in Belize, viewed from the Caribbean.

2. One of the temples at Cerros.

3. Diagram of monumental structures of the Cerros site northern zone.

4. Structures in Uaxactún, Guatemala.

5-6. Maps of the main monumental complexes in Uaxactún.

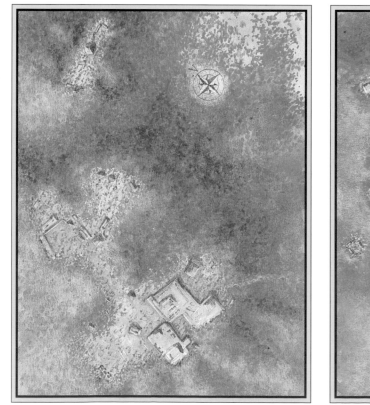

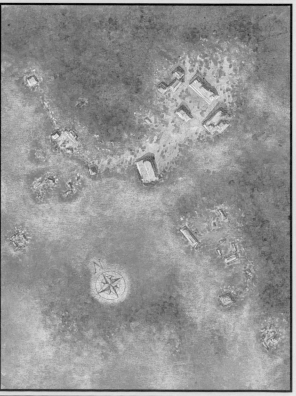

7. View of Uaxactún. Structure
E VIIsub, on the right.

8. Reconstruction of Structure
E VIIsub, based on an etching
by T. Proskouriakoff.

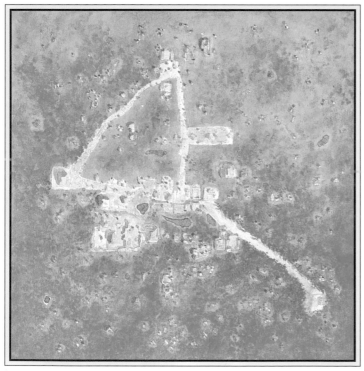

9. Aerial view of Tikal, Guatemala. Temples I and II of the Central Acropolis can be seen.

10. Map of Tikal.

11. Summits of the temples of Tikal in the Petén jungle.

*front page*:
12. Temple II, Tikal. Temples III (*left*) and IV (*right*).

13. Central Acropolis at Tikal.

# CALAKMUL

*previous pages*:
14. The plaza of Tikal, with
Temple I, the Great Jaguar.

15. Map of Calakmul, Campeche.

16. View of adornments on the
Toniná Acropolis, in Chiapas.

17. Map of Toniná.

18. A temple at Toniná.

# PALENQUE

22. The Temple of the Inscriptions.

23. Map of the central area of Palenque.

*front page*:
19. The Palace of Palenque, Chiapas.

20. Engraving that shows D. Charnay's "kitchen" in one of the buildings at Palenque.

21. Detail of one of the Palace buildings.

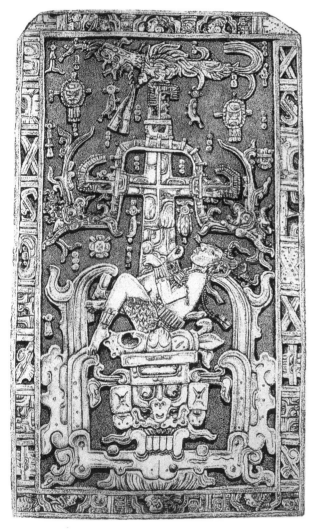

24. The Temple of the Inscriptions.

25. The gravestone on the tomb of Pacal II.

26. Side view of the Temple of the Inscriptions.

27. Temple of the Cross.

28. The Temple of the Foliated Cross.

*front page*:
29. Temple of the Sun.

30. General view of the Group of the Crosses.

31. Temple I at Comalcalco, Tabasco.

32. Map of Comalcalco.

33. Another view of the Temple at Comalcalco. Note the use of brick.

34. The top part of a building at Comalcalco.

# YAXCHILÁN

35. View of the Usumacinta River.

36. One of the temples at Yaxchilán, Chiapas.

37. The Yaxchilán Plaza. The ball court can be viewed in the background.

38. Map of Yaxchilán, on the banks of the Usumacinta River.

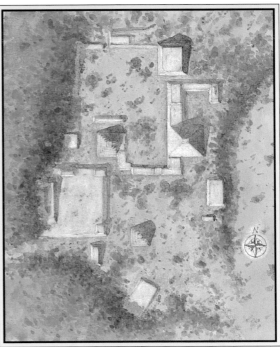

39. A-3 Building at Seibal, Guatemala.

40. Stele 10 at Seibal.

41. Map of Seibal.

42. View of the Nohoch Mul pyramid in Cobá, Quintana Roo.

43. Detail of the stairway of Structure I of the Cobá Group.

*front page*:
44. Structure I of the Cobá Group, also known as the Temple of the Churches.

45. Map of the Cobá Group, one of the sets of buildings that form the archaeological area of Cobá.

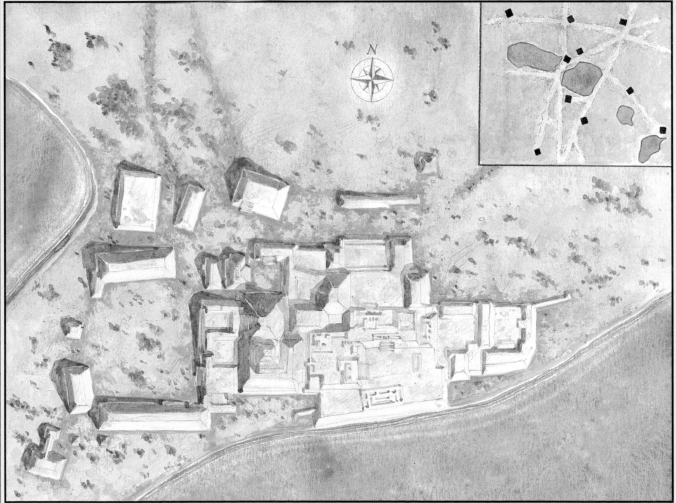

# LAMANAI

46. Pyramid of Lamanai, Belize.

47. Map of Lamanai.

48. Structure N10-43 of Lamanai, with mask friezes at the side.

*front page*:
49. View of structure A-6 at Xunantunich, Belize, also known as Benque Viejo.

50. Structure A-6 at Xunantunich with mask friezes.

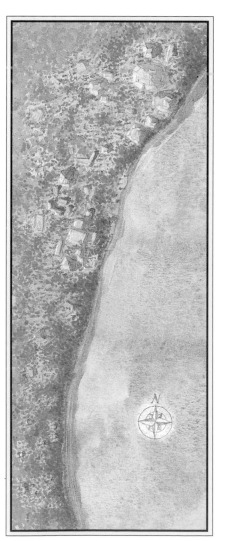

# COPÁN

51. Building at Copán, Honduras.

52. Map of Copán.

*front page*:
53. Hieroglyph stairway at Copán.

*next pages*:
54. Ball Court A-III and Copán's Great Plaza.

55. Detail of sculpture in Copán.

56. Structure I of Xpuhil,
Quintana Roo.

57. Map showing the location
of the Río Bec sites.

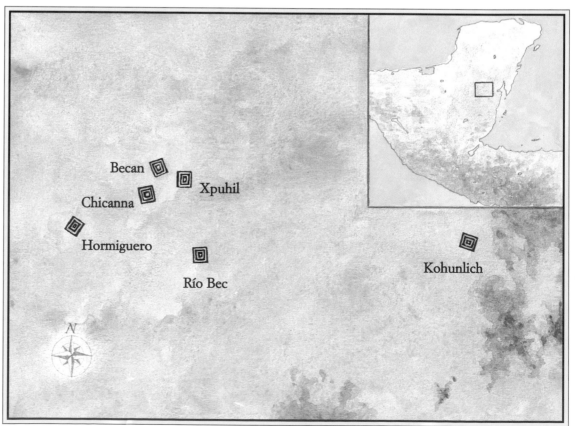

Becan

Chicanna

Xpuhil

Hormiguero

Río Bec

Kohunlich

58. Temple with zoomorphic façade, at Hormiguero, Campeche.

59. Structure at Kohunlich, Quintana Roo.

*next pages*:
60. Zoomorphic façade at Chicanná, Campeche.

# EDZNÁ

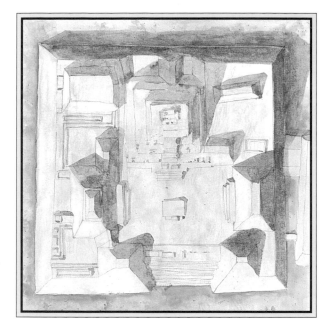

61. Building at Edzná, Campeche.

62. Map of Edzná Acropolis.

63. Monumental center of Edzná.

64. Palace of the Governor of Uxmal, Yucatán.

65. Map of Uxmal (drawing by Martinelli).

*front page*:
66. Temple of the Turtles, Uxmal.

67. Pyramid of the Fortuneteller, Uxmal.

68. One of the buildings at the Quadrangle of the Nuns.

69. View of the Quadrangle of the Nuns.

*next pages*:
70. The monumental center of Uxmal with the Pyramid of the Fortuneteller, the Quadrangle of the Nuns, and the Ball Court.

71. The façade of a building in the Quadrangle of the Nuns.

# LABNÁ

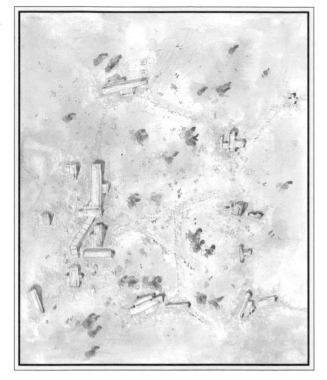

72. Map of Labná, Yucatán.

73. The *sacbé* of Labná.

74. The Arch of Labná.

# SAYIL

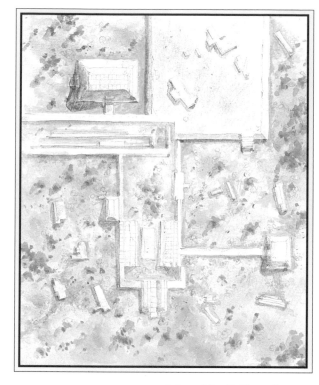

75. Map of Sayil, Yucatán.

76. Detail of the façade of Sayil Palace.

# KABAH

77. Façade of Codz Pop in
Kabah, Yucatán.

78. The Arch of Kabah.

79. Map of Kabah.

*front page*:
80. Detail of a mask frieze of
the Codz Pop.

# CHICHÉN ITZÁ

81. The Church of Chichén Itzá, Yucatán.

82. Map of Chichén Itzá.

*front page*:
83. El Caracol, at Chichén Itzá.

84. The Sacred Cenote of Chichén Itzá.

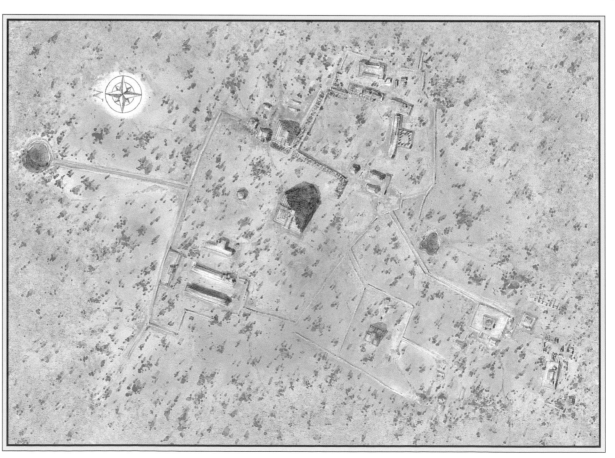

85. Xlapac building, Yucatán.

86. Another view of the same building.

(*Ananas comosus*), among others. In view of their economic importance, it is very likely that products such as cacao, cotton (*Gossypium hirsutum*), and tobacco (*Nicotiana tabacum*) were grown following special procedures within plantations located in restricted areas, for their cultivation requires specific conditions.

The animals most commonly hunted by the Mayas to complete their diet were deer, tepezcuintle, and peccary. They also caught and ate rabbits, monkeys, armadillos, quail, pheasants, wild turkeys, iguanas, frogs, turtles, etc. A very important part of their food intake consisted in marine resources such as fish and seafood, as well as fresh-water mollusks.

The Mayas carried out their productive activities with a very simple technology, using tools and weapons made out of cut and polished stone, wood, and bone. These included granite, basalt, rhyolite and flint projectile heads, axes, knives, chisels, mallets, drum-sticks, and mortars (figures 43, 44, 45, 46); obsidian razors and arrowheads; hoes, planting rods, and possibly blow guns made with hard rainforest wood such as mahogany (*Swietenia macrophyla*), sapodilla (*Maniklara zapota*), and ceiba (*Ceiba petandra*); deer horn or bone drills. Notwithstanding this basic set of tools the achievements of the Mayas were outstanding, thanks to a strict social organization of labor which compensated for the lack of more sophisticated instruments or draft animals.

As mentioned above, the proximity to, as well as the adequate exploitation and administration of strategic resources were key factors in the growth and greater development of certain cities in the Mayan area. These resources possibly included raw materials such as salt, sea-shells and conches, obsidian, rhyolite, flint, granite, basalt, serpentine, jade and jadeite, used in making utensils, tools and luxury objects. Important also was the existence of soils apt for the specialized cultivation of cotton and cacao, as well as the accessibility of maritime, fluvial, and terrestrial communication routes, since interregional

40. Glyph meaning «war» formed by a shield and a flint knife on top of the sign «earth» (from Marcus, 1992).

41. Two hypothetical reconstructions of the political organization of the Mayan Lowlands during the Late Classic. On the left is R. Adams' proposal and P. Mathews' on the right (from Mathews, 1991).

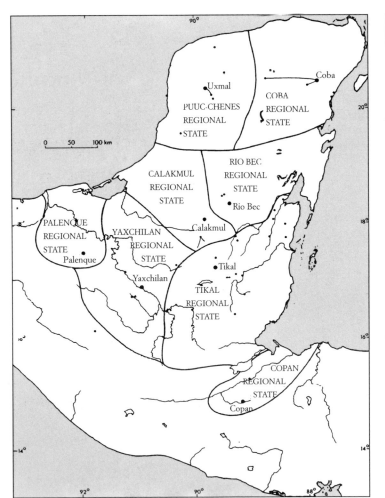

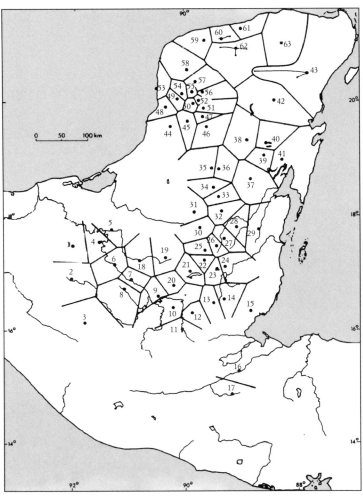

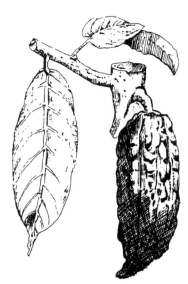

42. The cacao.

43. Stone metate and *mano* or grinding stone (from Willey, 1966).

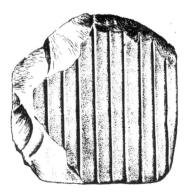

44. Instrument for crushing bark in paper production (from Willey, 1966).

and long-distance trade of the above mentioned raw materials, and the products made with them, was the main cohesive factor among the great capitals of the Classic. Goods circulated in two ways: by means of a barter system –trading salt for honey, for example– or through payment with goods that, having a pre-established value, were used as money –cacao beans, cotton cloth, or oyster-shells.

Benavides (1995a), for example, mentions that the confluence of rivers that communicate two shores, the flood lands apt for intensive farming, and the flint deposits located in the hilly area of Tikal, were natural resources administered for the benefit of this great capital's development. Río Azul, who for some time formed part of the territory dominated by Tikal, prospered more than other secondary centers due to its role in protecting the important Azul and Hondo rivers' trade route. It is probable that the importance of Caracol had to do with the fact that it profited from its easy access to flint stone deposits while controlling the production and distribution of basalt objects such as *metates*, axes, and chisels. Lubaantún was founded during the Late Classic as an administrative center for the regional production of cacao; Altún Ha distributed the high-quality flint instruments made in the workshops of Colhá (figure 46); Yaxchilán, after being a subject to the state of Tikal, became a capital of great relevance when it took over control of commercial traffic along the Usumacinta from its strategic location. It is most likely that Palenque exerted economical and political control over neighboring cacao producing centers such as Tortuguero and Comalcalco; while in the Motagua river basin Copán dominated for a long period of time over Quiriguá and other minor centers in the region thanks to its control of the trade route along this river, taking over the distribution of the highly valued metamorphic rocks found there, and which included jadeite, serpentine, and a most esteemed apple-green jade. In the Highlands, Kaminaljuyú was a site that during the Early Classic profited from the ecological diversity of the surrounding area by controlling the exchange of a great variety of resources available in territories relatively near but quite different from each other. Moreover, thanks to its geographical location, this center controlled access to resources from nearby mountains, coasts, and valleys, establishing thus its dominion over the South Zone while at the same time providing the Lowlands with products such as cacao, obsidian, jadeite, cinnabar, hematite, leather, feathers, fish, shells, snails, etc.[22] Products and ideas were imported to many cities in the Mayan area through this important center, a center which was instrumental in spreading Teotihuacan commerce and ideology.

Besides the importance of war on the political and ideological level, it is evident that it played a fundamental role in the economy. On the one hand, the resulting encroachment upon resources and the tribute extracted from the conquered area increased the wealth of the victor; on the other hand, a great majority of the captured prisoners ended up working as servants in the palaces of the nobles, or as farmhands, public workers, or slaves. As is common in other agriculturally-oriented societies, the season most often preferred by the Maya for warring was the dry season (Winter), which helped them avoid leaving the land empty of workers during the time dedicated to planting and sowing. And of course, the economical objective of war was always veiled with ideological propaganda advocating war as a means of taking prisoners which would be offered in sacrifice to the gods.

## Social Classes and Political Propaganda

As any other civilization, the Maya constituted a complex society hierarchically organized. Two endogamous layers can be distinguished within it: the upper level included the nobility, while the inferior encompassed the plebeian or common people. Each of these groups was similarly divided in hierarchies according to family ties and to the occupation of each individual, factors which determined access to wealth and services.

The highest level of Mayan society was occupied by the dynastic elite, which was composed by the supreme ruler (the *ahau*, a hereditary title) along with the main branch of his family. The *ahau* held complete political, economic, and religious power, and ruled over the whole region from his residence in the capital city. His political authority was absolute, his right over the wealth obtained through the work of the community, and his role as universal distributor of goods, reflected his power over the economy; and his position in the religious system was fundamental, since he had to guarantee the continuity of order within his world through a series of complex rituals. In the Mayan world the *ahau* was likened to the Sun, and the dynastic succession to the solar cycle; the new ahau was compared to the rising Sun, while the deceased ancestor represented the Sun of dusk in its descent into the netherworld.

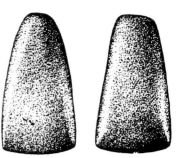

45. Two stone axes (from Morley, Brainerd and Sharer, 1983).

Other members of the superior stratum were the rulers of dependent cities or secondary centers, who had to belong to the royal lineage and be subordinates to the *ahau*; the political and religious city officials (bureaucrats, priests, war chiefs), and just below them, the full-time specialists such as long-distance tradesmen, diviners, scribes, architects, artists, and artisans, whose occupations allowed them to separate themselves from the peasantry and, in many cases, to enjoy enormous privileges within the court. Members of this social class lived in housing complexes surrounding the monumental centers where the *ahau* and the royal family had their residence. Gradually, this sector of society began to acquire greater power, to the point that in some cases they managed to bring about the downfall of entire ruling dynasties.

At the lowest level of the social scale were the plebeians –the productive sector of society, composed of peasants, manual laborers, stevedores, and slaves, who occupied modest living quarters at the periphery of the sites. The plebeians were required to pay in kind for the support of the nobles, and in services for the construction of buildings and public works.

To ensure their permanence as the class in power, the aristocracy developed

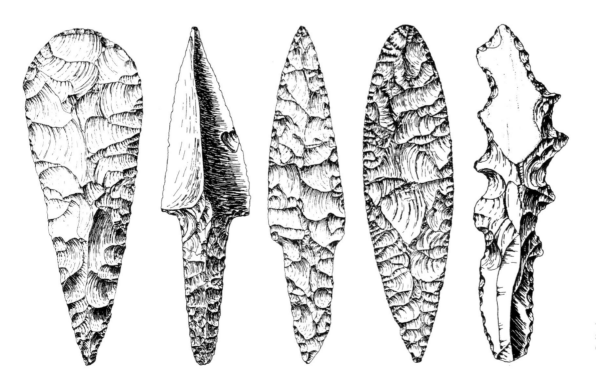

46. An axe, three spear points and a flint eccentric from Colha, Belize (from *Colha e i maya...*).

47. Throne shaped like a jaguar. Detail from Stele 20 at Tikal, 751 A.D., Late Classic (from Marcus, 1992).

certain mechanisms aimed at reinforcing the social differences between them and the plebeians. For example, they reserved for themselves the use of writing and esoteric knowledge, while conveniently keeping the rest of society in ignorance. They manipulated the calendar, determining which days were the most or least favorable according to the social level to which one belonged. But the most effective social innovation of the Classic period, the one that deepened the gap between the people and the aristocracy, was the institution of the ruling dynasties (or lordly regimes based on lineage), established with all certainty in the year 292 A.D. in Tikal, but whose deepest roots may be traced back to maybe a century before this date. With this political system the social differences which since the previous period had been exacerbated were finally declared not only legitimate, but necessary and intrinsic to the order of the cosmos, since the ahau had the divine right to govern, a right inherited directly from his real or mythical ancestors. His absolute power, inherited from father to son, guaranteed a social order in which the subjects accepted unquestioningly their complete submission.

Nevertheless this institution nurtured within itself the seeds of its own destruction. Since it was a system strictly dependent on rules for succession, the moment came when difficulties arose in the process of the transference of power among the generations belonging to the royal lineage. When a dynasty came to an end and the following ruler was unable to legitimize his position, the community abandoned the place, ritually burning the masks of its gods and ancestors, «killing» the objects so as to suppress the power accumulated in them, covering the monuments with lime, and returning to its previous, more rustic, way of life.

Many early dynasties failed and fell, but the institution itself lived on for centuries thanks to the political propaganda put into circulation by the elite through art, the calendar, and writing, which in the Mayan zone reached a complexity and splendor unmatched in other parts of Mesoamerica where royal lineage systems were not in use.[23] Progress in Mayan epigraphy has revealed that the texts contained in the steles and in other monuments reflect the intent of the rulers of emphasizing their genealogy as a means of legitimization, and to demonstrate that historical events were the inevitable result of cosmic and divine necessity.

The *ahau*, with the support of the clergy and of the whole governmental apparatus, had to be very skillful in order to validate his divine ascendancy, and produce convincing proofs of his blood-ties with the deified ancestor who had founded his royal lineage, since dynastic power as well as his right to rule depended on this.

The deities transmitted their instructions to the people only through the *ahau*. For this reason a way in which he could legitimize his genealogy was by carrying out

48. Decoration on a polychrome vessel found in Burial 196 at Tikal, Late Classic. The scene portrays two noblemen before the *ahau* (from W. Coe, 1977).

periodical rituals to establish communication with his divine ancestors. A fundamental ingredient of these rituals was the ritual self-sacrifice by blood-letting practiced by the *ahau* himself (figure 53) and other members of the royal family, such as wives or mothers (figure 101; plate 99). Blood was offered to the gods, since this was the necessary means by which one could communicate with them. This ritual was enacted by the royalty to commemorate the 5th or 25th anniversary of the *ahau*'s enthronement; to celebrate the birth of a heir, or the 20th anniversary of the death of an ancestor.

49. The glyph of a Tikal ruler's name: Jaguar's Claw (from Marcus, 1992).

Another way of establishing a bond with a divine ancestor consisted in manipulating the calendar in order to artificially make an important event in the life of the *ahau* –the date of birth, of enthronement, or of the inauguration of a building commissioned by him– coincide with the anniversary of some event in which his mythical ancestors had taken part. The most surprising case has to do with the triad of temples in Palenque –the Temple of the Sun, the Temple of the Cross, and the Temple of the Foliated Cross (plates 27-30). The construction of these three splendid edifices (among the most beautiful in the Mayan area) was ordained by *ahau* Chan Bahlum, the son of Pacal. In each of the temples there's an inscription that refers to the birth of three individuals whose mother was 754 years old the moment she gave birth to them. This event had taken place 3000 years before the inauguration of the temples. It is most likely that the intention of the *ahau* in commemorating the birth of these characters in such a spectacular fashion was to prove that they were the deified mythical ancestors from whom the rulers of Palenque (i.e. him and his father) claimed to descend.[24] The ahau had in his favor the fact that nobody questioned his word, and that everybody would believe, if he so affirmed, that he was in fact the descendant of a divine being who had lived 3000 years ago.

The dynastic history of the sites was registered on the objects and monuments of the whole Mayan area.[25] But the rulers also used hieroglyphic writing to refer their own personal histories, leaving written constancy of their bond with the founding ancestors of the royal lineage, and of the most important events in which they participated –their enthronement, the acquisition of honorary titles, the expansion of their territories, and their victories in war. Propaganda, myth, and history were inextricably combined in the Mayan inscriptions.

Even though only the nobles were able to read, the texts inscribed on the monuments were almost always brief, and what astonishing, both for the literate as for the illiterate, were the sculpted or painted scenes, in many of which were represented events such as the transmission of power, the consecration of a heir, rites of self-sacrifice, or images of prisoners subjected by the ahau, whose message could be understood immediately by anyone. This was due to the employment of certain icono-

50. A further scene painted on a vessel from Burial 196 at Tikal. The *ahau* is sitting on a throne covered with a jaguar's skin (from W. Coe, 1977).

graphic conventions that could be identified as emblems of power by the whole community, even if the majority could not understand their real meaning: the *ahau* sat on the «Jaguar's Matting», an expression incorporated to plain language and which meant that he occupied the highest level in society, that of the supreme ruler. The other nobles and lords also «sat on the matting» to indicate their political position, but only the ahau's was made of jaguar skin, and was thus represented in the Mayan plastic arts (figures 47, 50). The supreme ruler was the only one to carry the ceremonial band or manikin scepter with the representation of the God K, symbol of sovereignty (figure 51). There were certain iconographic conventions used to identify political acts such as the transference of power —in some cases the image of the successor is larger than the *ahau*'s who is transferring the political office. Or the dead ruler, or some close relative of his, is represented in the symbolic act of handing over the paraphernalia of power to the successor. The people could confirm that their su-

51. Stele 4 at Machaquilá, Guatemala on which a ruler is seen carrying a scepter-manikin (drawing by I. Graham, from Schobinger, 1994).

52. The Oval Slab from the Palace of Palenque. Lady Sak-K'uk' delivers the power insignia to her son Pacal II, who is sitting on a double jaguar throne. 652 A.D. Late Classic (from Schobinger, 1994).

preme ruler descended from the divine lineage just by looking at certain images on the monuments, especially those in which the ancestors appeared in the same scene next to the ahau and other members of the royal family. Sometimes these supernatural beings can be seen as small figures flying on the top section of the monuments. In other places the ancestors were outlined with circles that seem like blood drops, implying their consanguinity with the members of the royal family that appear in the scene (figure 54). These beings were also represented as characters materializing themselves in front of the ahau –or in front of his mother or wife (figure 101; plate 98), who could also invoke them through the blood self-sacrifice– after emerging from the jaws of a fantastic serpent, which was the Mayan style for representing the appearance in the world of a being that inhabited another world.

53. The Lintel 2 at La Pasadita, Guatemala. The scene portrays the lord of Yaxchilán «Bird-Jaguar» who is performing the self-sacrifice before his *cahal*, the manager of the Guatemalan site where the ritual took place. 766 A.D., Late Classic (from Schele and Miller, 1986).

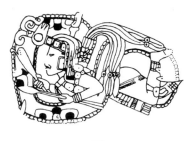

54. Images of ancestors framed by dotted lines carved on the upper part of Stele 4 at Ucanal, 849 A.D., as well as on Stele 1 at Jimbal, Late Classic (from Marcus, 1992).

Towards the year 800 the splendorous cities of the Mayan Central Zone began their decline. The great regional states started to dissolve into less centralized political units, and some secondary centers tried to consolidate in power their own royal lineages. Other steles in other places mention new centers of power, closer to each other, with smaller territories, and populations ruled independently of each other. The area of the regional states shrank gradually until the latter disappeared, some forever, others with brief revivals. Such would be the case of the Petexbatún Confederation, who after intense warring among its members began to consolidate into a regional state with Seibal (plates 39-41) as its capital, and possibly with the participation of Putún groups from the Gulf Coast.[26]

While in a great part of the Central Zone the rulers suspended the erection of steles, the construction projects ceased or whole cities were abandoned. In the North Zone a number of sites of the east coast and the Puuc region of northern Yucatán flourished, such as Kabah (plates 77-80), Uxmal (plates 64-71), or Sayil (plates 75, 76), which began to compete for power over the region.

But why the collapse of the Central Zone? Despite the great number of hypothesis advanced to explain the phenomenon, none has done so altogether satisfactorily, maybe because it has been visualized as a process which occurred violently and rapidly throughout the region, and furthermore because it has been attributed to sole causes. Now we know that this is not true: some cities were completely abandoned after the destruction of the monuments of the ceremonial centers, but others were not, and the reasons that could explain the phenomenon in certain places cannot be applied to others. Furthermore, if we analyze the historical development not only of the Southern Lowlands but taking into consideration at the same time the North Zone as part of the Mayan area —as indeed it was—, we will note that the same history repeats itself in different moments. For a few centuries some sites of the Central Zone had the power and political ability to put under their dominion great expanses of territory, and we have seen that this was done through a powerful governmental institution based on dynastic succession. When this system collapsed the great regional capitals fell and the sites were eventually abandoned. This power vacuum was counterbalanced in time by attempts at regional integration in the Northern Lowlands, where splendid city-states such as Uxmal flourished. Mayan culture did not disappear, and proof of this is the refinement it achieved during the 9th century in sites such as this.

55. Altar Q from Copán. The altar portrays the rulers of the city. Yax-K'uk'-Mo', the founder of the dynasty is seen in the scene bestowing the power onto the last lord of the dynasty, Yax-Pac. 763 A.D. (from Marcus, 1992).

Now the fall of the dynastic regime in the Central Zone was due most certainly to diverse causes and not only to one. What is more, everything indicates that in each site the conditions were very different. Among the factors most frequently adduced is the uncommon increase of the non-productive population for a great part of the region during the Late Classic. This fact implied a great demand of food, which the peasants had to meet in some form or another. It has been discovered that in some places the Mayas exhausted the productive capacity of the soil when they significantly shortened the periods of rest between sowing, and degraded the ecosystem with deforestation and the consequent erosion of great extensions of land. In other cases the practice of intensive systems caused the salification of the land, thus making them unproductive. On the other hand, the population growth of the nobility and its each day greater power drove the peasants away from their lands since they were required for their services in the palaces and lands of the aristocracy. The gap separating peasants from nobles widened each day more, the taxes paid by the former were enormous, and undoubtedly there came a moment when they rebelled and destroyed the urban centers where the power of the *ahau* was concentrated. In some cases, after overthrowing the ruling class, the people continued to live in the place for a long period of time before abandoning it altogether, as happened in Copán.

The generalized state of war in the region weakened the political system. Apart from the peasant revolts there were constant wars among sites for large territories, for

56. Images of prisoners carved on the bottom part of some steles at Naranjo, Guatemala, Late Classic (from Marcus, 1992).

57. Lintel 1 at La Pasadita, Guatemala. The figure on the right is Bird-Jaguar from Yaxchilán, who is grabbing a prisoner of war in a submissive attitude. The *cabal* of La Pasadita, subordinate to the lord of Yaxchilán, is watching the scene. 759 A.D. Late Classic (from Marcus, 1992).

gaining control over strategic resources, or for gaining independence from a capital. Many rulers were taken prisoners and sacrificed. In other cases whole dynasties fell and their thrones were occupied by usurpers.

The combination of these and other factors brought about the decline of the dynastic regime en the Central Zone, a fall which was irreversible. This did not mean only the disappearance of the hereditary political offices, but of a whole ideological system implemented for the perpetuation in power of the ahau, a system which gave rise to an exceptional culture. The cultural nucleus shifted towards the north, but in the Southern Lowlands the decline was permanent, and Mayan civilization came to a close officially towards the year 910 with the last declaration of the rulers of the Classic inscribed on a monument at Itzimté.

Notes

[1] Since its publication these documents have been an invaluable source of information for the researcher on Mayan culture. Most prominent among them are the accounts of the conquistador Bernal Díaz del Castillo contained in his famous *Historia Verdadera de la Conquista de la Nueva España*; the *Cartas de Relación* by Hernán Cortés, written to the emperor Charles V between 1519 and 1526; the *Carta de Relación* by the magistrate Diego García de Palacio to the king of Spain (written in 1576 but not published until 1860); and of course, the work of Fra Diego de Landa titled *Relación de las Cosas de Yucatán* (1566).

[2] These books were: *Incidents of Travel in Central America, Chiapas and Yucatán*, 2 vols.; and *Incidents of Travel in Yucatán*, 2 vols., published for the first time in New York in 1841 and 1843 respectively.

[3] *Incidents of Travel in Central America...*, vol. 2, p. 442, New York, 1962.

[4] The best known works by these authors, and which synthesize their theoretical model on Mayan civilization, are: *The Ancient Maya* by Sylvanus G. Morley, published in 1946; *The Civilization of the Mayas* (1927), and *The Rise and Fall of Maya Civilization* (1954) by J. Eric S. Thompson.

[5] A magnificent comparative study between the traditional model and the new perspective on the Mayan world is Sabloff's in *The New Archaeology...* (1994).

[6] The discovery of the historical nature of some of the inscriptions and important progress in linguistics that has allowed the decipherment of a great number of glyphs has been possible thanks to the investigations of Heinrich Berlin (who in 1958 identified the emblem glyphs) and Tatiana Proskouriakoff (who in 1960 published her discovery of the historical content of the inscriptions she had studied at Piedras Negras and Yaxchilán, in which dynastic successions had been registered).

[7] For a more thorough discussion on this subject, refer to J. Marcus, «Lowland Maya Archaeology...», (1983), where the author analyzes with great clarity the cyclic return to old postulates.

[8] See *Arqueología. Memoria e Identidad*, 1993; *Proyectos Especiales de Arqueología Mexicana*, 1993; *Arqueología Mexicana*, vol. II, no. 10, 1994.

[9] Nalda, E., Luz E. Campaña and Javier López Camacho, *Arqueología Mexicana*, vol. II, no. 10, 1994, p. 14.

[10] Although the dates inscribed on this monuments very clearly mark the limits of the Classic, to simplify the organization of the literature some authors register the begining in the year 250, and others in 300 A.D., while the year 900 A.D. has been generally accepted to indicate the end of the period.

[11] A transcendental change, not yet thoroughly explained, began towards the year 534 A.D. when the carving of inscriptions and the construction of monuments were temporarily suspended. This hiatus was archaeologically registered in Tikal, and some authors explain it as a result of the terrible defeat suffered by this great regional capital after six years of war with Caracol. Years later this event was registered in the inscriptions of this latter site, the victor. Other researchers have suggested that the crisis or hiatus was due to the as yet unexplained interruption of commerce between Teotihuacan and the south and central regions of the Mayan territory.

[12] In the last decades important archaeological projects have been carried out in order to better understand the Pre-Classic period in the Mayan area. Most important have been: the Cerros project directed by David Freidel and Robin Robertson of the Southern Methodist University between 1974 and 1981; the

Lamanai project directed by David Pendergast of the Royal Ontario Museum in the decades of 1970 and 1980, a period in which research was also carried out in Cuello under the direction of Norman Hammond of the University of Boston.

[13] Not long ago Norman Hammond of the University of Boston reported the finding of a ceramic phase in Cuello, Belize, known as Swasey phase, which was dated in 2500 A.D. by radiocarbon, and which would suppose a very unlikely antiquity for the beginning of village life in the Central Zone. Later studies have given this ceramic a later date, 1000 and 800 B.C., that is at the beginning of the Middle Pre-Classic. What is clear though is that a very old ceramic phase has been found for the Southern Lowlands, and this, together with findings of pre-ceramic phases in the diggings directed by MacNeish in Belize also, proves that the area had been inhabited thousands of years before our era, and that possibly the ceramic villages developed in that very area until the rise of the splendid civilization of the Classic.

[14] See note 11.

[15] It is worth mentioning Yaxhá as an exception. It is a small Mayan city to the southwest of Tikal which presents an urban design combining the amorphous Mayan pattern with Teotihacan-style road planning.

[16] In this case we also have as exceptions certain sites that do have established limits, surrounded as they are by defensive pits or walls, such as Becán in the Northern Lowlands, Punta de Chimino, and Dos Pilas in the Southern Lowlands, among others.

[17] It has been estimated that in the moment of greater splendor, towards the mid 8th century, the domains of the powerful state of Tikal extended over 2500 square kilometers, with a population close to 425000.

[18] See J. Marcus, *Ancient Maya Political...* (1993), where the author proposes her model of dynamic political organization, and makes a synthesis of recent progress in this subject.

[19] Expounded here is only a model for explaining the territorial and political organization of the Mayan area during the Classic, and it is worth mentioning that there are other hypothesis, such as Mathews' (1985), who believes that the sites with emblem glyphs were independent, an opinion which takes us back to Thompson's model who imagined the Mayan area dotted by myriad autonomous city-states. It is also foreseeable that, as a result of recent investigations in the Mayan area, other explicative models will appear, based on a greater quantity and quality of information.

[20] Sanders (in the PBS documentary Artisans and Traders, 1993) mentions that the members of the archaeological project in Copán discovered a series of housing complexes near the rhyolite mines where peasants lived in small mud adobe huts. Around the whole area they found pieces of *metates*, some broken, others in the process of making, which indicates that these were workshops dedicated to the production of these utensils. Through ethnographic analogy he concludes that the peasants involved in this did not live from the manufacturing of these products, but that it was a half-time occupation. This discovery contrasted with the Teotihacan complexes, in which the families living there specialized in the full-time production of certain types of household goods.

[21] Before this it was thought that the Mayas had only practiced extensive slash-and-burn agriculture. But thanks to studies around settlement patterns we now know that the high density of population in the sites left very little space for practicing this system in a scale that would have permitted to meet the demand of food, for which reason it is probable that other intensive agricultural systems were employed, creating other niches apt for cultivation since at least the Late Pre-Classic. This was proven by the archaeological discovery of pre-Hispanic terraces, troughs, and canals in various sites of the Maya region.

[22] Many authors affirm that Kaminaljuyú exerted a monopoly over the exploitation of obsidian mines at El Chayal, but this is an unlikely supposition, since there is still much research needed around the mines themselves. First of all it is necessary to establish the limits of their total extension, and the dimensions of their exploitation at different times. The same can be said about the exploitation of Ixtepeque, in Guatemala, another important source of obsidian in the Mayan area. The most that can be said today is than Kaminaljuyú administered the circulation of this mineral during some time (A. Pastrana, personal communication, 1996). Similarly, research is needed on the exploitation of the metamorphic rock mines in the region of Motagua.

[23] A superb analysis about political propaganda in pre-Hispanic Mexico is the one carried out by Joyce Marcus in her work *Mesoamerican Writing Systems...*, 1992.

[24] The magnificence of Pacal's tomb and of the building that contains it (the Temple of the Inscriptions), as well as the three splendid edifices built by his son Serpent-Jaguar (Group of the Cross) have made some researcher think that maybe Pacal and his son had been usurpers that needed these tremendous statements of power to legitimate their supposed royal lineage.

[25] A magnificent example is the Glyph Staircase in Copán, which constitutes a veritable encyclopedia for the history of the city.

[26] The Putunes were groups of tough merchants from the coastal plains of Tabasco and the south of Campeche who had great mobility. During the 9th century they invaded sites of the Central Zone of the Mayan area, taking advantage of the crisis that the latter were experiencing, and established an interesting flux of ideas and goods with Central Mexico. Most likely it was they who were responsible for introducing powerful Mayan influence in places such as Cacaxtla and Xochicalco.

# The Sacred Forces
# of the Mayan Universe

*Mercedes de la Garza*

*Introduction*

All cultural creations of the Mayan people were based on a religious conception of the world and life, according to which the universe is filled with sacred energies that manifest themselves in numerous ways and in diverse natural beings. For the Mayan people, the supernatural beings created the cosmos with a precise purpose: to preserve their own existence. A special being, man, would be in charge of such a task because he was considered the motor and axis of the cosmos. Based on this conception, the Mayan people made ritual activities the core of their existence.

The Mayan people expressed their religious thought in all of their cultural creations, among which the most outstanding examples are their cities, their art –generally accompanied by texts–, and their myths or sacred tales. These are preserved in Latin characters thanks to the eagerness of Mayan leaders during the Colonial era to preserve their identity against the invasion of the western culture. The myths, as in any other religious culture, not only explain how the world began (cosmogony), but also why men and all other beings are the way they are and why they behave they way they do. This is due to the fact that myths are living history for them, real history, not fiction; they are their truth and their guideline for action in the world because they are the reason of their inmost being, accounting for their place within the cosmos.

That is why the basic Mayan myths about the creation and the structure of the universe have survived to this day in the indian communities. At present and despite the Spanish conquest, most indigenous groups preserve them –perhaps adding a few changes– as were collected by the Mayan people in the Colonial books. It is believed that if the essence of the myths was able to survive colonization, as well as all of the changes operated since then, they could have easily arisen in the Pre-Classic period. There is sufficient evidence that allows us to know the age of the basic religious concepts as expressed by the indians of the Colonial era, all of which have been helpful in understanding and clarifying the meaning of Mayan myth.

The surprising survival of pre-Hispanic Mayan religious concepts about the world and life has varied explanations. However, a basic explanation regarding the nature of religious phenomena, is that people tend to preserve myths that express the main con-

58. Stele 2 at Izapa. It represents a celestial dragon coming down on a tree; on each side, two men are worshipping it; the earthly dragon is found at the roots. Late Pre-Classic (from Lowe, Lee, and Martínez, 1982).

cerns and facts of human life. This obviously takes place within the American Indian cultures only five centuries after they were conquered.

This fact in mind, and the use of a comparative method of sources from different ages for the understanding of Mayan religion, has been helpful in historical research on Mayan culture. Fortunately, this method has been adopted by other disciplines. Now the epigraphers, for example, perform comparative analysis of the glyph texts from the Classic period and the Colonial books, such as the *Popol Vub*. This has produced greater knowledge than the one which had been acquired through an isolated interpretation of the inscriptions.[1]

We will not of course analyze the religious content of the Colonial books nor of the three surviving codices. Since these belong to the Post-Classic period, our analysis will focus mainly on the Mayan religion of the Classic. However, we have taken into consideration the beliefs and ritual ways of the Post-Classic period as well as the Colonial myths and the etnographic information in order to support our interpretations of the classic sources, which are limited to material vestiges. We believe these cannot be fully understood if we do not consult what the Mayan people said about themselves and their ideas, because their conception of the world and of life differs very much from ours.

On the other hand, in our opinion, a universal knowledge of symbols and religious phenomena is a basic support for understanding any religion. And this has been demonstrated through the comparative history of different religions and through the phenomenology of religion, methodological procedures essential to our work.

### Pre-Classic Manifestations of Religious Symbols in the Classic Period

The symbolic analysis of the ways in which supernatural beings and forces were represented in Classic Mayan sculpture have been found in sites in the Highlands of Guatemala and Chiapas, and especially in Izapa, all of which seem to have been built by non-Mayan peoples during the Pre-Classic period.

Aside from discussion on the ethnic identity of this people, the creators of the «Izapa Culture» undoubtedly reveal through their sculpture an essential precedent of the religious symbols and ritual practices found later among the Classic Mayan peoples of the Central Zone. Thus a brief reference to these representations has been included here.

The steles of Izapa include figures such as man-bird and dragon deities;[2] representations of a man or a god inside the fauces of a serpent or jaguar; of a serpentine rain-god with an axe in hand, and of men worshiping the gods. These also became the main motifs of Mayan art during the Classic period.

The Izapa-style dragon is a fantastic animal that has serpent, bird, jaguar, alligator, and crocodile features. These animals were chosen to symbolize the sacredness of the universe, represented by the natural forces which man as a farmer depends on for his material existence. That is why the context in which the dragon is found generally refers to fertility, and the deity can either be heavenly, terrestrial, or aquatic.

Among the figures which can be considered depictions of the Classic Mayan dragon are: in Stele 2 a descending being, that is with its head upside-down, a human body, wings with the St. Andrews cross —which will become one of the glyphs of heaven among the Mayan peoples—, and a helm with the head of a serpent (figure 58). Here we can also see a man worshiping the heavenly god, next to the axis tree of the world. On Stele 21 there is a human sacrifice by decapitation, performed before a lord sitting on a public throne (figure 59). This type of sacrifice was the most common among the Mayas of the Classic.[3]

On Stele 25 (figure 59) there is a convergence of symbols essential to Classic Mayan religious thought: the Bird-serpent, the terrestrial dragon, the *axis mundi*, and man as supporter of the gods, placed at the center of the cosmos. At the bottom of the stele we can appreciate the what may be considered the oldest plastic representation of the terrestrial dragon in the shape of a crocodile. The head is upside down, and its body, positioned vertically, is being transformed into a tree on which a bird is perching. In order to complete the cosmological idea of the *axis mundi*, in the middle of the stele there is a man standing over a rectangle (which might be the symbol of the surface of the earth), holding a mast, on which the Bird-serpent can be seen. This Bird-serpent, as we have previously mentioned, is the antecedent of the Mayan Bird-serpent, while the crocodile-tree is the prefiguration of the terrestrial dragon, the great crocodile Itzam Cab Ain, the symbolic image of earth in Mayan religion. The alligator or terrestrial crocodile also appears on Stele 6 and Stele 11 (figures 166, 60).

Man is represented on Stele 25 as is standing in the center of the world holding its axis. It expresses the essential anthropocentrism of the Mesoamerican religion. Here man is another *axis mundi*, and at the same time the being who, due to his consciousness and capacity to enter into all of the cosmic spaces, links all other beings with the gods. He is able to achieve and maintain the balance and existence of the entire universe through ritual and through his own vital energy, in other words, his blood.

In Izapa the probable ancestor of the Mayan rain-god, Chaac, can also be found in the guise of a man-like dragon which is holding its ray-axe before another gigantic, serpent-bodied dragon (figure 60). These are the sacred forces of cosmic fertility in dialectic play by which the fertility-dragon becomes a symbol of death, signifying the dynamic forces of death and rebirth that govern the universe.

*The Spatiotemporal Cosmos*[4]

The Mayans were outstanding among all the ancient cultures because of their deeply original ideas about time and space, although they coincide in various aspects with the views of other ancient peoples. For example: they understand time as the order of

59. On the left: Stele 25 at Izapa showing the earthly dragon in crocodile shape and the Bird-serpent at the top. On the right: Stele 21 at Izapa. Its subject is a sacrifice by beheading. Late Pre-Classic (from Lowe, Lee, and Martínez, 1982).

movement, as in the east. Mayan thought conceives temporality as cyclical, much as the philosophies of India and China, suggesting that the temporaly order of the universe alternates with periods of chaos and repose.

As in many other religious traditions, for the Maya, time is basically related to the Sun and the heavens; the transit of the Sun is understood as a circular movement around the earth which determines the changes of space; consequently, time is understood as a cyclic movement. Temporality thus is not an abstract concept for them, but the evident and eternal dynamism of space, which grants all beings with multiple and sometimes contradictory qualities. Such movement is orderly and stable as the regularity of nature and human life itself demonstrates. So for the Mayas as well as for other cultures, time is order and, consequently, independence from time is chaos.

The Mayan ideas about space-time are found in all their beliefs and cultural creations, but mainly in their prophetic and historical texts, in their calendaric and astronomical knowledge, in their cosmogonical myths (regarding the origin of the cosmos), and in their cosmological conceptions (about the structure of the cosmos).

Here I will emphasize the ideas about space-time only in cosmology and cosmogony, but not without referring first to the Maya's understanding of mathematics, astronomy, and chronology, the most outstanding among ancient cultures. They were the first to conceive the standing value of symbols and the use of the zero. Their solar calendar is the most precise ever created. Its margin of error is only of 17.28 seconds in relation to the tropic-year.

It should also be mentioned that the Maya's knowledge about mathematics, astronomy and chronology can also be considered as an objective science according to the conventional western concept of «objective» science. However, from the perspective of the creators these «sciences» are a way of establishing contact with the gods, while the heavenly bodies and becoming itself are divine energies which have influence over the world and men. The purpose of this knowledge is to protect man, helping him to physically survive, forecasting his future, which is why it is part of their religion. The sacred forces generated during each lapse of time act either beneficially or malevolently over men. But man is not passively subjected to the gods because as their movement is cyclical –and knowing what

60. On the left: Stele 11 at Izapa where we can see the earthly dragon as an alligator, from whose fauces a winged deity comes out. On the right, Stele 3 at Izapa, which represents the dragon as a rain god, brandishing his axe-lightning in front of another dragon. Late Pre-Classic (from Lowe, Lee, and Martínez, 1982).

has happened in the past– he can know what will happen in the future and look for the best way to change his fate. In this way, scientific achievements imply a creative and free attitude mainly concerned with human fate before the gods.[5]

## Cosmogony

The cosmogonical myths of the Mayas which can be read are those found in the Colonial texts of the indians. The main ones are: the Quiché's *Popol Vuh*, the Cakchiquel's *Memoriales de Sololá*, and the Yucatán Maya's *Books of the Chilam Balam*. However, in pre-Hispanic codices and works of art we find representations and texts that agree with these myths and help to confirm their age.

A comparative analysis of the myths contained in these colonial manuscripts allows us to synthesize the Mayan cosmogony, bringing forth its Classic expressions.

Generally speaking, cosmogonic myths relate a process of creation and destruction, a chain of cycles or cosmic eras in which the world and man were constructed. Thus according to Mayan thought the universe is being created and destroyed following a qualitative evolution, an idea which implies that it is infinite. Mayan creation myths are very complex and rich in details; I will only synthesize the most representative.

The cosmogonical myth of Guatemalan Quiché indians,[6] the most comprehensive among Mesoamerican cultures, tells us that the gods of creation, settled on indifferentiated pristine waters, during a «static age» or a lapse of chaos, decided to create a world that would be inhabited by a conscious being whose mission would be to workship and feed them. The gods of creation had different names, but all of them are Gucumats, «Quetzal-Serpent», a symbol of the primeval waters, and «Heavenly Heart», original center, the initial point from which the cosmos would evolve. The deities caused the earth and its inhabitants to emerge through the word, which is the creative energy. Later, they formed, in consecutive stages of creation-destruction, clay and wooden men who, unable to fulfill the expectations of the gods, were destroyed, in the first case by a flood, or turned into monkeys, in the second, their world disappearing under a burning resin rain. Finally, the gods found a sacred plant, corn, which they mixed with serpent and tapir blood (sacred animals symbolically related with fertility and water) in order to create a new man, who is aware of the gods and of his mission on earth. In this way the Quichés expressed their idea about the basic union of man and nature, and its peculiarity.

In the consequent stages different Suns appeared, but since they were as imperfect as men they were destroyed. Together with man of corn, our Sun and Moon appeared as a result of the apotheosis of two twin heroes who played ball with the gods of death and then died and were reborn in the netherworld: Hunahpú and Ixbalanqué. The stars remained motionless in the sky until the newly created men offered them human sacrifices; with this they began to move, or in other words, the history of man on earth began,[7] profane time.

The Yucatán Maya myths included in the *Books of the Chilam Balam* are formally different and we only have a few fragments. They also express the same cosmogonical idea, narrating cosmic creations and destructions, as well as communicating the main cosmogonical ideas of the Mayas, that is, their conception of the structure of the cosmos. One of the fragments, titled «The Book of the Ancient Gods» expresses the idea that after various stages of creation and destruction of men, the heavens collapsed. The Bacabe gods, sustainers of heaven at the four cosmic points, rebuilt it again, putting the four cosmic ceiba trees on each direction, with its bird on the branches, and the «Great Mother Ceiba» or green ceiba at the center of the universe.[8]

Among both the Quichés and the Mayas of Yucatán, the men of the last age, the corn men, are the result of a spiral progressive perfection of the human being, determined by

the substance from which they were formed, which had also been improving until it reached the form of corn. The men of the last age[9] are qualitatively different because they had within them another sacred substance: the blood of the gods, and that new quality is conciousness, which reveals to them that their mission is to sustain the gods.

The version of the Mayan cosmogonical myth in the *Popol Vuh* and in the *Sololá Memorial* seems to be expressed in hieroglyphic texts, reliefs, and ceramic works from the Classic period. It has survived until today with few changes among some Mayan groups such as the Tzotzil, Tzeltal, Lacandon, Mayan Indians of Yucatán. This corroborates that this myth persisted during the pre-Hispanic age among maya groups and that it was common to them.[10]

One of the favorite parts in the myth, both among current Mayan groups as among those of the Classic, are the adventures of Hunahpú and Ixbalanqué. We see them in diverse Classic ceramic and sculpture works performing actions such as killing birds with their blowguns. Freidel and Schele state that the Mayan myth of creation included in the *Popol Vuh* is not different from the one that was inscribed during the 6th, 7th and 8th centuries on the stone monuments of the great Mayan cities.[11]

«There is no book of the Classic period equivalent to the *Popol Vuh*, which was written by the Quiché people after the Spanish conquest. But we have the history of Creation as was written by the Mayan rulers on their royal monuments –they say–.»[12]

These authors performed the interpretative reading of three texts from the city of Cobá, according to which the present world was created on 13.0.0.0.0, day 4 *Ahau* 8 *Cumhú*, which in our calendar corresponds to August 13, 3114 B.C., and functioned as the Era Date in Classic calendaric calculations.[13] Likewise, they found this same date on Stele C of Quiriguá and interpreted the inscription as the record of the birth of the present world (figure 61). The text expresses that on 4 *Ahau* 8 *Cumhú* «the image appeared and the three stones were set...» These seem to be related with the three stones which the Mayas put at the center of their houses, and in this cosmogonical text they are clearly a symbol of the center of the world.

The rear or northern side of the stele represents for us god Itzamná, «the Dragon», supreme god of the Mayan religion in its human form. He carries the heavenly crossed bands (figure 62) and is the creator of the cosmos, according to the Colonial texts, which confirms that the text of Stele C refers to creation.

Another work where the epigraphers find the cosmogonical myth is the panel of the Temple of the Cross in Palenque. Creation started with the birth of the First Father (June 16, 3122 B.C.), who «ascended» to the center of heaven over the world's axis-tree. This father was called Father Wak-Chan-Ahaw «(Six or) Elevated Heavenly God.» Then the First Mother was born (December 7, 3121 B.C.).

On the attached image (figure 64) we see the axis-tree, identified with the supreme heavenly god Itzamná. It is formed by two-headed serpents, and over them there is the Bird-serpent, which we interpret as an aspect of the heavenly dragon.[14] Thus, the First Father would also be Itzamná. In Palenque it is called the god G1, and the Temple of the Cross is dedicated to him. This agrees with the fact that the sculpted deity on the northern side of Quiriguá's Stele C is also Itzamná.

Cosmology

Three religious symbols of a universal character play a significant role in the Mayan conception of space: the cross and the square, which cannot be separated, and the pyramid.

The Mayas understood the universe as formed by three great areas: heaven, earth, and the netherworld. Heaven was subdivided into thirteen horizontal strata in the form of a scaled pyramid, as Eric Thompson suggested.[15] It is very likely that the heavens were imagined in this way, because the pyramid-shaped[16] constructions which supported the temples and which represented the sacred mountains, symbolized the heavenly space, the topmost level of which constituted the abode of the supreme deity. In a correlative manner, the netherworld was also visualized as a pyramid, but with nine bodies[17] and maybe in an upside down position. And earth was thought of as a quadrangular flat plate divided into four sections, each of which had as symbols a color, a tree (ceiba) on which a bird is perched, a variety of corn, and a variety of bean. The trees sustain heaven, next to anthropomorphous deities known as Bacabes.[18]

Mayan myths also mention a great ceiba tree in the center of the universe –the Great Mother Ceiba which grows through the three levels. This image of the Cosmic Tree located in the center of the world is one of the most common in the universal symbolism of the center.

The conception of terrestrial quadruplicity, so clearly expressed in the Mayan cosmology, seems to have been the result of experiencing the natural phenomenon of sunrise and sunset on the horizon during the Sun's annual cycle. This determines the appearance of the four regions of earth, the four cardinal points, as well as the four seasons, with space and time merging together in this quadruplicity.

Alfonso Villa Rojas published in 1968, well before archaeo-astronomy made its first contributions, an innovative and well founded interpretation of quadruplicity in Mayan thought. He states that the four directions correspond to the four houses of the Sun: two to the east, two to the west. These are inter-cardinal points which represent the extremes that the Sun will reach over the horizon during the year: sunrise in the summer solstice, and in the winter solstice, sunset in the summer solstice, and in the winter solstice. The central position or zenith would come to be the Sun's fifth house.[19] In this way, the north would be the course to the right of the Sun's path. The south would be to the left of the Sun's path, and the «four corners of the world» would be located at the NE, NW, SW, and SE positions.[20]

The four directions thus do not seem to have corresponded exactly to the cardinal points. But even when the religious meaning given to the East and the West in Mayan thought was the essential one, due to the sacredness of the Sun, the North and the South were not eliminated from their cosmological thought, as has been stated, undoubtedly, by some researchers.[21] Miguel León-Portilla shows that in Mayan religious thought the four cardinal points had an important religious meaning, though the main points were undoubtedly the east and the west. The consideration about the four cardinal points is corroborated by the existence of glyphs representing each (figure 63) and by the discovery of a tomb in Río Azul by Richard E. W. Adams in 1985, on whose walls we can see the glyphs of the four cardinal points, *precisely in the real directions.*[22]

However, there are two other points which the Mayas seem to have considered in their cosmology: the highest at the center of heaven: the zenith; and the lowest at the center of the netherworld: the nadir.[23]

Thus, in Mayan thought terrestrial space cannot be understood independently of time, and both are determined by the solar cycle. The four «Year Carriers», as they called the first day of the year in the ritual 260 day-calendar, tread the four sectors and the three cosmic levels, bequeathing space with an orderly movement, and filling all existent beings with their positive or negative influence.

During the Mayan Classic we find many ceremonial centers which reveal such cosmological ideas,[24] but in addition to this each of the cosmic levels is symbolized in sculpture by a reptile-like monster. This is what we have termed dragon because it is a

62. Northern side of Stele C at Quiriguá. The god Itzámná in an anthropomorphous representation and holding a sky glyph. Classic Period (drawing by M. Aguirre, based on Maudslay, 1974).

*Previous page:*
61. Southern side of Stele C at Quiriguá. The inscription tells the Cosmogonic myth. Classic Period (Freidel, and Schele, 1993).

hybrid creature with the features of many sacred animals, mainly those of a serpent. This being, as we have mentioned, is the supreme deity which governs all levels and dimensions of the universe.

In religious symbology the square represents the material world, that which is solid, perceptible, tangible; but it derives from the cross –so the sacred number is not four but five, which is the result of the convergence of the two lines of the cross, in other words: the center of the universe. The four sides cannot be considered independently from their relationship with the center or with the point of intersection of the cross axes. The center is exactly the same for heaven, for earth, or for the netherworld, because it is a juncture and communicating point of the diverse cosmic spaces. Thus, the center is not only a point but an axis which unifies the two poles of the cosmos.[25] And because it is an axis, an umbilical cord of the world, the center is the threshold where a rupture of levels, or a jump into another world, becomes possible.

The Mayan symbols of quadruplicity and of the fifth direction, or center of the cosmos, inscribed within this general meaning, are diverse. In the first place and most important is the glyph of the Sun, which is a four-petalled flower[26] (figure 63). It is the Sun who governs time, and determines the division of space. Another glyph which geometrically represents the quadruple cosmos and its center is the *quincunce*[27] (figure 63).

And one of the most outstanding Mayan symbols of the cosmic quadruple system and of the *axis mundi* is the cross, which can be found on diverse Classic plastic works. For example, on the gravestones of the temples of the Inscriptions (sarcophagus) (figure 65), of the Cross (figure 64),[28] and of the Foliated Cross (figure 67)[29] in Palenque, as well as in the lintels 2 (figure 69) and 5 (figure 68) in Yaxchilán. In the first two works, the cross is formed with the body of the heavenly dragon, leaning on a figurehead related to the terrestrial dragon and finishes at the top with the Bird-serpent, which is a variety of the heavenly deity. At the Foliated Cross Temple, the cosmic tree is a corn plant in the shape of a cross, leaning on a mask of the solar god, as a terrestrial dragon, and at the top of the vertical axis there is a Bird-serpent. Thus, in these works the four directions, the three cosmic levels, and the *axis mundi* appear simultaneously.

On the lintels 2 (figure 69) and 5 (figure 68) from Yaxchilán, the rulers hold cross-shaped staffs finished with flowers at the edges of the horizontal bar, with a descending quetzal at the top, which likewise symbolizes the heavenly divinity at the top of the *axis mundi*.

But in the Mayan world quadruplicity is not only seen at the terrestrial level, it also comprises the heavenly and the netherworlds. Myths speak about the four regions of heaven –corresponding to the four sides of the heavenly pyramid–, which share the

*Following pages:*
64. Panel in the Temple of the Cross at Palenque, where the celestial dragon and the *axis mundi* are represented. 692 A.D. Late Classic period (drawing by L. Schele).

65. Gravestone of the sarcophagus in the Temple of the Inscriptions at Palenque. There, the symbols of the three cosmic levels and the *axis mundi* were carved. 615-683 A.D. Late Classic (drawing by A. Villagra).

66. Panel in the Temple of the Sun at Palenque. It represents the Sun God as a shield and as a jaguar that is coming down to the Netherworld. 690 A.D. Late Classic (drawing by L. Schele).

67. Gravestone from the Foliated Cross Temple where the *axis mundi* is a maize plant. 692 A.D. Late Classic (drawing by L. Schele).

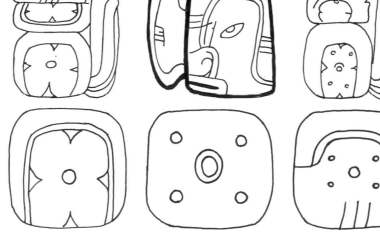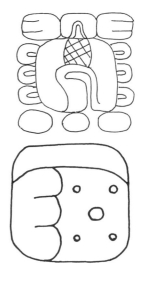

63. Top: glyphs of the four cardinal points. From left to right: East (Palenque, Inscriptions), North (*Matritensis Codex*).

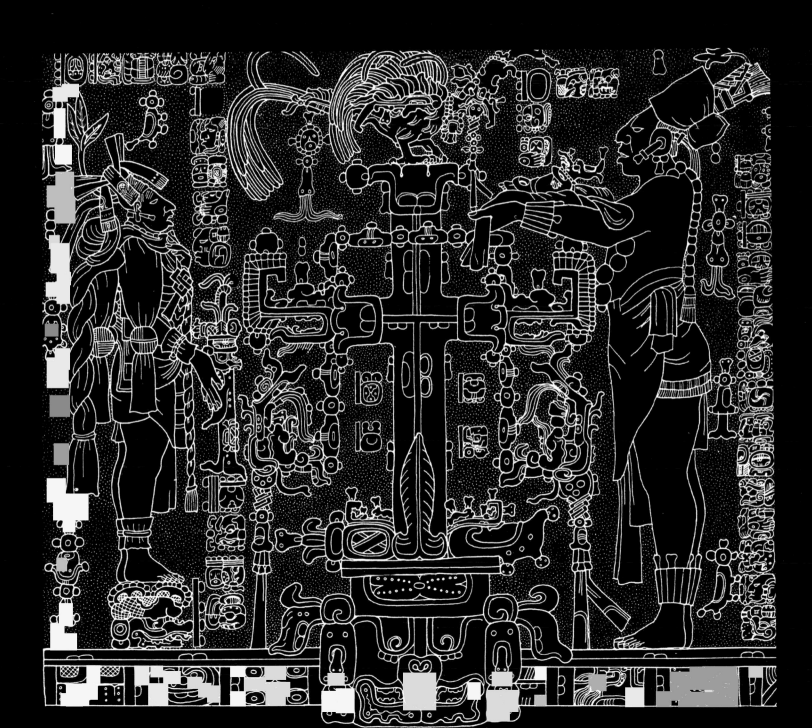

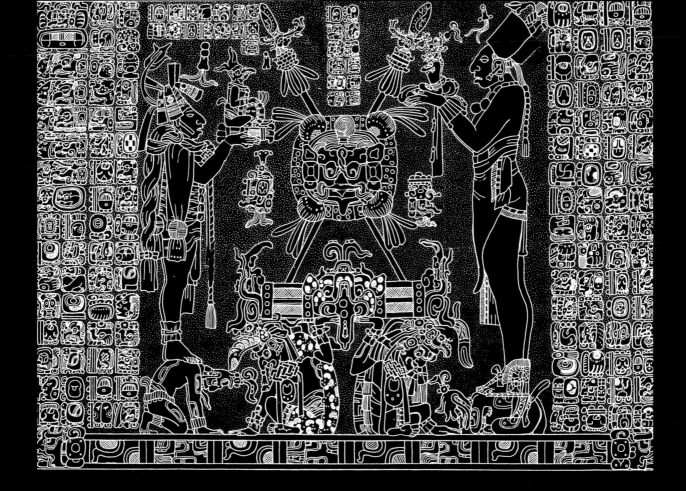

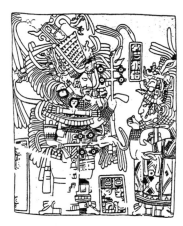

68. Lintel 5 at Yaxchilán, *ca.* 760 A.D. Late Classic (from Freidel, Schele, and Parker, 1993).

colors of the terrestrial regions, as well as about the four regions of the netherworld. Even the supreme heavenly god Itzamná is at the same time one and four, in consonance with the four cosmic colors of corn: black, white, red, and yellow.

The pyramid is one of the universal symbols of the cosmic quadruplicity and of the center of the world. It represents the mountain and is a perfect figure: a volume oriented towards its apex, where it becomes unified. Thus it comes to mean, totality. It is limited by opposed sides which are a materialization of cosmic polarity. Resting on a quadrangular platform attached to the earth –with which it is identified–, its apex represents the heavenly level.[30]

In Mayan thought the heavenly pyramid symbolizes the progressive ascent from earthly multiplicity towards unity, represented by the apex, where the supreme god Itzamná, «the Dragon» –vital principle of the cosmos– dwells. Thus, the heavenly pyramid symbolizes the progressive deification of cosmos. And that supreme point is also the Sun, because it would correspond to the zenith. This is why the Dragon and the Sun are identified.

And the upside-down pyramid of the netherworld thus comes to mean the descent from the quadrangular terrestrial level, the seat of multiplicity and transformation, to the sacred unity of death, the end of temporality, and consequently of the earth. There, within the lowermost stratum of the netherworld is where the god of death resides, a dialectical counterpart of the supreme god of heaven. That is why the god of death is also identified with the Sun at its nadir, the dead Sun.

Thus, the apexes of both cosmological pyramids symbolize the two opposing sacred principles, located on the two extreme vertical axes of the Sun's position. Both points symbolically represent life and death, they rule over the balance of the cosmos, and their alternation results in the earth's existence.

These Mesoamerican symbols are of a universal nature. The pyramid, or triangle with an upward vertex, represents the mountain, the ascent to heaven, while the pyramid with the downward vertex symbolizes the cavern, which is an entrance to the netherworld.

69. Lintel 2 at Yaxchilán, where the ruler Bird-Jaguar IV holds as a scepter a cross that symbolizes the *axis mundi* and the four cosmic directions. Mayan date: 9.16.6.0.0, 757 A.D. Late Classic (from Graham, vol. 3, part 1, 1982).

Likewise, the former embodies the active and masculine principle, while the latter is passive and feminine.[31] For the Mayas, the netherworld is the womb of the mother earth, where it keeps seeds and treasures, alongside the dead, who can give birth to new life.

Thus, in Mayan thought quadruplicity extends over the heavenly plane and the netherworld, unifying them. The unity of the sacred opposite principles is the culmination of a progressive spiritualization, of a progressive departure from materiality and a concretion of the terrestrial level, in a movement towards life and death.

These ideas reveal an unparalleled awareness of cosmic unity: earth, heaven, and the netherworld are different realities, but they participate in the reality of the sacred, sharing a structure in which the cross, the square, the triangle, and the sphere coexist, that is, where space and time form a unity.

Cosmological ideas, as well as the astronomical knowledge, determined the construction of sacred spaces on earth: the ceremonial centers. The temples were built following the position of the stars,[32] mainly during equinoxes and solstices, and were set on pyramidal foundations. These buildings could only be climbed by the priests, while the people remained at the main squares during the religious ceremonies.

This tells us that climbing the pyramid, which represented the sacred cosmic mountain, was tantamount to ascending the heavenly regions to communicate with the sacred. Once the uppermost terrace of the temple was reached by the priest, there was a rupture of levels: he went beyond the sphere of man, entering the sphere of the gods.

There are many works in architecture and sculpture which reflect Mayan cosmology and prove that the ideas expressed in the myths were already in use during the Classic period. We will mention only a few examples.

The facade of Temple 22 at Copán, in Honduras (figure 70) is adorned with an extraordinary high-relief which represents the three vertical levels of the cosmos. At the base, under the temple's entrance, there is a frieze with skulls, and on both sides, two large masks of the death deity which symbolize the netherworld. Over them there are two half-kneeling human figures which seem to represent the Bacabes, deities located at the four cosmic directions which support heaven, and who symbolize the terrestrial level. They carry on their shoulders a great two-headed serpent, a representation of the heavenly dragon.

70. Temple 22 at Copán, whose facade represents the three cosmic levels. Classic Period (from Freidel, Schele, and Parker, 1993).

One of the best Classic examples of Mesoamerican architecture is found in Palenque, a Mayan city located in Chiapas.[33] There a nine-level pyramid symbolizes the netherworld (although it is not an inverted pyramid), and another thirteen-leveled one represents heaven. These buildings serve to corroborate the idea that those cosmic spheres were conceived in pyramidal fashion.

The pyramid of the netherworld, also known as the Temple of the Inscriptions (figure 127; plates 22, 24, 26), contains the sumptuous tomb of Pacal, lying inside at the center, in the lowermost point, symbol of the tenth stratum of the netherworld. The entrance is located at the top of the pyramid, and the ten-level descent, starting from the terrestrial level, symbolizes the entrance to the netherworld. This descent was a journey that most of the immortal spirits of men had to take after their death.

In Dzibanché, Campeche, there is a temple called the Owl, which was also built as a funeral monument; it includes several death chambers and a main tomb, which remains as yet unexcavated, and is located at the level immediately following the level of the plaza.[34] Its entrance is at the top of the pyramid, as in the Pacal tomb at Palenque, but the base has four, instead of nine, components. Thompson said that the pyramid of the netherworld was formed with four steps on one side, four steps on the other, and the bottom step, which was the ninth. Maybe this is why this foundation represents, as in Palenque, the sphere of the netherworld to which the spirit of the dead descends.[35]

The heavenly pyramid in Palenque is the Temple of the Cross (figure 71; plate 28), which is considered the best example of the architectural representation of heaven. It rests on a 13-level base, and at the pinnacle there is an enclosure dedicated to the supreme god of the heavens Itzamná, «the Dragon», here called god G1. Besides, this temple forms a triangle with the Temple of the Foliated Cross, and the Temple of the Sun (plate 29), respectively located at the northern, eastern, and western sides of a courtyard (plate 30). They symbolize the sacred cycle of corn harvest and the daily and annual cycles of the Sun. They are associated with the cosmic directions and with the equinoxes and the solstices, as well as with the initiation rites of the rulers.[36] Thus, the three temples, together with the Temple of the Inscriptions, constitute an outstanding artistic expression of the Maya's notions of time and space.

And the great lord buried at the Temple of the Inscriptions was represented on a sculpted monolithic gravestone which covers his sarcophagus, and which also sym-

71. Temple of the Cross (692 A.D.) at Palenque, where the solar cycle is recorded. Late Classic (picture by M. de la Garza).

bolizes temporal space (figure 65; plate 25). The figure of the ruler, at the center, is the symbol of the terrestrial level; over him rises a cross formed by two-headed serpents, a representation of Itzamná, who symbolizes heaven and the *axis mundi*. The infraterrestrial region was represented underneath with images of bones and the lean mask of the god of death. The cosmological scene is surrounded by a band with star symbols, expressing the superiority of heaven, the temporary nature of the universe, and cosmic unity.

## *The Gods*

The gods of the Classic Mayan religion are artistic representations of supernatural beings with highly stylized features of various animals and plant elements which sometimes appear in combination with human figures. To arrive at the meaning of these fantastic beings it is necessary to direct our attention to similar figures in the surviving manuscripts, which belong to the Post-Classic period, and to the Spanish and Indian Colonial texts. These confirm the nature and the manifestations of the sacred beings and give us their names, whose meanings allow us to delve deeper into their characterizations.

Written sources tell us that the gods were conceived by the Mayas as invisible and untouchable energies manifested in different natural beings. For instance, they are manifested in the stars, rain, thunder, and powerful animals, such as the serpent, the jaguar, birds and bats, as well as in plants such as corn, and hallucinogenic plants and mushrooms. They also appear in minerals such as quartz. Likewise the spirits of outstanding men were deified upon their death.

Besides those natural beings, the images of the gods made by men were also their epiphanies. These images often acted as incarnations of sacred energies during the rites, in order to receive the offerings of men.

Among other authors from the 16th century, Fra Diego de Landa confirms the ethereal nature of the gods when he says:

«They well knew that the idols were dead and godless works of theirs, but they revered them because of what they represented and because they had been made with many ceremonies, mainly the ones made of wood.»[37]

Another feature of the Mayan gods is that, despite being superior to men, and capable of creating, they were conceived as imperfect beings that are subject to birth and death, and that had to be fed in order for them to survive. This idea is clearly expressed in the cosmogonical myths, rites, and hieroglyphic inscriptions of the Classic period, such those found in Palenque, where according to the epigraphic interpretations the births of some of the gods are registered.[38]

Each of the sacred beings has diverse epiphanies and multiple names, in accordance with its attributes, and above all with temporality. The Mayas do not conceive static beings, everything is moving, changing. Thus the gods and their influence are different in each period. That is why one god can be at the same time heavenly and terrestrial, good and evil, masculine and feminine, the energy of life and the energy of death. Besides, the gods can be one and many; above all they can multiply into four every time they encompass the four directions of the cosmos. They also multiply into thirteen, the heavenly deity, called Oxlahuntikú in Yucatán, «Deity Thirteen», or into nine, the deity of the netherworld, Bolontikú, «Deity Nine». This determines diverse artistic representations of each god. To this we must add the different artistic styles characteristic of each region.

72. Side view of the Stele D at Copán. Late Classic (drawing by C. Ontiveros, based on Robicsek, 1972).

All of which makes the study of the Mayan gods much more difficult. However, the deities can be identified by some symbolic elements, which remain constant in all the regions of the Mayan territory, and even in all phases.

Here, basing ourselves on Schellhas' classification of the gods in the codexes,[39] we will present the main deities of the Classic Mayas, identifying them with their Yucatán Mayan and Quiché names give to us in the written sources, as well as with the letters which were assigned to them. The gods of the Post-Classic and their names as they appear in the Colonial written sources allow us to better identify and understand those of the Classic, because even when their representation is different, they present the same symbolic elements. Thus we have decided to use those names.

Many different interpretations of the Mayan gods have resulted from the different viewpoints adopted in Mayan studies. Many of them coincide, others do not. We prefer to consider as the most credible those which have resulted from a comparative analysis of the different sources. Among the Indian written sources, besides the Quiché *Popol Vuh*, we have considered other texts in that same tongue, the Cakchiquel texts, Spanish versions of texts originally written in a Mayan language, and sources in Yucatán Mayan such as the *Books of the Chilam Balam*.

### The Dragon

In most of the Classic figures of deities we find serpentine features. Stylized representations of serpents prevail in Mayan art, thus proving that the ophidian was an essential symbol of sacredness. An analysis of the symbolic importance of the serpent among the Mayas[40] has allowed us to know that the serpent, transfigured into a dragon[41] and enriched with elements from other powerful animals, symbolizes a universal sacred power, a vital force. Thus, this generating principle of the universe is linked to the Sun, to water, earth, blood, semen, and corn, which are presented as diverse deities or manifestations of the supreme sacred principle.

The dragon is essentially the combination of serpent and bird. The Mayas chose outstanding creatures: the bird, a quetzal (*k'uk'* in Yucatán Maya; *kekchi* in Tzeltal and other languages; *guc* in Quiché and Cakchiquel), and the tropical rattlesnake, (*ahau can, tzabcan, zochch,* and *cumatz*). They gave them features and qualities of other

73. Top: Altars G1 (800 A.D.) and G2 (795 A.D.) at Copán, which represent the celestial dragon (drawing by C. Ontiveros).
Bottom: Altar O at Copán, image of the celestial dragon and the feathered serpent. Contemporary with altars G. Late Classic (drawing by G. Bustos, based on Maudslay, 1974).

sacred animals, like the jaguar, the alligator, the crocodile, and the deer, to create the dragon, the supreme symbol of sacredness. Thus, the dragon embodies the vital force of earth (serpent and deer), from the womb of the Mother Earth, that is, the netherworld (jaguar), of the waters (alligator and crocodile) and of the heavens (bird).

The dragon is then a polyvalent and multiple being, the sacred figure *par excellence* in Mayan art of the Classic period. Thanks to some descriptions of deities found in the Colonial written texts, and which coincide with the symbolic elements in the works of art as well as with the images found in the manuscripts, we now know the names given to them by the Mayas of Yucatán. Itzamná, «The Dragon», for example, in its heavenly aspect; Itzam Cab Ain, «Terrestrial Crocodile-alligator», or Chac Mumul Ain, «Great Muddy Crocodile», in their terrestrial and infra-terrestrial aspects. The god was also known as Canhel, «Dragon», in its function as deity of creation in cosmogonical myths, which corresponds to Gucumatz, «Quetzal-serpent», in the Quiché *Popol Vuh*.

Furthermore, there are other deities which we consider as aspects or derivations of the dragon, due to their serpent-like nature and to their close affinity with this creature. Examples of these would be Chicchan, god H, «Biting Serpent», symbol of the night sky; Kinich Ahau, god G, «Solar Eyed Lord»; Chaac, god B, god of water, and Bolon Dz'acab, god K, «Nine Generations», which symbolizes and sacralizes the human aspects of fertility, such as blood and semen, and is likewise linked to the corn plant.

74. Stele D at Copán where the ruler is seen and, on top of him, a bicephalous serpent. Late Classic (drawing by C. Ontiveros based on Robicsek, 1972).

### The Heavenly Dragon: Itzamná, God D

The heavenly dragon is mainly the combination of attributes of bird and serpent. Represented as a two-headed dragon, plumed serpent, winged serpent, and Bird-serpent, the celestial dragon appears in artistic representation throughout the regions of the Mayan area and during the whole pre-Hispanic period.

As a two-headed dragon it can be found at the altars G and the altar O in Copán (figure 73). In these works the feathered serpentine body is outlined and bears symbols of water; it has alligator legs or jaguar paws. Anthropomorphous figures of gods emerge from the open fauces of the two serpent heads. At Altar O we can see two representations: on one side, the two-headed dragon with jaguar paws; on the other side, the feathered serpent with a dragon-like head. This corroborates that it is the same deity. Itzamná was even represented in ceramics, like the container in the form of a two-headed dragon with human faces emerging from its fauces found in Chacchoben, Quintana Roo.[42]

Various works in Yaxchilán, Palenque, Piedras Negras, Tikal, Copán, and Uxmal, often represent the dragon as a two-headed plumed serpent, with very stylized heads and open fauces, like on Lintel 3 at the Temple IV in Tikal (figure 80). It is also found on Stele D in Copán (figures 72, 74), and on the gravestones of the Temple of the Cross (figure 64), and the Temple of the Inscriptions in Palenque (figure 65).

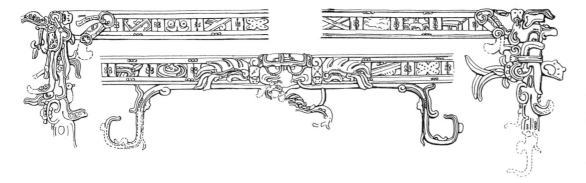

75. Stucco relief in the house E at the Palace of Palenque, which represents the celestial dragon and the Bird-serpent. Late Classic (drawing by M. Aguirre, based on Maudslay, 1974).

76. Bird-serpent on the stucco panel at Toniná, Chiapas 790-849 A.D. Late Classic (drawing by M. Aguirre).

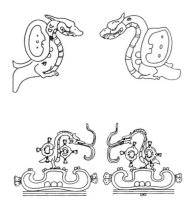

77. Winged dragons. Top: detail of a headdress from the Panel of the Slaves. Bottom: stucco fretwork in the house B at the Palace of Palenque. Late Classic (from Hellmuth, 1987).

78. Altar 41 at Copán. It represents the celestial dragon. Contemporary with the altars G. Late Classic (drawing by G. Bustos, based on Maudslay, 1974).

We also find winged dragons, like the ones which appear over the headdresses of Pacal, the ruler, and his wife Ahpo Hel on the Panel of the Slaves, and over a scaled plaster fret at the Palace of Palenque (figure 77).

Another way of representing the celestial dragon is with a large, sometimes fleshless mask, and carrying the glyph of the Sun on its forehead, and over it, the so called «triadic symbol». It is formed by a cross of St. Andrew, which is one of the glyphs of heaven; a shell, the symbol of origin, and a thorn for self-sacrifice, which represents blood. These elements, such as the aquatic (jade circles) show us that the heavenly monster symbolizes the fecundating energy of the heavens. But at the same time, the fact that the mask is lean reveals the monster's ties with the earth and the netherworld. This refers to the duality of the dragon as a symbol of life and death. The glyph of the Sun on the forehead of the mask shows that the star is one of the aspects of the dragon. Thus, in the panel of the Cross Temple in Palenque (figure 64), each side of the large mask has a band with symbols of the stars, showing the heavenly nature of the deity. The planetary band as the body of the heavenly dragon, which can also be found in the codexes, shows us that the great serpent from heaven was identified with the Milky Way.[43]

The Altar 41 from Copán (figure 78) represents the two-headed dragon as a four-legged and two-headed serpent-alligator. One of the heads bears the «triadic symbol», a fact that confirms that the mask at the Temple of the Cross in Palenque and others that bear this symbol also represent the heavenly dragon; the god of corn emerges from the fauces of the other head.

Another sacred image that we have identified with the heavenly dragon is the Bird-serpent. Unlike the feathered serpents, the birdlike nature predominates in the Bird-serpent. It is a bird with stylized serpent heads over its wings, and sometimes the head of the god K with serpentine features. This representation appears in different shapes and contexts; it is often related with the two-headed dragon and the feathered serpent, or with its humanized aspect.

The Bird-serpent with the head of the god K, Bolon Dz'acab –another aspect of the dragon–, appears on the great plaster panel of Toniná (figure 76) and on the panels of Palenque. In these works it can be seen in profile. But there are others on which it appears with the face of a bird and is represented facing the front, with wings open on both sides, and on which there are serpent-heads. We can see this on the incense burners recently found in Palenque (figure 82; plate 115).

The Bird-serpent is often represented over the serpentine dragon, as in Lintel 3 of Temple IV in Tikal (figure 80). Above the ruler, who is at the center, there is a great plumed two-headed serpent with circles of feather, jade, and water on its body. The god K emerges from one of its heads; at the top, perched over it, is the Bird-serpent, with its face looking to the front, and its wings spread out. It is wearing a headdress and earrings, as well as serpent tails under the wings, with crossed bands, to show it is a heavenly deity.

The union of these two manifestations of Itzamná, but in a very different artistic style, can also be found in the trapezoidal motif, formed by two-headed serpents, from the

Eastern Building of the Quadrangle of the Nuns in Uxmal, where the Bird-serpent is facing forward (figure 79).

An other example is the stucco relief at the House E of the Palace of Palenque (figure 75). Here, the body of the two-headed dragon is an astral band. At the center is the Bird-serpent facing front with its wings spread out and the serpent head on top. The two-headed dragon is a clear expression of the life-death, heaven-netherworld duality, because one of the heads is throwing water (like the famous dragon on page 74 of the *Dresden Codex*), and the other, fleshless, is looking upward.

Among the main artistic representations of the dragon as *axis mundi* and its identification with the Bird-serpent and the god K, we will focus on the best known, which are from Palenque.

The gravestone from the tomb at the Temple of the Inscriptions (figure 65) shows us an *axis mundi* cross, which is, at the same time, Itzamná, since its horizontal axis is a two-headed serpent with jaws made out of jade beads (which symbolize water and feathers). The top of its vertical axis finishes with another serpent head, and it is surrounded by a two-headed ophidian with a flexible body made of jade beads, and from whose fauces the God K emerges. At the top is a perching serpent-bird with the head of the God K, carrying a palm-leaf in its beak, a symbol of human power in allusion to the consecrated ruler. Over the headdress of the serpent-bird and under the tail and the head we can see *Yax* (blue-green-aqua) symbols, which corresponded to the celestial deity.

The central motif of the panel at the Temple of the Cross in Palenque represents the dragon in four different shapes: Below we see the dragon with the astral band covering its body. Above, there is a serpent-cross-tree, whose horizontal band is a two-headed serpent, over which there is another two-headed serpent with a flexible body made up

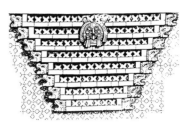

79. Trapezoidal motif from the East building of the Nunnery Quadrangle at Uxmal. It represents the celestial dragon and the Bird-serpent, Late Classic (drawing by C. Ontiveros).

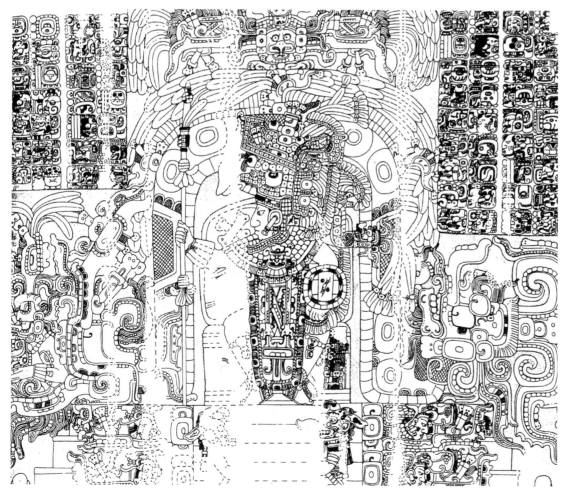

80. Lintel 3 in the Temple IV at Tikal, which represents the ruler surrounded by the celestial dragon (from Morley, Brainerd, and Sharer, 1983).

119

81. Large mask of the earthly dragon with the Sun inside his fauces. Toniná, Chiapas (picture by M. de la Garza).

of *Yax* glyphs. The top end of the vertical bar has a serpent-bird almost identical to the one at the Temple of the Inscriptions.

## Kinich Ahau, God G

A deity so closely related to the celestial dragon that it could be considered one of its outward manifestations is the Sun, which was known in Yucatán as Kinich Ahau, «Lord Solar Eye», and as Itzamná Kinich Ahau, «Lord Solar Eye of the Dragon». In its artistic representations, the solar Lord has large quadrangular crossed-eyes, a filed tooth or protruding tongue, a twisted fang at the edge of the mouth, and sometimes a kind of 8 figure on the forehead, which is the body of the serpent.

In some images, such as the clay incense burners from Palenque, the deity is wearing a large mask, and has a serpent-bird on its headdress (figure 82; plate 115), thus confirming the god's relationship with the celestial dragon; and sometimes large masks of the terrestrial dragon can be found below them.

Another link between Itzamná and Kinich Ahau is that the latter's glyph appears under the triadic symbol located on the celestial dragon's head, as we mentioned before, which corroborates the identity of both deities. But the solar god is also associated with the earthly dragon, from whose fauces he emerges in the mornings and into which he disappears in the afternoon. This can be appreciated in some works from the Classic period; for example, on a large mask of the earthly dragon located on the ground floor, at Toniná, which has a sphere within its fauces, a clear symbol of the Sun (figure 81).

The animal epiphanies of the solar god are deer, jaguar, hummingbird, eagle, and macaw. The latter was known as Kinich Kakmoo, «Fire Macaw of the Solar Eye», in Yucatán. It was said that the Sun, incarnated in this bird, came to receive man's offerings at Izamal. At the ball court in Copán (plate 54) the score-markers have the form of a Macaw's head (figure 83), showing that from the Classic period macaws were linked to the Sun, because the game has astral symbolism.

Recently, a great acropolis –possibly part of the neighboring city of Dzibanché– was found in Quintana Roo. It has been called Kinichná, the «House of the Sun» on account of its reliefs related to the solar deity. It is thought that it might have been dedicated to a cult of the Sun.[44]

Very close to this city and sharing this same style, we find Kohunlich, whose main temple is also dedicated to the solar god, to judge from the large masks of the deity flanking the stairs of the pyramid. The masks have all the symbolic features of the solar god. Besides, some of them have the *Chuen* glyph, which is related in many other contexts to the solar deity. The meaning of *Chuen* is «monkey, artisan, creator», and is identified with the Sun, not only because it is an astral deity (the brother of the Sun in the *Popol Vuh*), but because both are associated with artistic creation. Moreover, the head of a monkey sometimes replaces the head of the Sun god as can be seen in the *Kin* sign, thus indicating their connection.[45] The Mayas saw in the Sun, among other aspects, the patron of song and music. This is where his relationship with the monkey arises, a relationship that is clearly expressed in the masks of the main temple of Kohunlich. Under them, there is a mask of the terrestrial dragon, such as have been found in some censers in Palenque.

The Sun was the major deity because it generated temporality: its daily and annual cycles determined movement, days and nights, the four regions of the universe and the four seasons. Thus, he is the patron of the number 4, and his glyph is a four-petalled flower (figure 63). The cycles of the Sun are of a double nature: when it crosses the sky during the day, the deity represents light, life, day, order, and welfare. It is his beneficial

82. Incensory at Palenque that represents the Sun god, in his association with the celestial dragon. Late Classic.

and vital aspect. But when he enters into the netherworld at sunset, he becomes death energy transmuted into a jaguar. These ideas are expressed in the panel of the Temple of the Sun in Palenque (figure 66), whose central motif is a mask of the solar god in the shape of a shield, crossed over which are arrows symbolizing thunder; it has an eight-shaped serpent on its forehead, jaguar ears, serpentine eyes with volute-shaped pupils,[46] protruding tongue, a filed tooth, and a serpent fang wrapped at the mouth. Under the solar shield is a two-headed serpent (Itzamná, the heavenly dragon), in whose center there is a jaguar face seen from the front. The jaguar is the Sun descending into the netherworld during the spring equinox; it is associated with the western direction (the sunset) which is the same direction of the temple with respect to the main plaza. Some researchers have given the name of GIII to the patron god of the temple, who is precisely the Sun in its aspect of jaguar god of the netherworld, that is, a death god.

83. Marker in the shape of a macaw head by the ball court at Copán (picture by M. de la Garza).

It was the solar cycle which served as a guide to the construction of this and the other main temples of Palenque. Hartung says:

«The facade of the Temple of the Sun faces the rising Sun during the winter solstice, while this same star, during sunset on this same day, also shines over a very characteristic area of the Temple of the Cross. A sight from the Temple of the Foliated Cross passing over the center of the Temple of the Sun arrives at a point at the Temple of the Inscriptions (its main door)».[47]

## Chaac, God B

The god known as Chaac in Colonial texts –the god most depicted in the three pre-Hispanic Mayan codices is mentioned as a cornfield deity, and as a manifestation of water. This includes rain water, lakes, rivers, and seas, which when vaporized ascends into the sky, concentrating in clouds, and coming down again as rain.

Chaac, the god B, is another anthropomorphous deity derived from the dragon, which is represented above all in the codices from the Post-Classic period. But we also find him sculpted in Classic works from the Yucatán peninsula in Bec, Chenes, and Puuc styles. Here he is represented as a large geometric mask made of stone mosaic decorating almost all of the buildings constructed in these styles (figure 84; plates 71, 76, 77, 80, 81, 85). The masks have clear serpentine features and a large «nose» which can be raised or lowered, and is sometimes decorated with circles of water, symbolizing the

84. Large mask of Chaac, the rain god, in the *Codz Pop* at Kabah (drawing by C. Ontiveros).

85. Altar of the Stele M at Copán, which represents the earthly dragon as the Cauac Monster. 756 A.D. Late Classic (drawing by C. Ontiveros, based on Spinden, 1975).

86. Top portion of the Zoomorphic P at Quiriguá: the earthly dragon as the Cauac Monster (drawing by M. Aguirre, based on Maudslay, 1974).

upper stretched fauce of the serpent. There are some large masks with stylized feathers or plants, which could represent either Chaac or Itzamná or Bolon Dz'acab (god which is related to corn), because these tree gods have a serpentine nature.

In the Central Zone, rain —and water in general— is associated with the heavenly and terrestrial dragons. For this reason, it is hard to find representations that correspond to Chaac. Maybe the *Cauac* Monster, which we consider to be a representation of the earthly dragon (besides the Cauac glyps he has plant elements), is a deity related to the earth's water.

The Terrestrial Dragon: Itzam Cab Ain

Considering its relationship with the earth, the dragon symbolizes the earthly surface, as well as the generating power hidden inside. Thus, it is linked with the death god who dwells there, and with the jaguar, who is a symbol of the dead Sun, the netherworld, and the night sky.

During the Classic period, it was sometimes represented with a large, and occasionally fleshless, mask, but with plants and aquatic symbols; it was also called earthly monster and Cauac Monster, because it has that glyph symbolizing water. Examples of the earthly dragon are the Cauac Monster at the altar of Stele M in Copán (figure 85); and the zoomorphic P at Quiriguá, where it was sculpted as a Cauac monster and as a great serpent from which the ruler emerges (figures 86, 87). Another example is the large mask appearing at the base of the *axis mundi* tree, with two serpent heads emerging from its fauces, and which is identified with the solar deity on the panel of the Temple of the Foliated Cross in Palenque (figure 67). Other examples are the lean figure, in this case with corn leaves and *Cauac* glyph which form the pedestal of one of the rulers represented there.

Likewise, outstanding representations of the earthly dragon can be found at the recently discovered Balamkú site (Campeche). Here there is a frieze with plaster reliefs, called House of the Four Kings, which has four large masks of the earthly dragon with plant elements and two serpent heads emerging from its fauces (figure 88). The terrestrial nature of these masks can be corroborated because over them, representations of the rulers can be seen emerging from the open fauces of reptiles which are looking upwards.[48]

The Balamkú reptile figures also represent the earthly dragon because in many plastic works from the Mayan area, from Izapa, as well as in Colonial texts, earth is

87. North side of the Zoomorphic P at Quiriguá: ruler coming out of the earthly dragon's fauces (picture by V.

symbolized as a great alligator or fantastic crocodile. Its Yucatán name is Itzam Cab Ain, «The Earth-Crocodile Dragon»,[49] and Chac Mumul Ain, «Great Muddy Crocodile». In the *Popol Vuh* we can find the equivalent of this crocodile in the caiman, Zipacná, son of Vucub Caquix (the imperfect Sun of the previous era), creator of mountains and of the whole earth, and who in the text symbolizes the earth.

One of the most outstanding works that represent the earthly dragon as a crocodile is the Altar T in Copán (figure 89), whose antecedent (an example of how old this symbol is), is the crocodile from Stele 25 in Izapa already described (figure 59).

The earthly dragon below the gravestone of the tomb at the Temple of the Inscriptions in Palenque (figure 65) is a large fleshless mask within a cavity formed by bones (a clear image of death and the netherworld); it has plant elements, and, on the forehead, the Sun glyph, and the triadic symbol of the earthly dragon. But instead of the glyph with the crossed band there is a glyph representing death. This image confirms that the heavenly and earthly dragons (in this case also underworld symbols) are the one sacred energy which extends to all levels of the cosmos.

Domenici).
88. Detail of the stucco frieze in «The House of the Four Kings» at Balamkú, with the image of the ruler coming out of the earthly dragon. Early Classic (from Baudez, 1996).

## Ah Puch, God A

Mostly identified with the earthly dragon, we find the god that symbolizes death, represented as a skull, as a skeleton, or as a rotting corpse. In the Colonial texts he is called Ah Puch, «The Fleshless», or Kisin, «The Fetid», and has been identified with the god A of the codices. His abode is the lowermost region of the netherworld, where the spirits of most men arrive upon death.

In Classic art works he appears with a necklace made of rattles, as in the codices, and with eyes –never with empty eye sockets. One of the most outstanding images is that of the great plaster panel in Toniná. There he can be seen holding the head of a beheaded victim (plate 107) offered in sacrifice, because the god of death was, of course, linked to human sacrifice.

89. Fragment of the altar T at Copán: earthly crocodile (drawing by M. Aguirre, based on Maudslay, 1974).

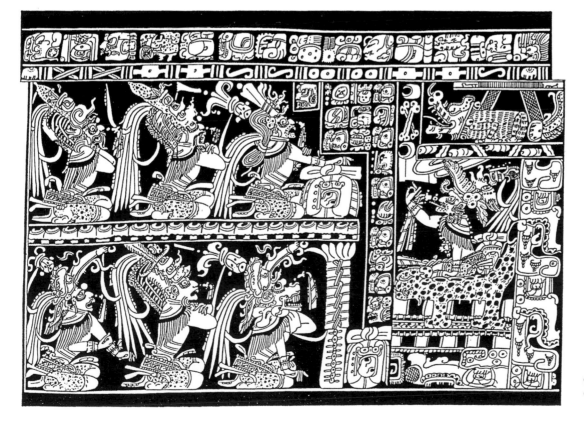

90. Glass of the seven gods (M. Coe in Friedel and Schele, 1993).

91. Altar on the Stele D at Copán which represents the god of death. *Ca.* 736 A.D.. Late Classic (drawing by C. Ontiveros, based on Spinden, 1913).

92. Deity of death in the shape of a skull, in the Temple XII at Palenque (picture by M. de la Garza).

93. God K in the ruler's arms. Temple of the Inscriptions, Palenque (drawing by M. Aguirre, based on A. Ruz, 1973).

Another image is the one at Temple XII also known as Temple of Skull (figure 92), where it is represented in stucco at the base of the door jambs, linking the temple to the netherworld.

And the altar of Stele D in Copán (figure 91) shows the deity's fleshless head, but whose eyes are the glyph of the solar god, who while crossing the netherworld becomes a god of death. In this way he is identified with the Sun at its nadir, that is to say, the dead Sun.

The *Popol Vuh* mentions many deities of death and disease, all headed by Hun Camé, «Death one», Vucub Camé, «Death seven». These deities also seem to have been represented in works from the Classic, such as the so called «Vase of the Seven Gods», in Naranjo, Guatemala (750 to 800 A.C.) (figure 90),[50] where the god L, which Thompson identified as the number 7 jaguar god,[51] can be seen smoking. He is sitting on a throne covered with a jaguar skin, facing six deities which can either be some of the lords of the netherworld mentioned in the text, or aspects of the god of death; although some of them have features that resemble those of the solar god, and have jaguar skins, and thus are associated with the evening Sun, whose epiphany is the jaguar. The background is black, and L, Vucub Camé, the main god, who clearly corresponds to Hun Camé, is under a crocodile which symbolizes the surface of the earth. These details indicate that they are in the netherworld. The number seven coincidence (seven gods, god of the number 7, «Death seven») in the vase and the text, confirms this interpretation. The date of the vase is 4 *Ahau*, 8 *Cumhú* –the date of creation–, so that the scene probably refers to the birth of the gods of the netherworld at the beginning of the present era.

Bolon Dz'acab, God K

One of the gods most represented in the art of the Classic period is the one known as god K, who has been identified with the Bolon Dz'acab mentioned in the written sources, due to a series of coincidences, particularly among the references of Fra Diego de Landa and the codices.[52]

Bolon Dz'acab means «Nine generations», in clear reference to the illustrious lineages of the rulers, the ancestors who dwell in the netherworld; and Classic representations show the deity always in reference to these characters. Despite this, it has recently been called «K'awil» (maybe because the god is associated with corn), based on epigraphic readings.[53]

Bolon Dz'acab is a serpentine, generally anthropomorphous god, with one leg transformed into a serpent, although his face sometimes appears as the face of a serpent-bird or in a serpent's body. The face is composed of a serpent's eye with a spiral-shaped pupil; a supra-orbital scale; the *Nen* glyph (mirror) on its forehead, from which corn leaves emerge (sometimes ending in a tassel), flames, or an axe; long bifurcated nose which derives from the serpent's upper jaw, and the serpent's fang wrapped around the edge of the mouth, a feature present in other serpentine deities, such as Chaac, the god of rain, and Kinich Ahau, a solar deity (figure 93).

During the Classic period this god was represented in reliefs or isolated sculptures, in ceramics and in figurines, walking sticks, and manikin scepters held by the rulers as a symbol of power. These figures have human bodies, a serpentine face, and a leg or the penis transformed into a serpent (figure 94), referring to the illustrious lineage of the ruler who holds it.

The Yucatec name for the manikin scepter is Canhel. Colonial texts use it in reference to the heavenly dragon, in its aspect of creator, thus expressing the correspondence between both deities. On the other hand, the manikin scepter god, due to the peculiarity of its leg, seems to correspond to Hurricane, «One-Legged Thunder», a heavenly Quiché god which is the rain manifestation of Gucumatz. He is also called «Heavenly Heart», which means «center, or axis, essence of heaven»; that is why he appears as ruler of the other deities in the Quiché's divine council.[54]

Bolon Dz'acab also symbolized the offering of blood to the gods, one of the ascetic rites of the ruler. His image appears on the handles of the knives used in self-sacrifice, as can be seen in some lintels of Yaxchilán. While the scepter, walking cane, or manikin figure, symbolize the male masturbation rites performed by the Mayan rulers for the offering of semen, and which are also represented in Yaxchilán and in the plaster reliefs at the entrance of the Temple of the Inscriptions in Palenque.[55]

An extraordinary image of god K appears in a drawing of a codex-style cylindrical vase in the Nakbé region of Guatemala (figure 96).[56] The god's serpent-leg surrounds a woman's voluptuous body, and from the enormous open fauces of this serpent emerges another deity whose arms are stretched towards the woman. The scene has clear sexual connotations, which corroborate the relation of god K with semen.

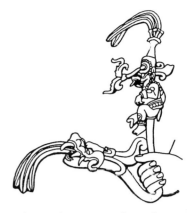

94. Manikin sceptre from the altar at Quiriguá (from Spinden, 1913).

The god is also related with corn, because plant leaves emerge from his forehead. This link is clearly expressed in the panels of the Cross group from Palenque, where god K is a figure sitting in oriental position, in the hands of the rulers, representing the corn, whose cycle is recorded in those reliefs. On the panel of the Temple of the Sun, whose main subject is the corn plant in the shape of an axis mundi (in celebration of its coming to the world), we can also see god K (also called god GII) being born from a snail, with corn leaves emerging from his hand, among which we can see an ear of corn with the shape of a human head (figure 95). All of this confirms god K's nature as a corn deity during the Classic period. This is another reason why he became a god so closely related to men, who had been formed with corn dough by the god of creation according to the cosmogonical myth.

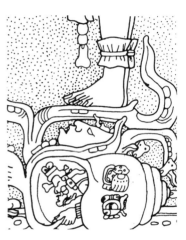

95. The god K being born from a conch shell with maize leaves. Detail from the Panel in the Foliated Cross Temple at Palenque. 692 A.D. (drawing by L. Schele).

The kinship between Bolon Dz'acab and Itzamná is revealed in multiple images where we can see it emerging from the fauces of a two-headed heavenly serpent, as on the gravestone at the Temple of Inscriptions, in Palenque, on Stele D in Copán, and on Lintel 3 of the IV Temple in Tikal. In other representations his face is the Bird's-serpent (mentioned earlier as a variation of the heavenly dragon), such as in the plaster panel in Toniná, and the panels of the Crosses in Palenque. This is why the god K is undoubtedly another aspect of the supreme deity; it seems to symbolize the manifestation of the sacred power of the dragon in the human world.

## God E, Corn God

We have seen how the god K is related to corn. However, there is yet another divine figure that seems to be a manifestation of corn, because its head ends in a corncob. This image is similar to the representations of the corn god, called god E in the Post-Classic codices, with which it has been identified. This deity does not present animal features

96. Bolon Dz'acab. Codex-style glass from the Nakbé region, Guatemala. Ca. 672-830 A.D. (from Reents-Budet, 1994).

97. Copán sculpture representing the young maize god (from Gendrop, 1972).

–his face is that of a young man, and Thompson relates the god K'awil, mentioned in the written sources, with the corn god, because it meant «Plentiful daily bread».[57] Itzamná, the supreme god, is sometimes called Itzamná K'awil, which also shows that the corn god was closely linked to the heavenly dragon. The corn god is the patron of the number 8 and his glyph is Kan (corn) day.

As Classic examples of representations of the corn god, we can mention the well-known Copán sculptures (figure 97); a fragment of Stele 1 from Bonampak, where the corn god emerges from the earthly dragon in the aspect of the Cauac Monster (figure 98), and various ceramic items, where the deity emerges from a turtle shell.[58] Because corn is the plant of man par excellence, the Quiché cosmogonical myth says that man was made out of corn dough, and this is why this god is represented as a human figure without animal features.

## Feminine Deities

From the Classic period, epigraphers mention the reference to ancestral feminine deities in the texts, mainly those of Palenque, such as the one they call First Mother, who appears in the cosmogonical text, and who was born a year after the First Father.

However, there are no stone or plaster sculptures from the Classic, that can be identified as representations of the mother goddess. They do however appear in clay figures from various sites, such as Jaina (plates 111-114), an island located on the coast of Campeche. Here we have found a series of feminine figures with sacred features, such as the two-headed serpent on their back, and hands folded on their chest, in a ritual position. The two-headed serpent, symbol of the godhead, presents the mother goddess in her feminine aspect, and is possibly related to the Moon, as is the mother goddess from the Post-Classic codices.

There are many more deities, or many other aspects of the main gods, represented in the art of the Classic. We have only centered on the great cosmic deities, and on those related to fertility, a prime concern of the Classic Mayas.

## *The Rites*

### General Characteristics

As in many other ancient and modern religions, Mayan religious rites were fundamentally aimed at establishing contact with the sacred forces to attain happiness,

98. Maize God being born from the earthly dragon on Stele 1 at Bonampak, Late Classic.

power, material wealth, relief from ills, forgiveness for errors, and in an even deeper sense, it pursued the survival of man and nature.

The priests, who generally considered themselves chosen by the deities to intervene between man and the gods, were the ones responsible for carrying out the rituals. Their place within society was of prime importance, because the life of the community as a whole was directed to the service of their gods. The Mayas were convinced that without ritual the earth would become sterile, there would be no rain, living beings would not give birth, and the Sun would stop moving and die, prompting the death of the entire cosmos. Thus, the main task of man on earth consisted in feeding and worshiping the gods, as is expressed in the cosmogonical myths.

Rites were complex public celebrations related to calendaric periods, ceremonies for accession to power, and to other events carried out by rulers: agricultural, guild, healing and initiation rites, as well as life-cycle rites: pregnancy, birth, childhood, puberty, marriage, and death.

There are multiple expressions of Mayan ritual from the Classic period, beginning with the ceremonial centers themselves; the heart of the cities, which included temples with pyramidal foundations or pyramids set over platforms, temples for idols, plazas, ball courts, tombs, and innumerable sculptures that speak to us about the rites.

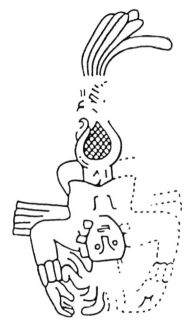

99. Human sacrifice by heart removal. Details from the steles 11 and 14 at Piedras Negras (drawing from C. Ontiveros in Nájera, 1987).

## Sacrifice

Acts common to all rites were prayers, dances, songs, dramas about myths and stories of illustrious ancestors who had been deified. But the central event of ritual were the sacrifices.

Sacrifice means to «make sacred», and it includes all those gifts which were offered to the divinities. There were multiple and varied offerings. Since to the Mayas the gods were invisible and impalpable, they were offered subtle substances, such as the perfume of flower and incense, and food and drink flavors. But the most important offering was the vital energy or the spirit contained in the blood of animals and humans.

That is why the most prized gifts were those which implied the spilling of blood and the death of the victims, an act which allowed the liberation of vital energy. In most rites, bloody self-sacrifices and the ritual death of human beings and animals were observed.

## Human Sacrifice

Human sacrifice did not only serve as a means for communicating with the deities to thank them for their favors, but also as a way of securing them. During the Classic period there were diverse ritual deaths, such as heart removal. Because the heart is the place where vital energy resides the gods would eat it at the very moment it abandoned the body. This can be seen in steles 11 and 14 from Piedras Negras (figure 99). Other death rituals included beheading (plates 107) and arrow shooting, for the fertilization of the fields, because the head is linked with the corncob, and arrow shooting (figure 100) with sex.[59]

Bloody sacrifices among Mesoamerican peoples are mainly explained in their conceptions about the gods and the meaning of blood, especially the blood of man. The Mayas considered human blood sacred because it came from the gods; it contained the spirit or vital energy of the deities, which the latter gave to man when they created him, as the cosmogonical myths say. Thus, there is an essential consanguinity between man and the sacred. Blood is the cosmic vital energy that comes from the gods and will return to them through sacrifice. Blood is life itself; for which reason bloody sacrifice

100. Scene of human sacrifice by bowshooting on a rock carving in the Temple II at Tikal (from Henderson, 1981).

means giving life back to the gods so that they, in return, may prevail and sustain the life of the cosmos. Without blood, the gods die and the universe is comes to an end.

And in another sense, sacrifice also meant feeding men with the essence of divinity. In many sacrifices, the human victim became the god during the rite; he was dressed up and worshiped; and after being sacrificed, he was eaten by the faithful. This communion with the god, besides transforming man into a sacred being, tended to strengthen ties among the community members. In diverse rites, the incarnated deity was killed in front of the temple, at the top of the pyramid. Then, it was thrown down the front steps of the pyramid to the plaza, where it was cut into pieces and eaten by the faithful. The meaning of this rite was that the god had descended from the sacred heights of the heavens (symbolized by the pyramid) to the world of man, where it established a consubstantial tie with him.

## Self-sacrifice

Following the basic idea of the need to feed the gods with blood, self-sacrifice was a ritual practice in the Mayan world. This consisted in making a sacrifice of blood but without killing the volunteer.

Blood was extracted with boring tools made of animal bone, strings with thorns, and other objects. It was then generally poured on papers or into containers and offered to the gods' images. Various works of art –the Yaxchilán lintels (figure 101; plate 99), and the Bonampak frescoes (figure 158), for example– show that this rite had been practiced since the Classic.

But self-sacrifice was also an essential part of the ascetic rites, which, on the one hand, were preparatory rituals for the religious ceremonies, and, on the other, initiation rites and customary practices of priests and sorcerers. Many cultures considered that ascetic practices conferred supernatural powers that allowed a closer link with the godhead.[60]

Besides blood, semen was another sacred liquid. Considered a recipient of vital energy, it was offered by the ascetics to their deities in onanistic rituals. The gifts of blood

101. Self-sacrifice scenes on the lintels at Yaxchilán. On the left: Lintel 17. Lady Balam-Ix celebrates the birth of Lord Bird-Jaguar's (who is sitting at the front) and his other wife's son. 770 A.D.
On the right, Lintel 15. Lady 6-Tun, a third wife of Bird-Jaguar, during the vision following the self-sacrifice performed at the same date as the happening on lintel 17. 770 A.D. Late Classic (from Schele and Miller, 1986).

and semen were accompanied by insomnia, fasting, sexual abstinence, purifying baths, or bath abstinence, prayers, dances and rhythmic chants, and either ingestion or application of psychoactive substances such as tobacco, hallucinogenic plants or mushrooms, as well as intoxicating drinks.

## Idea of Man and Canonization of Rulers

In the Mayan universe, suffused as it is with the sacredness born of movement, of life and death, man stands forming an harmonic whole with nature. According to myth, man belongs to the universe because his being participates of plant, divine, and animal substances. But at the same time, he is a being apart from others, because he is conscious and is able to know and handle the spatiotemporal cosmos through his ritual actions. These ideas are also expressed in the archaeological remains of the Classic period; for example, the extraordinary gravesite at the Temple of the Inscriptions in Palenque, where the skeleton of the ruler, now known as Pacal, has a jade sphere in one hand, and a dice in the other: both are basic cosmological symbols of heaven and earth, time and space. This shows that this man was aware of his universe and lived in harmony with it.

Being responsible for the existence of the cosmos, man acts as an *axis mundi*. This is evident in many pre-Hispanic works, among which some of the most impressive are Stele 25 at Izapa (figure 59), which we have already mentioned, and the gravestone on Pacal's tomb (figure 65). Here the ruler is depicted at the center, between heaven and the netherworld, on the surface of the earth, and just at the foot of the cross, the axis of the universe and one of the artistic representations of Itzamná, the supreme god.

The men represented in Classic works are generally rulers, called *Halach uinicoob*, «True men», by the Yucatán Mayas. Although in some pictures and sculptures we can also see the common folk, they are generally depicted in relation to their rulers, many times in an act of submission, as can be seen in the paintings of the Bonampak Temple.

The main symbol of the ruler is the dragon, as a celestial, creative, organizing force, which grants him the powers he needs in order to rule over the people, and as an earthly force, which turns him into a supernatural being. The ruler, represented in multiple steles and lintels from the central Mayan area, carries the heavenly dragon (in the aspect of a two-headed serpent) over his chest as a ceremonial band (figure 102). He holds it in his hand as a scepter or manikin stick (figure 94), and it also appears in his headdress and other accessories, such as belts, bracelets, and sandals. Thus, the dragon symbolizes the omnipotence of the ruler, on whose face the features of a dragon are noticeable. This was meant to express the ruler's assimilation to the supreme deity (figure 103).[61]

The rulers also carry scepters that symbolize the *axis mundi* with the heavenly deity. For example, on lintels 2 (figure 69) and 5 (figure 68) from Yaxchilán, where the characters hold cross-shaped scepters with flowers on the ends of the horizontal bar, representing the world axis tree, from whose top branches quetzal birds are descending. This is another way of expressing that the ruler has in his hands the power granted by the heavenly deity, a power which extends to the four directions of the cosmos.

## The Rulers' Initiation Rites and Shamanic Practices

Mayan rulers practiced strict initiation rites to reach the throne, as well as constant ascetic practices as long as they were important. That is, the Mayan rulers of the Classic age, like many Mayan healers and diviners of today, were sorcerers or shamans.

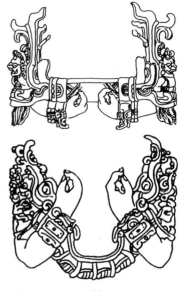

102. Ceremonial bars representing a bicephalous celestial dragon. Top: Stele N at Copán. Bottom: Stele P at Copán (drawing by G. Bustos, based on Robicsek, 1972).

103. Stele I at Copán. Ruler with dragon-featured face. 668-731 A.D. (drawing by C. Ontiveros, based on Robicsek, 1972).

104. Markers from the ball court at Copán, where gods playing the ball game can be seen. 731-751 A.D. Late Classic (from Fash, 1991).

105. Frieze on the Temple of the Cross at Palenque (drawing by M. Aguirre, based on Maudslay, 1974).

Various sculptures, among them many lintels of Yaxchilán, show us the monarchs emerging from the fauces of gigantic serpents (figure 101; plate 98). The character either carries the necessary tools for self-sacrifice –one of the most important shamanic rituals–, or receives them from a woman. Sometimes the woman gives the man the sacred package of the shaman's paraphernalia,[62] which is the symbol of supreme power. The ruler also emerges from the fauces of the terrestrial monster, in the same manner as with the zoomorphic P from Quiriguá (figure 87), and thus, he is likened with the sun, whose image can also be seen emerging from the dragon's fauces. The ruler is the Sun of the human world.

Claude Baudez, in his iconographic analysis of the frieze at the House of the Four Kings of Balamuk, says with respect to this:

«Besides illustrating in detail the opposing and complementary aspects of the netherworld, the icon shows that the dynastic cycle was compared to the solar cycle. In this conception, access to the throne is represented with the king emerging from the fauces of the terrestrial monster, just as the Sun emerges from the mouth of the earth. The king's death is seen as the setting of the Sun, when it falls into the mouth of the terrestrial monster –as with king Pacal from Palenque, represented on the lid of his sarcophagus».[63]

The idea of the Sun coming out from the fauces of the earthly monster also refers to an initiation of the gods, which is compared to that of the rulers, for it comes from the netherworld; in other words, he is being reborn each morning. Let us not forget that in the *Popol Vuh*, the characters destined to become the Sun and the moon have to go through an initiation in death and rebirth in the netherworld, in order to ascend to the heavens.

These representations of the Classic rulers are undoubtedly expressions of some initiation rites appearing in the written sources,[64] and which have survived until today among the Mayas and other Mesoamerican cultures.

Initiation rites begin with a long apprenticeship; the iniciate goes to a dark and remote place in the mountains or the woods. There he will stand near an anthill, from where a great boa emerges (symbol of *chthonic* forces) and swallows him, grinds him between its fauces, and after digesting him, finally excretes him. This is the way in which the shaman appears. He is a consecrated man, who has acquired supernatural skills through the serpent in order to exert his power over men. The serpent's role here is that of demiurge or «Master of Initiation». Once consecrated, the shaman may practice static trance and use the sacred plants (hallucinogenic and medicinal) to cure and foretell.

At the Temple of the Crosses in Palenque, next to the solar and the corn cycles, there is the representation of the initiation cycle of the rulers. Schele and Freidel say that the three sanctuaries symbolize the entrance into the netherworld, and compare them with the journey to the netherworld of the twins in the *Popol Vuh*.[65] Plaster reliefs decorating the northern and eastern friezes at the Temple of the Cross (drawn by Maudslay), of

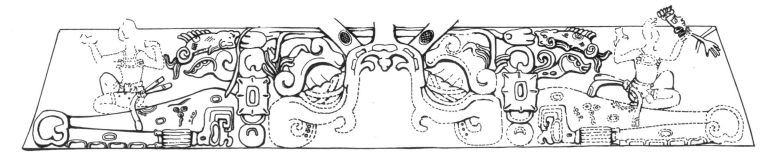

which now only fragments exist, represent a front view of the dragon with open fauces (figure 105). Thus, this is a monster-temple whose main facade probably had dragon's face as an entrance; it is therefore an initiation temple.[66] This confirms that the rites represented within are those of initiation of the rulers.

The transfiguration of all those who ruled, the ancient *Halach uinicoob*, the «True Men», and the present shamans, is linked with the terrestrial serpent or dragon, for it is an animal of the netherworld, a personification of death, and initiation implies dying in order to be reborn a consecrated being. Because the serpent is an animal that transforms itself, that has abandoned its old skin, cyclically springing up again, much as plants do, he becomes immortal. The serpent can make man a sacred creature because she is a being linked with the divine and cosmic forces, with the great Mother Earth, with water, with the phallus, and with knowledge. That is why the man who is linked to her acquires her qualities. The man who is swallowed by a serpent dies only to return to life as a man capable of entering into the hidden mysteries of the cosmos, the secrets of life and death, and of the future.[67]

106. Ball player represented on a polychrome glass. Late Classic (from Hellmuth, 1987b).

## The Ball Game as the Rite of the Rulers[68]

One of the most common and important pre-Hispanic rites was the ball game, because courts can be found in all the Classic Mayan cities and are all located at the ceremonial centers (figure 113; plates 54, 70). The symbolic sense of the game is evident in the reliefs found at the ball courts, mainly in the markers. It almost always has a cosmological significance, as a comparison between these reliefs and the myth of creation included in the *Popol Vuh* demonstrates.

The religious import of the ball game can be associated to one of the basic concepts in Mesoamerican thought: the struggle between opposing forces, which makes the existence of the cosmos possible. This is expressed in various myths which refer to the battle of heavenly and luminous beings against dark beings from the netherworld, a combat that is recreated at the ball court.

The game of men and the sacred war reproduced the war between the gods themselves. Maybe this is why during the Classic period the game had the ritual function of propiciating, through sympathetic magic, the movement of the stars, which was the same as safe-guarding the life of the universe. This is why the ball game always appears in relation to the earth's fertility. The Classic reliefs seem to represent the game of the gods as well as the ritual game of men, in which during the Classic period the rulers themselves participated.

An example of the game of the gods can be seen on the reliefs decorating the markers at the ball game in Copán –three works which date back to the 6th century, and which were found at Structure IIb (figure 104). The analysis of the different elements in these discs, shows that the game took place at night, at the moment when the Sun is in the netherworld. And it seems that it was there where they represented the initiatory episode of the appearance of the Sun and the moon in the *Popol Vuh*, in

107. Step VII from the Hieroglyphic Staircase of Structure 33 at Yaxchilán. Bird-Jaguar plays with a ball containing a prisoner's body. 744 A.D. Late Classic (from Schele and Miller, 1986).

108. Ball player with the characteristic belt and with a headdress shaped like a deer head. Painting on a polychrome glass. Late Classic (from Hellmuth, 1987b).

which the ball game between the twin heroes and the gods of the netherworld is a central event.[69]

The markers at Copán show that among the Mayas of the Lowlands, as early as the Classic, the ball game constituted a mythic explanation of the origin of the stars and their movement, as well as of the oppositions in nature, and illustrated the continuity of this belief until the time of the *Popol Vuh*.

Due to its religious significance, the nature of the ball game was that of an initiation rite, that is to say a rite of passage from profane to religious life, as well as of acquisition of supernatural powers which would allow direct communication with the gods. Just as the gods of the heavens in the *Popol Vuh* reached their apotheosis through the ball game, in the same manner the rulers from the Classic period participated in the ball-game ritual to go through their initiation rites as shamans.

Many art works from the same period, such as the reliefs in the rises of the arches at Temple 33 in Yaxchilán (figure 107), the Cancún marker, and the gravestones at the American Indian Museum in New York (figs. 109, 111), show the priest-ruler playing ball. The players are wearing luxurious headdresses, various representations of the god K (the deity of the rulers), and sometimes of Itzamná, the supreme god. The characters were represented either playing, or motionless, but always wearing the game implements. Their names appear in the associated hieroglyphic inscriptions: Jaguar-Bird, in Yaxchilán; Jaguar paw in Seibal, etc. Indigenous Colonial texts corroborate that the ball game was practiced by the rulers.[70]

In the reliefs of some Post-Classic ball courts we can also see beheading or decollation sacrifice rites symbolizing fertility. These symbols appear also in various Classic works, the most outstanding of which is the gravestone of the Temple of the Foliated Cross in Palenque, where the ears of corn are depicted as human heads (figure 67). The head is associated with the game because of the formal relationship (the sphere) between the head, the ball, and the stars. The latter were imagined as the heads of decapitated gods, and were identified with the ball. Likewise, the movement of the ball within the court was seen as the movement of the stars in the heavens.

None of the sources mention that the players were sacrificed or beheaded; so it seems that sacrifice by decapitation in the ball court or in association with it occurred with prisoners of war or slaves.

109. Scene of a ball game carved on a panel from an unknown Mayan site (Site Q, Calakmul?). The player on the left is dressed as Xbalanqué, while his opponent represents a god from the Netherworld. It seems as if the two Lords are representing the Twin Brothers Myth, known through the *Popol Vuh*. Late Classic (from Schele and Miller, 1986).

The reliefs and texts associated with the ball game, as well as the location of the courts at ceremonial centers, are an indication that the game symbolized the idea of cosmic struggle between opposing forces –a fundamental concept in Mesoamerican thought–, and that it also served as an initiation rite performed by the shaman-rulers as a part of their consecration. Likewise, they show that the purpose of the game was to propiciate, through sympathetic magic, the movement of the stars, which in turn gives rise to temporality, and contributes to fertility in nature and in general to life in the cosmos.

110. Pacal's skeleton, the great ruler of Palenque (picture by A. Romano, at the time when it was discovered).

### Beliefs about Life Beyond the Grave and Funeral Ritual

The various burial sites from the Classic period which were found by archaeologists, tell us about complex funeral ceremonies, corroborating the beliefs on human fate after death expressed in Colonial written sources. According to these, the spiritual portion of man is immortal. When it leaves the body upon death, it will dwell eternally in one of three main regions depending on the type of death. These regions are: the lowermost level of the netherworld, called Xibalbá by the Quichés, and Mitnal by the Yucatán Mayas; Heaven; and the «Ceiba Tree Paradise», a terrestrial place where there is a great ceiba tree.[71]

There were various techniques for disposing of the dead body: primary and secondary burial, cremation, and maybe air exposure and abandonment.[72] The skeletons often appear accompanied by human or animal remains, such as dogs and felines. Likewise, there are many types of graves –from a simple hole in the ground, to great funerary chambers built with domes, or even covered by a great pyramid that served as a funerary monument. This is the case of Pacal's grave in Palenque (figure 110) and the one at the Owl Temple in Dzibanché, from the Early Classic.[73] And there were also graves under temples and houses, in caves, cracks or even rock holes, or in abandoned chultunes (grain or water deposits), buried pots or urns, and cenotes.

At Uaxactún and other places there were childrens' skulls buried together with the phalanxes of an adult, supposedly the mother's, showing that she in some way accompanied her child.[74] Buried children are most of the time in fetal position inside pots, which obviously symbolize the mother's womb and which are undoubtedly related to the idea of rebirth.

111. Panel with a scene of a ball game which might come from the same staircase to which the panel in the figure 109 belonged. Both players are dressed as warriors. The one on the right has various elements that define him as the one who was beaten at the battle (from Schele and Miller, 1986).

Mortuary bundles have also been found, that is, the remains of a body which was covered with cloth prepared with a resin or liquid, that was petrified, as the one found in 1994 by Ramón Carrasco at a burial site from the Late Classic, at Structure 15 in Calakmul. And various graves were also found, with secondary burials of bones and other parts of the body which had previously recieved different treatment, such as ingestion, exposition, or even inhumation. Generally, these are multiple burials, most certainly of sacrificed victims.[75]

The graves contain several objects, such as tools, weapons, ceramics, sea-shell ornaments, obsidian, flint, bone, jade and other semiprecious stones, copper rattles, musical instruments, figures of deities, complete skeletons, and parts of animals, and other objects symbolizing the sacred energies that would protect the spirit. The objects that the deceased used when alive were included, and consisted of working tools, codices and other ritual objects –if they were priests–, and if they were shamans, their paraphernalia.

All of these things illustrate the belief that the spirit would live as it had lived on earth, preserving its identity during the journey towards the region predestined for the victim according to the type of death. We prefer not to call them offerings because properly speaking they are not part of a cult of the dead, but a gift from those alive to help the dead during a period after the death of the body.

Since the Mayas believed that animals, plants, minerals, and even man-made objects were also possessed of a spirit, it is clear that this invisible part of the objects was the one which would be used by the spirit of the deceased. This is why in the graves we can find pots which have been intentionally broken, or «killed».

The objects with the greatest significance in burials were jade or other stones, which were put inside the mouth of the corpse; an inverted pot, turtle shells, or pieces of stone protecting the head; stingray spines over the pubis and bones; feline teeth and claws. The object over the head serves as protection for the immortal spirit, because it was considered that the latter emerged from the body through the top of the head. Maybe this was a way to keep it from being stolen or destroyed while it travelled to the beyond. We know that the stingray spines were used for self-sacrifice, so maybe their being set over the corpse symbolized the offering man makes of himself to the gods after his

112. Temple-monster at Chicanná, Campeche (picture by T. Pérez).

death; in other words, that in the beyond he would keep worshiping and supporting them. But we don't know the meaning of their relation to the genitals, unless they refer to the sacrifice performed on them during fertility rites. The jaguar symbolizes the Sun on its journey through the netherworld, so that the portions of its body in the graves might refer to an identification of the man who descends to the netherworld, with the star in its nocturne transit. But we also know that the jaguar was the animal *alter ego* of rulers and priests, and that they were shamans who practiced self-sacrifice with stingray spines, so maybe the Mayan burial sites with remains of both animals belong to shamans. Others, such as the ones at Kaminaljuyú, have sculptures in the form of mushrooms indicating the use of hallucinogenic mushrooms, and thus probably belonging to a shaman.

The dog's skeleton confirms the belief that this animal led the spirit towards its final abode –a belief which is not only Mesoamerican, but universal.

The stone, according to Colonial sources, was placed when he was about to die, so that his spirit would incarnate in it; this is why it was preserved carefully and offered sacrifices. It was because of the hardness and the durability of the stone that it symbolized the immortal spirit, called *ol* by the Yucatán Mayas, a spirit which transcended the body's destruction.

Vermilion red powder was also commonly used. The body was painted with it during the primary burials (when the flesh disappeared, the powder adhered to the bones, much like in Pacal's tomb), or it was sprinkled over the bones during the secondary burials. Red was the color of birth, because of its association with the east, where the Sun rises, and therefore with the origin of life; so that its use in corpses indicates a sympathetic magic rite to propiciate life in the beyond, that is, immortality.

Archaeological data also indicate a great veneration for the dead that had been deified, but only for those who had been important during their lifetime. This fact is corroborated, for example, in the steles of Copán which represent rulers, and underneath them have chambers strewn with offerings.

113. Ball game court at Tikal, Guatemala (picture by M. de la Garza).

135

Sacred spaces or places where the gods manifested themselves, may have been special spots uninhabited by man such as woods, water sources, or mountains. But they were also the ceremonial centers built on sites with outstanding features that placed them apart as abodes of divine beings. The ceremonial centers, which constituted the core of Mayan cities, were erected as images of the cosmos. The centers were built following cosmogonic and cosmological models, as ocurrs with most ancient cities of religious peoples. Federico González says:

«Every city is located in the center of the universe; construction is not possible without the absolution of profane space and time, and the establishment of sacred time and space. The city is always an *imago mundi*, a world image».[76]

Mayan cities were built following astral orientations,[77] which filled spaces with sacred energies from heavenly beings during their trajectories. Thus plazas, temples, pyramids, ball game courts, arches and paved roads, patios, and other buildings symbolize the primordial spaces where time originates, and the three great levels of the universe, a well as the paths of the stars.

For example when Carrasco describes Calakmul, Campeche, he says:

«Classic Mayas, when configurating their urban space, sought to reproduce the sacred landscape in the myth of the world's creation. The design of the north-south axis of the Calakmul central plaza is a symbolic arrangement in which the surface of the plaza represents the primeval sea and the pyramidal foundations, the sacred mountains where ancestors and deities dwelt.»[78]

Carrasco adds that the duplication of the space of creation in Mayan architecture sanctified the activities carried out here; activities which were not only ritual but also political, for both had religious import for the Mayas of the Classical.

114. Ritual arch at Kabah, Yucatán (picture by M. de la Garza).

The plazas were the spaces where the people participated in official religious ceremonies (plates 14, 54), while the temples on top of the pyramids were reserved for the priests, the *sancta sanctorum* which only they could enter perform a variety of ceremonies, among them human sacrifices (plates 14, 22, 29, 67).

The temples that were erected over the pyramidal foundations can represent both the last stratum of heaven as the terrestrial level, from where one descended into the netherworld. The pyramids that sustained the temples symbolize the heavenly and the netherworld strata, such as the Temple of the Cross, and the Temple of the Inscriptions in Palenque, cosmological images of the heavens and the netherworld.

Likewise, groups such as Toniná's acropolis (plates 16-18) have been interpreted as cosmological images. Juan Yadeum says that the acropolis has seven platforms on whose extremes the thirteen cosmological levels are represented, and which symbolizes the ascent into heavens and the descent into the netherworld. The sacred mountain, he adds, is oriented according to the movement of the Sun, with its two equinoctial extremes.[79]

At Dzibanché, facing Temple I, there is a plaza limited to the north and to the south by two elongated and identical buildings, each with two galleys and nine openings in the exterior walls, symbolizing the nine levels of the netherworld.[80]

On the other hand, the temples sometimes represent the serpentine monster through which the rulers ended their initiation rites. These are the so called monster-temples (or «zoomorphic facades»), which can be found in the Río Bec, Chenes, and Puuc styles of the Yucatán peninsula (figure 112; plates 58, 60). But they were also represented at Classic sites of the Central Zone, such as Copán and Palenque (figure 105). The complete facade of the monster-temples is a large central mask, whose mouth serves as the entrance, flanked as it is by rows of teeth, with spiralled eyes over the opening; on each side, they have earrings, and other decorative elements can be seen, such as serpents, huts, and frets.

The monster-temple seems to represent the divine site that can only be entered by the consecrated ones. This means, all those who have been initiated, because being swallowed by a serpent is the way in which one acquires supernatural powers among

115. Ritual arch at Labná, Yucatán (picture by M. de la Garza).

137

the Mayas and other groups. Thus, the temple's interior represents the entrails of the great serpent, the Master of Initiation, inside which men can become shamans.

The ball courts (figure 113; plates 54, 70), as we have already mentioned, represent heaven, and repeat the movement of the stars; the stucco paths repeat those followed by the stars on earth. These paths, found in many cities in Yucatán, are called *sacbeoob*, or «artificial, handmade roads», and «white roads». *Sacbeoob* are of different types; they communicate buildings within the same city (plate 73) and stellite centers with the capital city. Some also served as dikes for lakes, and it is possible that even these follow astronomical alignments.[81]

With respect to their meaning, several interpretations have been advanced. However, there is no doubt that they had a religious function and meaning, and this can be confirmed in various myths about sacred *sacbeoob* both ancient and modern.

In many cities in the Puuc region, such as Sayil, Labná, and Kabah, there is an internal road system that communicates the different groups of buildings following a north-south axis.[82] Moreover, on the outskirts of some cities huge arches rise at each of the ends of a *sacbé*, which joins two cities. For example, at the northern area of Kabah, there is a big isolated arch built over an independent platform (structure 1B1) (figure 114; plate 78); here is the starting point of a great *sacbé* which ends in a similar arch in Uxmal.

This great road seems to have had a basically symbolic and ritual meaning. That is, it represents a religious link between the two cities. Thus, this road could have served for religious pilgrimages, such as were carried out in other Mayan sites, because in order to walk, even carrying merchandise, a road as ample as the *sacbé* was unnecessary. The roads were carefully planned out and executed because the sacred journey had to be made on a road as sacred: a terrestrial reproduction of the great white road of heaven, the Milky Way, which is at the same time the body of the heavenly dragon.

The plaster floor generally had celestial significance, because it was applied over other divine spaces, such as ball game courts, which were also symbols of heaven, where the stars, represented by the ball, moved, and some patios and plazas, where many religious ceremonies took place.

The universal symbol of the arch —a transit from a profane state into a sacred one, such as the bridge between the terrestrial and the heavenly levels (the rainbow)– sheds light on our knowledge of the peculiar Mayan buildings that stood at the beginning and the end of the sacred roads (figure 115; plate 74). Thus, the function of the arches, which begin and finish in a *sacbé*, seems to have served to mark the limits of the sacred space of the ceremonial center, and to pass underneath them must have constituted an important rite of access.

In this way, the Mayan cities, dynamically and symbolically merged into the surrounding landscape (which also contained sacred elements), are the meeting points of men and gods. Both landscape and city, «are manifestations of internal forces liberated into shapes that reveal the qualitative and quantitative order of the invisible worlds behind them».[83]

The religious conception of the cosmos was, thus, the basis of life for the Mayas since the Classic period. All the outstanding works that have remained tell us about a great culture whose axis was the link between man and god, as their own words, directed to a supreme deity, express:

«Oh you, beauty of the day! You, hurricane! You, heart of heaven and earth! You, bestower of wealth, and bestower of sons and daughters! Turn your glory and your richness towards us; give my children and vassals life and growth; let the ones who shall support and feed you multiply; those who call your name in the fields, on the roads, and by the river banks, over the cliffs, under the trees, among the reeds...

«Let those who feed you and support you have a good life, in your presence, You Heaven's Heart, Earth's Heart... heaven's dome, surface of the earth, the four corners, the four cardinal points. Let only peace and tranquility be before your mouth, before you, Oh Lord!»[84]

## Notes

[1] Freidel and Schele, 1993, p. 60.

[2] The term comes from the Latin noun *dracon*, serpent, which derives from the verb *dercomai*, which defines the intensity of the serpent's fixed and paralyzing stare. *Dracon* is equivalent to *ophis*, ophidian. That is why the evil serpents in European Medieval myths are known as dragons. Such is the case also of the fantastic serpentine gods from Persia and other places in Asia, and of the auspicious Chinese and Japanese divinities, which have serpent and bird-like features. Thus «dragon» has become a universal term, the one which most precisely defines that Mesoamerican symbol, whose most notorious aspect is the plumed serpent that can be found in the most important cultures of that area.

[3] Nájera, 1987.

[4] See De la Garza, in press.

[5] See De la Garza, 1975.

[6] In the *Popol Vuh* and the *Sololá Memorial*.

[7] *Popol Vuh*.

[8] *Chumayel's Chilam Balam*, pp. 242-244.

[9] In Nahuatl cosmogony it is the fifth one, corresponding to the fifth cosmic direction or center of the universe.

[10] De la Garza, 1987.

[11] Freidel and Schele, 1993, p. 60.

[12] *Ibidem*, p. 64.

[13] On this date thirteen 400 year cycles, called *Baktunes* according to Mayan conceptions that hold that time is infinite, came to an end. According to the cosmogonic idea, there were other cosmic eras before, to which myths refer.

[14] Freidel and Schele call the Bird-serpent Itzam-Ye identifying it with Vucub Caquix, Seven Macaw in the *Popol Vuh*, the fake Sun of the previous era, an interpretation which differs from ours. See Bird-serpent analysis in the paragraph: *The gods*.

[15] Thompson, 1970, pp. 195-196.

[16] Contemporary tzotziles describe the sacred mountain, on top of which there are the divinized ancestors and gods, as divided into different strata and with a great staircase joining them. That is, with the image of a pyramid (Holland, 1978, p. 110). This reinforces the interpretation of the pre-Hispanic idea of heaven as a stepped pyramid. And in Colonial texts it is said that at the beginning of time the gods located themselves on the mountains («Título de los señores de Totonicapán», in De la Garza, 1980, p. 400).

[17] For the Mayas, 10 is the number of the god of death, so he would then be under the nine levels of the netherworld.

[18] *Chilam Balam de Chumayel*, pp. 88-89.

[19] See Aveni, 1980, and Villa Rojas, 1968.

[20] See Villa Rojas, 1968, p. 136.

[21] See discussion in León-Portilla,1994, Appendix II.

[22] Adams, 1986, pp.441-442. See León-Portilla, 1994.

[23] See Cohodas, 1974.

[24] See paragraph: *The Sacred Spaces*.

[25] Guénon, *op. cit.*, p. 57.

[26] Thompson, 1962, glyph 544.

[27] Thompson, 1962, glyph T585.

[28] Freidel and Schele call it Tree at the World and say its hieroglyphic name is *Wakah-Chan*, which literally means «Raised up to the Sky» (1993, p. 53).

[29] Freidel and Schele call this axis Na-Te'-Kán, «First-Precious-Tree» (1993, p. 54).

[30] Champeaux and Sterckx, 1989. p. 22.

[31] Guénon, 1969, pp. 186-7.

[32] As is shown in archaeoastronomy, the new science founded by Antony Aveni and to which Horst Hartung, and John B. Carlson, among others, have contributed.

[33] See De la Garza, 1992.

[34] Campaign, 1995.

[35] Thompson, 1970, pp. 195-196. This idea is about modern-day tzotziles.

[36] Cohodas, 1974, p. 19.

[37] Landa, 1966, p. 48.

[38] See Freidel and Schele, 1993.

[39] Schellhas, 1904.

[40] De la Garza, 1982.

[41] See note 2.

[42] Romero and Rique, 1995.

[43] See Sosa, 1984.

[44] See Nalda, 1944.

[45] Thompson, 1960, p. 80.

[46] Some have called this eye the «divine eye». It is the serpent's eye, which is carried by all deities related to it.

[47] Hartung, 1987, p. 19. See Carlson, 1976.

[48] Baudez, 1996.

[49] *Itsam* is not the name of an alligator, but of a god. They believe he is Itzamná in its earth-god aspect (*Diccionario Maya Cordemex*, p. 272).

[50] Reents, 1994, p. 236. Freidel and Schele, 1993.

[51] Thompson, 1970, p. 106.

[52] Thompson, 1970, p. 227.

[53] Fields, in Reents-Budet,1994.

[54] *Popol Vuh*, De la Garza, 1980, p. 13.

[55] See Coggins, 1988.

[56] Reents-Budet, 1994. Foundation for the Advancement of Mesoamerican Studies.

[57] Thompson, 1970, p. 289.

[58] See Freidel and Schele, 1993.

[59] See Nájera, 1987.

[60] De la Garza, 1990.

[61] De la Garza, 1982.

[62] According to Colonial texts, this bundle was a major symbol of power and contained self-sacrifice instruments, sacred stones, hallucinogenic and healing mushrooms and plants, as well as other objects used by sorcerers.

[63] Baudez, 1996, p. 40.

[64] See De la Garza, 1982.

[65] Schele and Freidel, 1990. p. 239.

[66] See Chapter VI.

[67] See De la Garza, 1982.

[68] De la Garza and Izquierdo, 1992.

[69] See detailed analysis in the works of De la Garza and Izquierdo, 1992.

[70] See «Testamento de los Xpantzay», in De la Garza, *Literatura maya*.

[71] De la Garza, 1978.

[72] See Ruz, 1968.

[73] Campana, 1995.

[74] See Ruz, 1968, p. 115.

[75] See Ruz, 1968.

[76] González, 1989, chapter IV.

[77] See Aveny, 1980.

[78] Carrasco and Boucher, 1994.

[79] Yadeum, 1994, p. 25.

[80] Nalda *et al.*, 1994, p. 17.

[81] See De la Garza, 1993.

[82] Pollock, 1980, p. 140.

[83] Ortega Chávez, 1992, p. 8.

[84] *Popol Vuh*, De la Garza, 1980, pp. 94, 95.

# Art
## Sentries of Eternity

*Beatriz de la Fuente, Leticia Staines Cicero,*
*Alfonso Arellano Hernández*

*A Tangible Cosmos*

Between the 10th century B.C. and the 16th century A.D. Mayan groups inhabited a territory with an approximate surface area of 350 000 km², that included the Mexican states of Campeche, Yucatán, Quintana Roo, Tabasco and Chiapas, and extended as far as Guatemala, Belize, and a portion of Honduras and El Salvador.

Throughout the vast geographical region there are noticeable differences concerning rainfall, topography, and all the natural resources that influenced their architecture, either in the distribution of the different buildings, or in the given solutions and materials.[1] The people adjusted to and sometimes even transformed natural conditions, so we can find cities over mountains or small hills, in savannas, islands, next to rivers, lagoons, or to the sea.

Due to their geographic location Mayan territory is traditionally divided into three areas: South Zone, Central Zone, and North Zone, or Northern Plains (figure 9).

The South Zone comprises the Highlands of Guatemala and Chiapas, Mexico, as well as the Pacific coast. It has high volcanic mountains and pine forests.

The Central Zone (Southern Lowlands) includes a portion of Honduras, the Petén area, of Chiapas and Tabasco, the southern area of Campeche, Quintana Roo, and Belize. It is a region were there is thick rainforest, lakes such as the Petén Itzá, large and flowing rivers, like the Candelaria, Usumacinta, Grijalva, Pasión, Lacanjá, and Motagua, which were also the main routes of communication.

The North Zone or Northern Plains (also known as Northern Lowlands) is located in central and north Yucatán, and is formed by a plate of limestone. The Puuc hills arise from northwestern Yucatán to central Campeche. Their estimated maximum height is 100 meters above sea level. There are natural water deposits (*aguadas*) and underground rivers. These subterranean currents are left exposed when the soil of a cave collapses, leaving natural wells (*cenotes*) above ground. Besides being important water resources they were sacred because they were considered a link with the netherworld. The Mayas also built the *chultunes* (cisterns) for storing rainwater.

116. Rebuilding of a Mayan hut and the stone basement ground plan (*Colha e i maya...*).

Architectural constructions are the most important cultural expressions of a civilization. They are spaces where multiple daily activities are carried out. That is why through different types of buildings we can interpret the way of life of its inhabitants, the political and economic conditions, social stratification, technological knowledge, and even their vision about the universe.

The Mayan people reproduced their cosmological knowledge and the legitimacy of their lineage through architectural monuments. In fact, certain buildings represent the entrance to a mountain or to a cave, believed to be passages into the netherworld. In the interior of some buildings chambers have been found containing the tomb of a ruler.

When referring to Mayan architecture of the Classic period (300-900 A.D.), it is important to mention formal features that indicate that even though the cities were distributed within a huge territory, Mayan groups shared architectural models and elements that point to the existence of a common cultural language.

The great urban centers were formed by patios, plazas, platforms, pyramid-temples, temples with overhanging domes and cresting, palaces,[2] ball courts, acropolis, quadrangles, structures over multi-level platforms, many aisles of rooms, and *sacbeoob*.[3] In some places defensive walls and hydraulic systems have been found.

On each of the great Mayan locations a precise planning of architectural monuments can be noted. Now it is possible to know the role some of these played.

Housing areas of the general population were located along the surrounding monumental area. Homes were made of perishable materials, but over stuccoed stone platforms (figure 116).

Concerning the temple, it has been mentioned that there was a constructive model based on three elements: a basement, a lower ornamental cover, a top ornamental cover, sometimes a cresting; all of these elements were articulated with moldings and cornices, creating a harmonious group (figures 117, 119).

Most of the buildings were painted on their exterior with one or several colors, or with images. Likewise, they had architectural sculptures and painted stone or stucco reliefs. The iconographic content of these expressions generally refers to the cosmos and to its three levels –heaven, earth, and the netherworld– representing the gods, the lineage ancestors, and the rulers, as well as their ritual activities. Through the integration

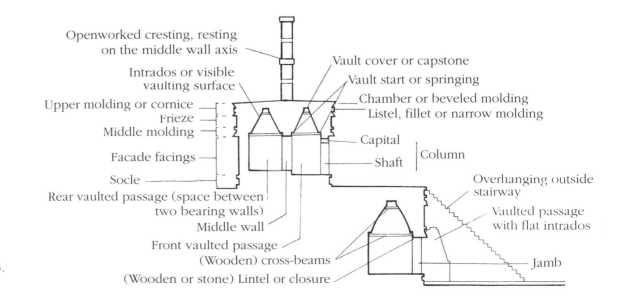

117. Elements of Mayan architecture (drawing by G. Ramírez).

142

of the plastic arts, their sequence and function, the rulers demonstrated their dynastic and religious power. This was a visual information media for the people.

Among the features that define and unify Mayan cities there are also some characteristics which make them different. There are several causes that gave place to particular characteristics in artistic expression. These local and regional aspects can be observed in certain architectural, constructive, and decorative elements, the same which lie at the root of the different architectural styles.

That is why the Mayan area is also divided into stylistic regions: Petén (northern Guatemala, Belize, the meridional edge of Campeche, and Quintana Roo, Mexico); Motagua (southwestern Honduras); Usumacinta (Highlands of Chiapas, Mexico, and Guatemala); Río Bec, Chenes, and Puuc (northern area of Yucatán), and northern Yucatán.[4]

We will briefly point out, with some examples, the most relevant features of the stylistic regions mentioned.

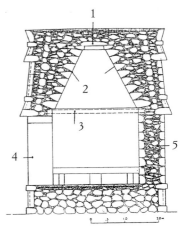

118. Constructive system of the Mayan vault 1. Vault cover or capstone; 2. Intrados; 3. Crossbeams; 4. Jamb; 5. Rear wall (drawing by E. Ramírez).

## The First Steps

The Mayan hut, such as can be seen in the present day, was basically the beginning of architecture; it was built over a rectangular platform, made of stone or levelled ground. The process of development continued, and the earliest proofs (Middle Pre-Classic 1000-300 B.C.) show us that the courtyard was the first unit of distribution, around which there were three to four buildings.

During the Late Pre-Classic (300 B.C.-300 A.D.), the architectural development of some sites at the South Zone —such as Izapa, Abaj Takalik, and El Baúl– is evident. These places show diverse constructive features: in Izapa the structures were made of packed earth. Pyramid-like foundations as well as elongated platforms set on plazas over a levelled terrain have been discovered.

Also during this stage the pyramid-temple architectural concept began to take shape, as a result of superimposing various platforms with a temple at the top.[5] This is an indication of intense activity in construction, demographic growth, concentration of political power, as well as a well defined social stratification. Examples of this can be found at monumental constructions such as Nakbé, in Guatemala, and Lamanai (figure 14; plates 46-48), Cuello, and Cerros (plates 1-3), in Belize.

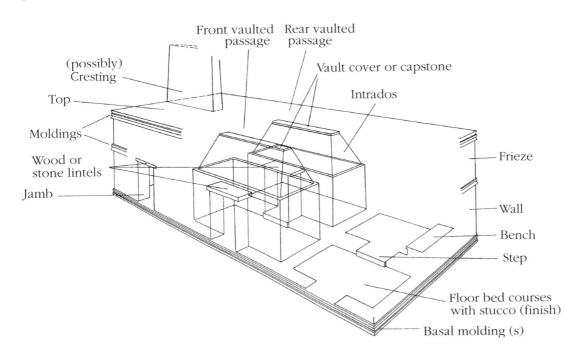

119. Elements of Mayan Architecture. Probable constructive sequence; according to G. Andrews and P. Gendrop (1985) 1. Foundations, floor bed courses, basal moldings. 2. Bearing walls, jambs, lintel, astragals, etc. 3. Soffit, middle molding, vault springing. 4. Scaffolding, transoms, and vault cradling. 5. Intrados, middle fillings, finishing moldings, and extrados. 6. Vault cover or capstone, and top sealing. 7. Upper facade finishings (frieze, cornice), roofing, probably cresting. 8. Middle walls, benches, stuccowork, and further inner finish. 9. Other finish (outside stuccowork, incorporated sculptures, paintings, etc.) (drawing by G. Ramírez).

143

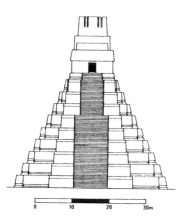

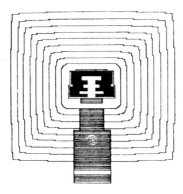

120. Temple 1 at Tikal. Facade and ground plan (from Miller, 1986).

On the other hand, the El Mirador site clearly shows the so called triadic complex. It consists of a large platform which serves as a support for a series of lateral temples, and of other platforms at the center; on the last one (the highest) there was a temple at the center, and two more temples, one on each side facing each other.

At the end of this period the palm roof was substituted by the overhanging dome,[6] which seems to have been used to cover graves, as well as being on antecedent of the cresting technique. This new technology produced a radical change in the building's appearance, and served to define the systems wed in construction.

Petén, the Center of the Universe

Mainly during the Late Classic period (600-900 A.D.), the Petén region —northern Guatemala, and Belize— was the location of many archaeological sites whose buildings show elements of a well-defined style.

Two outstanding cities are Uaxactún and Tikal. The buildings of both sites have opened our eyes to the constructive activity that had begun since the Late Pre-Classic period.

In Uaxactún (plates 4-8) the Structure E-VII-sub, located underneath E-VII, is one of the most ancient; it is a pyramid with inlayed front steps on its four sides; each body has salient moldings, and huge masks which belong to this period (figures 15, 16; plates 7, 8).

These Pre-Classic works were covered by several superimposed plates that belong to the next period. Group A-V (figure 122) is the best example for understanding the complexity of Mayan buildings. Here we find the different stages of construction and remodeling which were added since the construction of the traditional platform that supported three temples, until it became a veritable architectural complex.

Excavations in Group E in Uaxactún also revealed a group of astronomically aligned buildings, maybe to establish solstices and equinoxes. A similar case occurs in Structure 5C-2nd at Cerros, Belize.

Tikal is one of the most important urban and monumental centers (plates 9-14). More than 4000 structures are spread along a 16 kilometers range. It has been estimated that during the Late Classic period there were 90000 inhabitants.

Formed by various architectonic groups, the Central Acropolis (figure 121; plate 13)

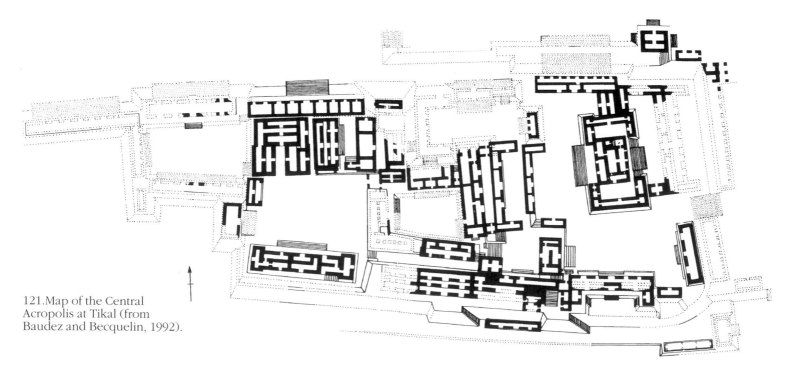

121.Map of the Central Acropolis at Tikal (from Baudez and Becquelin, 1992).

is an outstanding construction made up of elongated buildings with several levels each, and various rows of corridors or rooms. The high pyramids give the city a majestic air, transmitting a sense of verticality; the Building IV is 70 meters high.

One of the best examples that mark out Tikal and the Petén style is Building I (figure 120; plate 14). This style has stepped bodies, grooved moldings, receding corners, and a steep staircase leading to a temple. The latter's interior is narrow with thick walls for supporting the heavy crestings over which –as in the slightly inclined upper decoration–

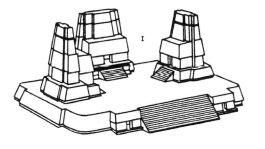
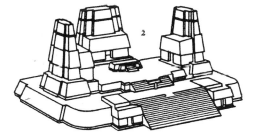
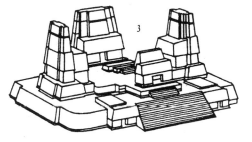
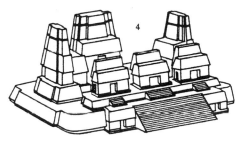
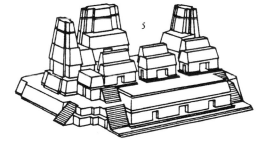
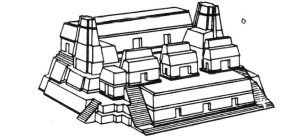
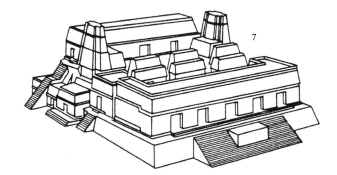
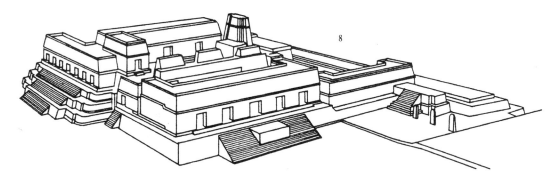

122. Group A-V at Uaxactún. Constructive sequence (from Kubler, 1984).

145

moulded plaster figures were placed. Undoubtedly, there was greater interest in the external appearance of the building. Other sites from this area are: Holmul, Naranjo, Altun-Há, Ixkún, Nakum, and Yaxhá.

In the Mexican territory, southwest of Campeche, there is Calakmul (plate 15) within the Calakmul Biosphere, one of the most important ecological reserves in Mexico. This is one of the most important cities in the Mayan area. Its location, as well as some of the stylistic elements of its buildings, place it within the Central Zone and in the Petén style. Its growth also begins during the Late Pre-Classic, and is formed by palaces, great acropolis and buildings surrounding the plazas and patios.

Likewise, it is worth mentioning the influences that come from the Mexican Central Plateau during the Early Classic period (300-600 A.D.) in architecture. These are notorious in Tikal, and Kaminaljuyú, because they express architectural concepts, such as the talus, and the panel, both from Teotihuacan.

Copán and the Water Way

Copán is located in a fertile valley, at the bank of the Motagua river (plates 51-55). It is one of the most splendid cities of the South Zone. The style of its architectural monuments is somehow different from that of Petén. It has very characteristic features and a unique way of organizing its spaces.

In recent excavations a series of substructures were found which had been covered by other buildings. An example is the Structure 10-L16, known as Rosalila (figure 123). Its good conservation allows us to appreciate the great reliefs of supernatural beings sculpled on its facade.

Another noteworthy construction is, on the other hand, the Hieroglyphic Staircase (plate 53), which measures 10 meters in width and has 62 steps with sculpted glyphs at its rises, and bulk sculptures which stand out in the middle of the staircase.

Temple 22, one of the most representative, is a palace built in several levels, with rooms, well carved ashlars, thick moldings and masks at the edges (figure 70). These are similar to those which form the buildings at the Chenes and Puuc region in Yucatán.

Other outstanding buildings are the Spectators' Tribune, and the ball court. This last one has a double T shape, which is one of the features of the building design of the court (plate 54), and markers with the form of a macaw (figure 83). Something peculiar

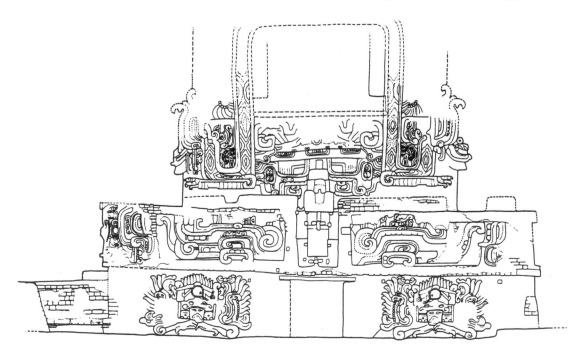

123. West facade of the Rosalila Structure at Copán with stucco decorations (from Fash, 1991).

is that at the end of the inclined wall, over a staircased platform, there are temples with stepped domes, a variant of the Mayan dome.

## River Cities

On the western section of Petén, on the banks of the Usumacinta and its affluents, there were various Mayan cities whose well-defined characteristics constitute an architectonic style in its own right. They were organized in such away that the buildings were adapted to the irregular terrain made up of slopes and hills.

Piedras Negras is an outstanding example and has some things in common with Petén. Similarities include: receding corners on each of the bodies of the pyramid, and salient sections on the walls of the temples, which sometimes have up to three openings. The interior is only slightly wider because thick walls are still used. The cresting is not so elaborate, but like in Tikal, it leans over the rear side of the ceiling.

Another majestic city of this region and in the Usumacinta style is Yaxchilán (plates 35-38), which spreads over long esplanades and hills. It has been said that this site combines some of the features of Petén and of Palenque. However, there are some differences, such as the temple-type buildings, which are built over hillsides and natural elevations, instead of on pyramids.

Structure 33 (figure 124) is undoubtedly a prototype that singles-out for us the characteristics of this site. It is made of huge limestone blocks; the rooms are not too narrow, and have three entrances; the cresting is a fretted wall that cuts back at the top, and leans on the central part. It still has remains of stucco figures that were placed there.

## Palenque: Residences of the Gods

It is located strategically at the northwestern region of the Central Zone because it is on the outskirts of the Chiapas mountain range overlooking the coastal plains of the Gulf of Mexico, an important commercial route to the Mexican Central Plateau.

Palenque (plates 19-30) is a city where architecture and fine sculpture relief are idea remarkably blended. It spreads over a series of artificial terraces, interrupted to the north by a hillside that still preserves the remains of what once were retaining walls used also

124. Facade of the Structure 33 at Yaxchilán (from Kubler, 1984).

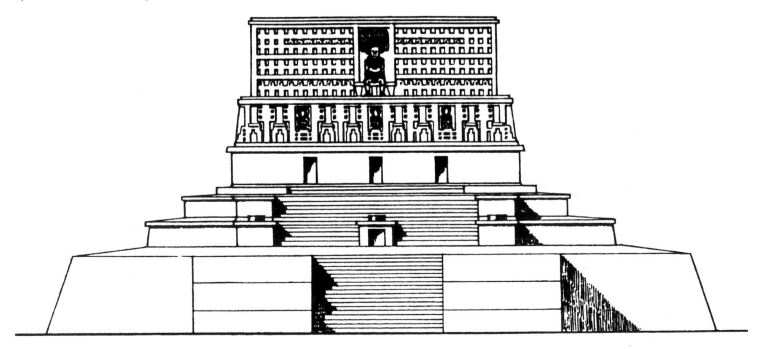

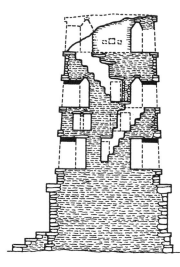

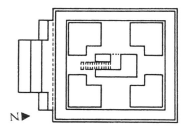

as defence. The Otolum river, a branch of the Usumacinta river that crosses the main plaza, was covered by a vaulted tunnel.

The Palace (figure 126; plates 19-21) was constructed over an artificial basement in different stages and levels. It is formed by the tower (figure 125) and several buildings (A, B, C, D, E, F, G, H) surrounding the patios, which were bounded by long parallel passages with wide openings and high domes. They form an almost continuous gallery and at the bottom level the rows of rooms form the so called «subways».

On the structures of the Cross Group (plates 27-30) (Temple of the Sun, Temple of the Cross, and Temple of the Foliated Cross) there are marked differences between the building systems and the aforementioned styles. The upper temples have a portico with three entrances, and in the central rear room, there is a roof-covered sanctuary containing the panels that tell part of the dynastic history of Palenque. The wide openings and narrow walls turn the interiors into ample and clear spaces. The ceilings become lighter with niches on the vault intrados. The three-lobed arch is also used. In the exterior there is an inclined frieze similar to the light cresting formed by two drafted walls on which there are figures molded in stucco.

Undoubtedly, the most important is the Temple of the Inscriptions (figure 127; plates 22, 24-26) in which the tomb of Pacal, the ruler, or Shield II, was discovered in 1952. Its construction is peculiar because the temple was built starting from the vaulted room in which the sarcophagus was covered by a very large gravestone. There is a staircase built with a vaulted ceiling leading to the crypt.

On the substructure, the western side of Temple XIII, during excavations carried out between 1992-1994 another sarcophagus was uncovered. This was completely painted in red, the natural color of cinnabar, containing the remains of a woman who might have been a relative of Pacal or Shield II.

Within the western region, the city of Comalcalco (plates 31-34) is worth mentioning. It is located on the western edge of the Mayan area, in what today is the state of Tabasco. Even when its features are like those of Palenque, its architectural style belongs to the one developed at the coastal flatland during the Classic period. Most characteristic

125. Cross section and ground plan of the Palace's Tower at Palenque (from Kubler, 1984).

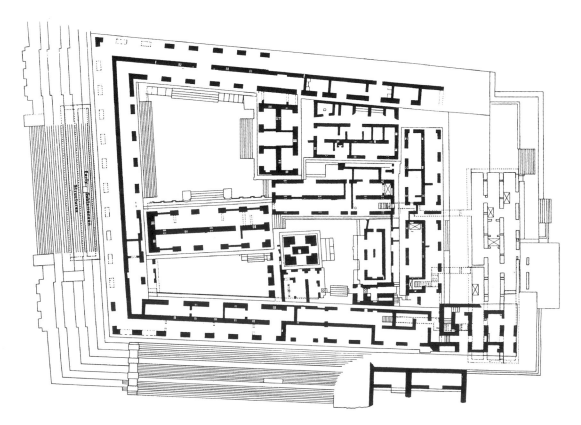

126. Ground plan of the Palace of Palenque (drawing by M. Greene Robertson).

here is the use of brick as building material, which makes the constructions different from those of other archaeological sites. The buildings mark the limits of the plazas and are built over high artificial elevations made of soil mixed with crushed oyster shell and covered with plaster.

### The Southeast of the Peninsula, a Special View

There are different sites in the southern area of Quintana Roo state. Information has increased thanks to the archaeological work carried out between 1992-1994 in sites such as Dzibanché, Kinichná, and Kohunlich. Although these sites evince local and regional characteristics of style, they do share some features with Petén.

The buildings are set around patios; the platforms support rows of passages; there are pyramidial basements, ball game courts, *sacbeoob*, and great acropolis.

Among the different buildings in Dzibanché, one of the most outstanding is Temple I, with its rounded corners, «apron» molds, and masks flanking the staircase. Likewise, Kohunlich is outstanding for the impressive masks in Building I.

### The Northern Plains

During the Late Pre-Classic period, in the Yucatán peninsula, places like Dzibilchaltún, Oxkintok, Yaxuná, Acanceh, developed in much the same way as the sites in the Central and South zones. And the latter, a well as Cobá, in the eastern portion (plates 42-45), and Becán, south of Campeche, present similarities with the Petén style. Their development during the next period can be seen in the changes in some of its architectural elements.

During the Late Classic, at the northern portion of the peninsula, original architectural features appeared, which have helped to define the existence of three distinct stylistic regions: Río Bec, Chenes, and Puuc.

### Río Bec Region: Towers and Caves

This region (plate 57) is located south of Campeche and Quintana Roo, close to the Guatemalan border. Its name derives from a specific location: the Bec river. Other important sites are: Xpuhil (figure 128; plate 56), Hormiguero (plate 58), and Chicanná (figure 112; plate 60), the three of which still retain, as has been said, some architectural elements from Petén: buildings with tall ceilings with rounded angles, and the use of heavy cresting.

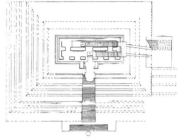

127. Cross section and ground plan of the Temple of the Inscriptions at Palenque, which encloses the crypt of Pakal II's tomb (from Miller, 1986).

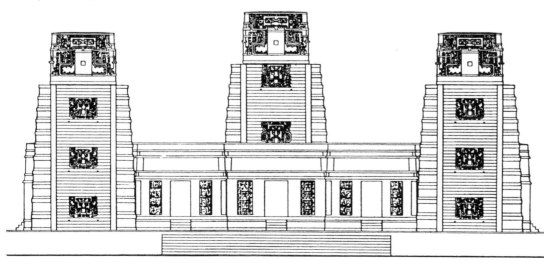

128. Xpuhil building with the typical towers (from Kubler, 1984).

The peculiarity of this style stands out in the use it makes of solid towers to complete the temple facade. These have staircases whose inclination is almost vertical, making them almost impossible to climb. The small superior temple with frieze and cresting has a fake entrance.

The decoration of the temple facades is a characteristic element of Río Bec just as it is in the Chenes region. It consists of a great mask whose open mouth, encircled by teeth or fangs, is the entrance (plates 58, 60) to its interior. It is the doorway to the mountain cave that leads to the netherworld. On the corners, vertically set, there are other masks, and inside the buildings we find low walls inlayed with geometric designs, crosses, squares, and rubblework benches.

## Chenes Region: Wells into the Other World

In the Chenes style –*Chen* is the Yucatán Mayan for water well– the sites of Hochob, Dzibilnocac, Tabasqueño, and Santa Rosa Xtampak are outstanding examples.

The temple facades (figure 129) have, as in the Río Bec region, zoomorphic masks, whose open fauces give access to the building's interior. Smaller masks also stand out on walls and corners. A distinctive element is the salient rocks on the middle moldings and the cresting which served to support sculpted human figures.

Dzibilnocac presents another characteristic: three temple pyramids were incorporated to Structure A-1, which is formed by aisles of rooms. Another peculiarity are the interior staircases –as those in the Palace of Santa Rosa Xtampak– which lead to different levels.

## Puuc Region, Cut Turned into Stone

Before delving into the main features of this style, it is important to mention Edzná (plates 61-63), because in its buildings are blended various stylistic elements, together with the local features.

In the substructures of some of the buildings it is possible to see Petén style features, but the Five-Floor Building, a palace-temple, has marked Puuc style characteristics. It stands out for its dimensions and location within the central axis of a huge acropolis. Each of its stepped buildings has an aisle of rooms whose ceiling serves as a terrace to the next floor. Running under each flight of the wide staircase are vaulted corridors.

The North Zone –the Puuc region, southwest Yucatán, and north Campeche–, is formed by splendid archaeological sites such as Uxmal (plates 64-71), Labná (plates 72-74), Kabah (plates 77-80), and Sayil (plates 75,76), and given the name *Puuc* (mountain range), because of the chain of hills that cross part of the peninsula. The Puuc style had

129. Chenes style building (drawing by C. Ramírez).

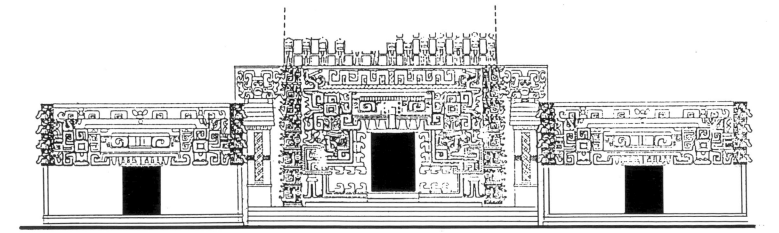

150

various stages of development, but we will mention only those characteristics that make it unique.

Elongated palace-type buildings stand on huge platforms. They have many stories and multiple rooms, such as the Sayil Palace, that has 90. On the other hand, the Quadrangle of the Nuns in Uxmal (figure 130) is a good example of the distribution of four buildings around patios, with vaulted corridors that serve as entrances.

The constructions are lighter and the walls are made of ashlar stones more carefully cut and fitted. There is a noticeable interest in making the interiors wider, and a knack for horizontality. Some sites carried on the custom of incorporating plaster figures to the cresting, or of using supports for sculptures, such as in the Chenes region.

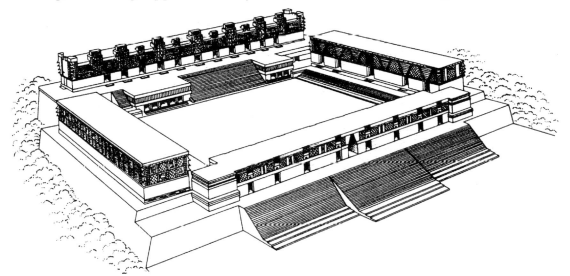

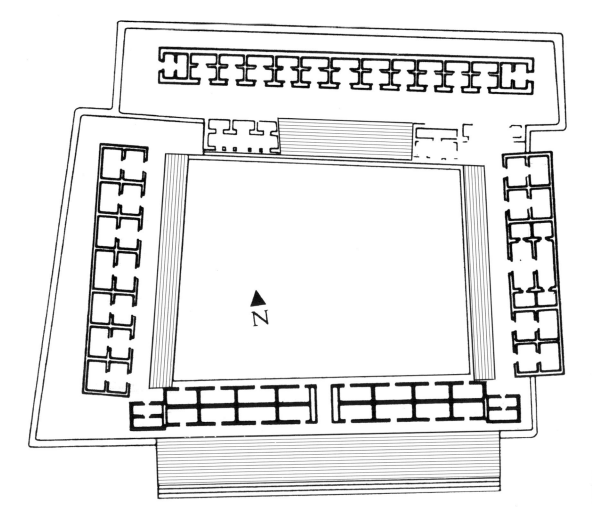

130. View and ground plan of the Quadrangle of the Nuns at Uxmal (from Kubler, 1984).

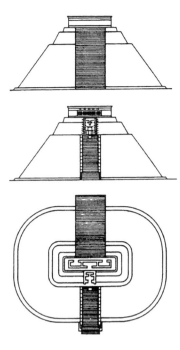

131. Views and ground plan of the Seer's pyramid at Uxmal (from Kubler, 1984).

Temples have various entrances divided by columns of masonry, either monolithic, or in overlapped reels with square-shaped capitals. The walls of the building facades are flat, and sometimes intercalated with groups of diamond-shaped cut columns or stones.

Most of the decorative elements cover the friezes, the entablature, and the cornices; in all of these the mosaic-on-stone technique –one of the most outstanding characteristics of the Puuc style–, can be appreciated. Their decoration has a range of geometric motifs: simple or stepped frets, window blinds, rhombs, huts, serpentine shapes, columns, crossed bands, indented stones or with human figures. The representation of the large mask or the large-nosed god over friezes or in corners is very common. Its maximum representation can be seen on the facade of the Codz Pop (plate 77) building in Kabah. Another distinctive feature of the Puuc architecture are the arches, such as in Labná, where the arch served to indicate the entrance to a patio.

## Chichén Itzá and the Confluence of Styles

In the city of Chichén Itzá (plates 81-84), the most important of the North Zone during the Late Classic period (600-900 A.D.) and the Early Post-Classic (900/1000-1250 A.D.), two architectural, sculptural, and even mural painting styles have been identified.

Despite being outside the Puuc region, the buildings that correspond to the Late Classic period are related to this style. This is particularly true of buildings such as the Temple of the Three Lintels, Las Monjas (The Nuns) and the Annex, the Church, the Akab Dzib, and the Red House.

In other constructions, maybe the best known of which are The Castle –a temple built over a pyramidal basement with radial symmetry–, the Temple of the Warriors –with its serpentine columns–, and the ball court the architectural elements –corresponding to the Post-Classic period– show the influence of Central Mexico.

## Sculpture

## The Mayas: Between Time and Space

In the broad territory we have mentioned there are many archaeological vestiges that indicate the existence of a magnificent tradition in sculpture. Peculiar features with respect to formal composition and treatment allow us to define a cultural and artistic unity which was characteristic of Mesoamerica.

During the era of greatest splendor many styles developed in accordance with precise criteria concerning temporality and space. The numerous works that make up Mayan sculpture are different from each other. This is why we can talk chronologically about an «Early Classic», or «Late Classic» art; or regionally, about the «Usumacinta», «Motagua», «Petén», «Puuc», or «Chenes» styles. Sometimes even the style of individual «artists» can be distinguished.

For example, it is possible to identify as «Maya» Stele 31 from Tikal (figure 27; plate 89: Early Classic, Petén style), as well as the gravestone of the sarcophagus at the Temple of the Inscriptions in Palenque (figure 65: Late Classic, Palenque style). These works are unmistakable and show us temporal and regional differences.

There are two great styles in sculpture: the first can be appreciated at the South (Pacific slope, and Highlands), and Central Zone (Lowlands of the south), and represents «historical» events, such as the adventures of a ruler. However, the human figure constitutes the main motif in sculpture, though it is not exclusive.

*previous page:*
87. Stele 50 from Izapa. Late
Pre-Classic.

88. Altar 1 from Izapa. Late
Pre-Classic.

89. Stele 31 from Tikal. Early Classic.

90. Detail of Altar 5 from Tikal. Late Classic.

*next pages*:
91. Stele C from Quiriguá. Late Classic.

92. Stele E from Quiriguá. Late Classic.

93. Altar Q from Copán. Late Classic.

98. Lintel 25 from Yaxchilán.
Late Classic.

99. Lintel 24 from Yaxchilán.
Late Classic.

*next pages*:
100. Back of a throne from
Piedras Negras. Late Classic.

101-102. General view and detail of the back of a throne from Piedras Negras. Late Classic.

103. Lintel 3 from Piedras Negras. Late Classic.

*next pages*:
104. The head of Chan Balum II, sculpted in stucco, from Palenque. Late Classic.

105. Mosaic, jade, shell and obsidian funeral mask of Pacal II, from Palenque. Late Classic.

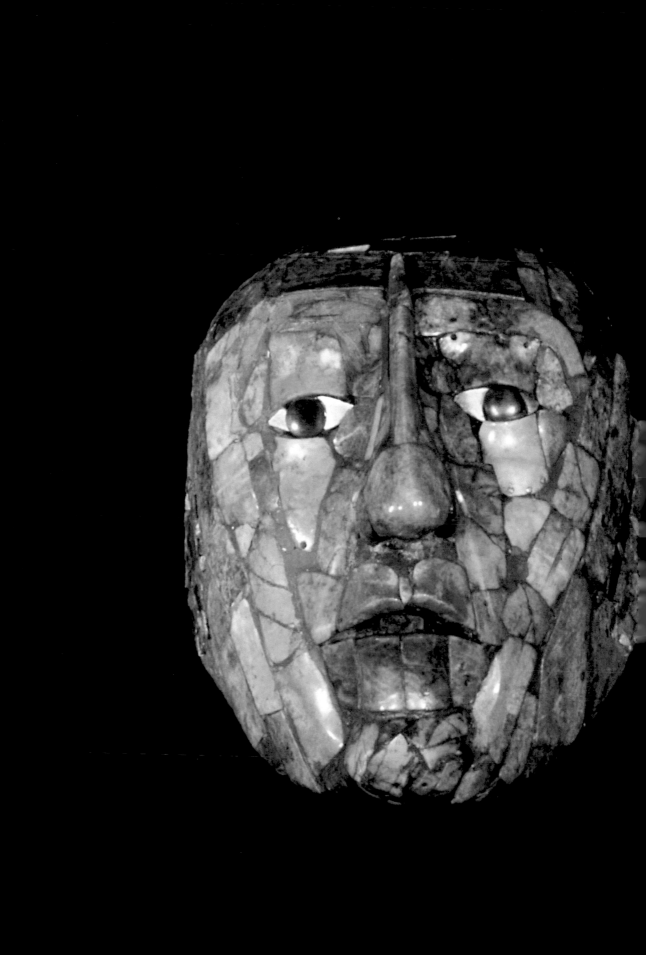

*previous pages*:
106. Detail of the great stucco
mural from Toniná. Late
Classic.

107. The god of death holding
the head of a victim sacrificed
by decapitation. Stucco mural
from Toniná. Late Classic.

108. The Queen of Uxmal.
Late Classic.

109. Column 2 from Oxkintoc.
Late Classic.

*next pages*:
110. Chac Mool from Chichén
Itzá. Late Classic.

111, 112, 113. Figurines from
the island of Jaina. Late
Classic.

114. Another figurine from the island of Jaina. Late Classic.

115. Clay incense-burner from Palenque. Late Classic.

*next page*:
116. Detail of wall paintings at Bonampak. Room 1. Late Classic.

117. East wall of Room 1 in the Temple of the Mural Paintings of Bonampak. Late Classic.

This reflects a conception of the world in which man plays the main role. It is the Mayan style par excellence and is the result of the combination of different abstract, symbolic, animal, and plant elements, and especially the human figure, around which all elements rotate.

The second style, which permeates the North Zone (Lowlands of the north, or Yucatán peninsula), can be considered as forming part of architecture. Forms become rigid, geometric, and evince aesthetic concerns quite unlike those of the first style.

Likewise, the evolution of the different stylistic groups can be fitted into the chronological stages. During the Late Pre-Classic period (300 B.C.-300 A.D.) the main subject –man–, has already been defined and becomes the stepping stone for the next period. Generally, the Pre-Classic period is characterized by a combination of features (subject matter, formal treatment, composition) and symbolic elements which tend to erase, to a certain degree, the human figure.

The art of sculpture reaches its apogee during the Classic (300-900 A.D), consolidating itself as anthropocentric, and directly related with the kings, court, and nobility. At the end of this period a new style arises whose main area of influence is the north, the Yucatán peninsula.

The Post-Classic (900/1000-1500 A.D.) sums up different aesthetic conceptions around man, plants, and animals. A certain influence from different centers of Mesoamerica can be appreciated.

Now, we will see, with some examples, how Mayan sculpture evolved.

The Pre-Classic: In Search of a Style

Recent excavations at various Mayan cities, such as Dzibilchaltún and Oxkintok (Yucatán), or Cerros and Lamanai (Belize), have allowed researchers to redefine the Late Pre-Classic period as the moment when the Mayan civilization and, consequently, Mayan sculpture began to take form.

In the beginning of the Middle Pre-Classic (1000-300 B.C.), the presence of Olmec tribes (whose central or «metropolitan» area was located along the coast of the Gulf of Mexico) spread throughout different regions in Mesoamerica, such as the Pacific mountain slopes. In fact, Olmec-style sculptures outside the metropolitan area indicate trading contacts among inhabitants of those regions. Cultural and commercial expansion increased, evidence of which has been located in the Highlands of Chiapas and Guatemala, in sites such as: Abaj Takalik, Bilbao, El Baúl, Izapa, Kaminaljuyú, Monte Alto, and Xoc.

Concerning huge stone block carving, the Olmec tradition was preserved in Monte Alto, Guatemala, together with a style of its own in sculptures representing the heads and chests of obese characters. There might have been a relationship between the spectacular Olmec heads and those of this center.

Another site in Guatemala, Abaj Takalik, still presents some formal Olmec features in its plastic representations. For example, the corners of the mouths are pointing down, but there is a pair of elements which would characterize Mayan culture from that moment on: 1) the steles (rectangular prism-shaped monuments) and the altars (block, drum, or animal-shaped monuments); and 2) the hieroglyphic writing system, which can be observed on Steles 2 (figure 21) (dated 41 A.D.), and 5 (dated 126 A.D.).

Kaminaljuyú (Guatemala) stands out for its carved images which are clear and well defined. Both factors allow us to speak of a local style characteristic of this city. Man's image began to be defined with a certain autonomy, despite the great symbolic elements that surround it. Thus, the importance of dynamic scenes and their related paraphernalia was announced. Examples: Steles 10 or «Black Altar», and 11 (figure 20).

132. Stele 1 at Izapa. Late Pre-Classic (from Willey, 1966).

133. Stele 27 at Tikal. 495 A.D., Early Classic (drawing by L. Gornto, from Michel, 1989).

In the first case, space is occupied by the remains of three people, one of which has an axe in his left hand. Behind the latter there is a fantastic and bearded (maybe masked) face of another person; underneath there is a small feminine figure. There are also some hieroglyphic texts.

The second case shows a person standing and seen from one side who holds some objects in his hands. He is also wearing a mask, and above him, there is another figure who seems to be floating, and which may be a god or an ancestor. This subject will recur in the iconography of the Classic.

However, the dominating style of this period is that of Izapa (Chiapas). Artistic language offers conventional representations of human figures; the bas-relief favors historical chronicles. These are mixed with a religious discourse: forms of expression range from naturalistic to abstract representations in human, plant, supernatural and animal figures.

Furthermore, the scenes evince an increasing interest in perspective, which divides space into three superimposed levels: below is the netherworld; in the middle, the domains of the terrestrial; and above is the heavenly world. Most of the events are beyond the visible and everyday reality. The beings and actions represented belong to another world, the sacred world of imagination and fantasy. Because of this, the most favored subjects from Izapa relate to primordial myths of nature's vital cycle.

We can mention anthropomorphous beings, wearing grotesque masks, sometimes wings, trees with animal-shaped roots, skeletal figures, or two-headed hybrids. Men, who appear with an impersonal expression, play secondary roles, though during the Classic period they began to leading roles. Examples of this are the complex scenes represented on the Steles 1 (figure 132), and 2 (figure 58), and on Altar 1 (plate 88), all from Izapa.

### The Classic Period Tile

The Classic period is divided into two stages: Early Classic (300-600 A.D.), and Late Classic (600-900 A.D.). Two dates recorded on the Mayan monuments determine the beginning and the end of these stages. The oldest is recorded on Stele 29 in Tikal, and it belongs to 292 A.D.; the most recent belongs to Stele 6, in Itzimté, and it is dated in 910 A.D. (almost one year after Monument 101 from Toniná: 909 A.D.).

During the Classic, sculpture has two tendencies, starting from relief, formal treatment, and the physical location of monuments within the cities.

On the one hand, sculptures include a variety of versions: from incision and bas-relief to high-relief, not to mention some cases of round bulk. Thus we have steles, altars, lintels, jambs, gravestones, or panels (group of scenes formed by one or more gravestones).

On the other hand, relief is also seen in architecture, which gives buildings a distinctive nature. It appears on facades of many constructions: stone carved or plaster-sculpted figures. There are anthropomorphous and animal-shaped masks over the body of the pyramidal foundations, human figures set on walls, columns (inside and outside the buildings), friezes, and crestings.

As for the North Zone of the Mayan area, geometric designs, which are mostly made of stone tiles, replace the voluptuous human shapes that belong to the Central Zone. Angular shapes substitute curved and sinuous lines, and dominate the architecture.

The different types of limestone that belong to the Mayan area constitute the main raw materials used in sculpture. However, there are also many other materials used, including gem stones such as jade, stucco, wood (generally from *sapodilla* trees), glass (obsidian), shells, and ceramics. The great images on the facades were made with sculpted plaster. Wood was carved and worked to form lintels. Clay was used to make different-size statues. At that time, all works were painted with a brilliant polychromatic design.

Another factor that gave Classic sculpture its identity, was the patronage of the rulers. The absolute power of an authoritarian and despotic elite favored the development of art. Thus the main «official» motifs were «historical», inspired by the activities of the king: coronation rituals; courtly scenes; wars and victories; sacrifices and self-sacrifices; plus the symbolic ball game. Some of the beliefs and ceremonies associated with death and the netherworld continued, as well as their complex vision of the cosmos, the gods, and their roles in the universe.

These elements were established during the Early Classic period (figures 133, 134), but their apogee was reached during the Late Classic period.

134. The sculpted image on the Hauberg Stele. It comes from an unknown site. 199 A.D. Proto-Classic (from Schele and Miller, 1986).

## Establishment of Sculptural Art

During the Classic Mayan period sculpture was characterized by various elements, especially stone carving with bas-relief.

The scenes most often represent human profiles disguised among adornments and symbolic characteristics where curved lines outnumber the straight ones. Men appear as conventional and stereotyped, lacking personal expression, but their identity can be known through emblems or inscriptions. The formal, plastic expression of human beings was not conquered once and for all: it was worked and re-worked following traditional conceptions about universe.

Likewise, it was at this time when the divine and earthly powers of the rulers were exhibited in all their splendor. The rulers tended to demonstrate their authority through a feverish activity in sculpture and building. These undertakings reveal the desire of the monarchs for «continuity» and their search for immortality.

In fact, Petén has produced the greatest quantity of sculptures revealing the art precepts of the time with regard to technical quality, the posture of the human figure and its proportions within the general composition. Steles become the most adequate means to celebrate the rulers' power. A meaningful example can be appreciated at Stele 29 in Tikal (Guatemala) (figures 10, 11), the most ancient Mayan inscription ever found.

A profile of a person can be seen –most probably the ruler Rizo Jaguar Lord– holding the anthropomorphous head of the Jaguar Lord of the netherworld on his left hand which may have been a royal attribute, while with his right arm he holds to his body a rigid ceremonial two-headed bar. At the top of the scene an ancestor is watching and protecting the king.

Another general custom is to carve the four sides of the steles with human representations and hieroglyphic records. And although they may be considered independent, from a plastic point of view, they can be read as one sole composition. This can be seen at Stele 31, also from Tikal (figure 27; plate 89), built in 445 A.D. in honor of the ruler Stormy Heaven.

Three of its sides have human representations. The one in the middle is Stormy Heaven, exuberantly dressed and surrounded by many symbols. Besides, there is a certain Teotihuacan influence in some of the formal elements of the paraphernalia of the characters. Particularly, the headdress of those who appear at the right and at the left (the predecessor Rizo Big Mouth).

Another example, a red painted plaster relief in Balamkú (Campeche), is a building whose frieze shows a complex scene and two (maybe four) sitting characters can be

135. Stele 30 at Tikal. 692 A.D. Late Classic (drawing by L. Gornto, from Michel, 1989).

seen facing front on top of great mythic animals with reptile features. These animals have themselves been placed over the head of monstruous beings surrounded by diverse elements, other animals, and aquatic bands. To the iconographic richness of the whole, then, is added a profound religious symbolic meaning.

## The Late Classic: Unity and Expansion

This period has many regional, local, and individual styles. They are distributed from northwest to southeast along the Usumacinta river basin, in the Petén forests, and in the Motagua river basin.

The carving techniques vary from the almost bi-dimensional bas-relief –such as on the gravestones of Palenque– to the high-relief volume, close to the sculpture in the round –on the steles of Copán.

The human figure predominates, representing rulers and courtty characters, artistically described while they are carrying out those activities which were basic in their life: enthronements, blood rites, political alliances, scenes of war and capturing of prisoners. In some cities faithful reproductions of the human body were achieved, such as in Palenque, Bonampak, Copán, or Yaxchilán. In others, such as in Tikal and Quiriguá, the conventional scheme is preserved. Besides, we now know the names of various «artists», sculptors, and painters that can be seen in various works, sometimes with the artist's working tools. The following are two examples of this.

At Stele 12 in Piedras Negras (figure 141), where some of the prisoners are identified as sculptors. The other one is a recently discovered plate at Emiliano Zapata, where a sculptor carrying a chisel is sitting in front of a carved stone whose shape is a monster's head.

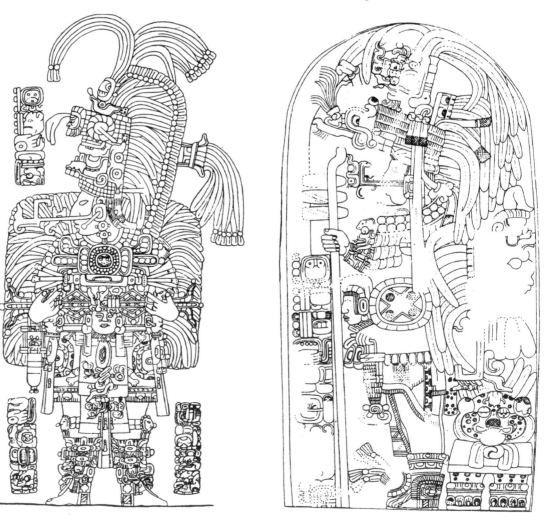

136. Left: The ruler Ah Cacao, represented on Stele 16 at Tikal. 711 A.D. Right: the sovereign Chitam on Stele 22 at Tikal. 771 D.C. Late Classic (from Márquez López, 1992).

## Tikal and the Attachment to Tradition

The Late Classic in Tikal (Guatemala) is characterized by diverse aspects: a lack of will for modeling and the search for planes that might give an impression of greater depth. Nevertheless, the surface is two-dimensional, and this impression is reinforced by the repetition of lines and signs that give a symmetric rythm to a perimeter's interior, defined by a molding that serves the purpose of a frame.

The motifs and forms seem to be in keeping with conventions of the Early Classic period. These include silhouettes of accurate, even subtle, lines. This formal and thematic tradition carried on for more than three centuries in Tikal.

The treatment of human figures remains almost the same. They appear in the foreground and in profile; occupying almost all the space, wich is limited by a frame. This is the most common model on the steles (figures 133, 135, 136) erected at the plazas and open spaces, in such a way that the spatial immensity acquires a specific order. In the steles, the public image of the ruler is reinforced and his sacred presence testifies to his authority. However, this privileged situation came to an end: the king's image would be changed for another. This explains the destruction of the rulers' carved faces, which were mutilated, and the deprivation of their sacred life and power.

On the steles war and military dominion are also recurrent themes, an aspect of

137. Sacrifice scene on Altar 5 at Tikal, which is linked with Stele 16 in the Complex N. 711 A.D. Late Classic (from Márquez López, 1992).

138. Wooden lintel from Temple III at Tikal (from Morley, Brainerd, and Sharer, 1983).

Mayan art which had not been understood until recently: war scenes reveal a people who was extremely conscious of war.

On the other hand, wooden lintels (figure 138), as well as some altars, were the only carved structures that expressed a real intention of dynamic expansion and of scenic complexity. Here one can appreciate compositions that incorporate two or more characters in different postures and attitudes: sitting, standing, kneeling down, half-kneeling, facing front, and in profile, with gestures that simulate dialogues and often accompanied by different objects of a ritual nature, or by gods with human and animal shapes. Two examples of this: Lintel 3 at the Temple IV (figure 80), and Altar 5 (figure 137; plate 90).

## Stone Giants at Quiriguá

The Quiriguá style (Guatemala) is unique if only for its height and colossal proportions. The city has the tallest steles in the Mayan world (plates 91, 92), measuring almost six meters in hight. This is a remarkable characteristic because of the treatment given to the stylized face of the ruler inside a niche located at the top of the monument. On the other hand, the body is carved as a very flat bas-relief. In this way a compositional and formal division of the steles is created, besides presenting a sharp contrast between the lower and upper sections.

It is no mere chance that the king's image, as a human and divine being, occupies an important place in the steles. He is effectively the main axis that serves as a basis for the Mayan political, social and courtly structure. The ruler personifies the supernatural powers as well as serving as intermediary for the immaterial gods so they may enjoy earthly life. He symbolizes the centralized political power, through which sacred authority is exerted over the community.

During the rule of Heaven Two Arms, who celebrated his victory over the 18 Rabbit Lord of Copán, these sculptures reached their maximum splendor and height.

Likewise, other original shapes adopted by monument-carvers in Quiriguá were of fantastic animals, who take the form of felines, reptiles, birds, or toads. The best example is called the Zoomorphic P (figures 86, 87): it shows a huge toad with open mouth and a ruler sitting within. His rank badges are in his hands, and he seems to be emerging from this mythical creature.

## Copán and the Three-Dimensional Wish

Artistic reality in Copán (Honduras) is in itself distinct. The characters represented rise impressively from a background profusely engraved with symbols and ornaments, which are mainly part of the attire. In fact, one receives the impression that they are «absorbed» by the paraphernalia they use to dress themselves (plates 94-96).

It must be pointed out that on every sculpture there is a dominant, almost obsessive presence of a sole figure. This figure is standing frontwards, with feet firmly on the ground and forming an angle of over 120 degrees. Its folded arms are holding a ceremonial two-headed serpent walking cane.

The human figure received a rigid and schematic treatment until the rulc of Lily-Smoke in the 7th century. During the first part of the 8th century it is less rigid, but between the 8th and 9th centuries –under the last rulers– it returns to its previous rigidity. Thus, as of 749 A.D. (under the rule of Smoke Shell), steles can undoubtedly be considered as pictures. Although they may not be real life images according to the conceptions of Western art, some of the most outstanding portraits in Mesoamerica were

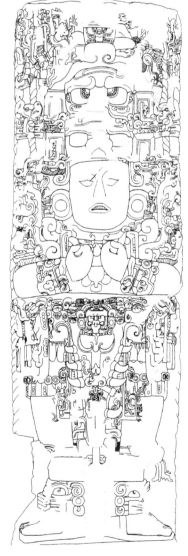

139. Stele C at Copán. Late Classic (from Fash, 1991).

executed here as the artists included in their work the particular features of their models in an attempt to perpetuate «the Mayan ideal of beauty» (almond-colored eyes, high and angulous cheekbones, thin lips, and high forehead).

This can be seen on Steles 8 and C (figure 139) (dated 763 and 782 A.D. respectively), wich reproduce the features of Smoke Shell, and his wife, Green Shark, who seem to be submerged in a variety of symbols associated with royalty and rituals.

Other examples of the importance given to the image of the ruler come from the reign of New Dawn, penultimate king of this city. Such is the case of Altar Q (figure 55; plate 93), on whose sides the sixteen kings of Copán were represented –including New Dawn–, with their bodies facing front and their faces looking to the right or to the left, and sitting over hieroglyphs that identify them, while they adorn themselves with headdresses.

## Gods and Warriors in Yaxchilán

During the Late Classic, Yaxchilán (Chiapas) was politically and militarily very important, and we know this because the rulers left an imprint of their power in numerous sculptures. Here there were two important trends in sculpture.

The first, and most ancient, is characterized by the figures that stand out sharply from the background. In contrast, the lines that define the attire, emblems and ornaments of the main character produce their effect by way of incisions: detail is generally very distinct. Hence the perfection in the formal finish in the designs of the hair, the textiles, and the jewels. The second form of expression in sculpture is a «pictorial» bas-relief that is barely detached from the rock.

Both expressions are most noticeable on the lintels. Besides, they are a good way of perpetuating the numerous subjects treated: scenes of submission, political rites and

140. Left: Lintel 26 at Yaxchilán, where Lord Shield-Jaguar can be seen, who is getting his war suit from his wife. 725 A.D. Late Classic (drawing by I. Graham, from Schele and Miller, 1986). Right: both sides of Stele 11 at Yaxchilán. On the rear side, Bird-Jaguar is subduing three prisoners, while on the front side, the same Lord is standing before his father Shield-Jaguar. 755 A.D. Late Classic (from Freidel, Schele, and Parker, 1993).

alliances, the exchange of insignia between rulers and heirs. Also worth mentioning is the importance of the noble women who usually appear carrying a package or bundle containing the emblems of self-sacrifice or of the government. Also noticeable is the history of a dynasty eager for power, especially under the rule of two noblemen: Jaguar Shield II, and his son, Jaguar Bird IV.

All of this can be seen on various lintels, some of which can be found in the British Museum, in London, and in the National Museum of Anthropology, in Mexico City.

Lintel 26 (figure 140; plate 97) (dated 723 A.D.) shows the effigy of Jaguar Shield II, dressed with his «armor». He has a knife on his right hand, and with his left he is receiving either an emblem or a headdress, which resembles a feline's head, from his wife, the powerful lady Shark.

At the same time, she appears as the main character in a scene of self-sacrifice on Lintel 25 (plate 98) (dated 723 A.D.). Dressed in her finest clothes, once she has offered her blood (plate 99), she has a vision, symbolized by an enormous half-fleshless bicephalous snake whose front head opens her jaws so that from them may issue a deity or an ancestor dressed in war apparel.

Jaguar Bird IV commanded a series of incursions in neighboring territories. The extraordinary Stele 11 (figures 8, 140) (dated 752 A.D.) shows the ruler's figure from both sides. He is the one who appears with a mask, like a god, standing above three prisoners. According to a tradition established since the Pre-Classic, the ancestors (Shield Jaguar II, and lady Skull Wind, mother of Jaguar Bird IV) observe from above (from the other world) the exploits of their heir. The other side of the stele shows Jaguar Bird IV dressed for war facing his father who is holding a decorated walking stick or scepter.

It is also worth mentioning that Yaxchilán is one of those places where many «scribes» have been identified. These are the sculptors or «workshop masters» in charge of making monuments narrating the history of the city's rulers.

The achievements of these artists can be appreciated in the details of the faces and extremities (especially the thighs) of the characters depicted: they evince to what degree the sculptors were familiar with the human complexion. This is the reason why we may judge a number of these figures as portraits of men and women of the highest category: the aristocracy.

141. Stele 12 at Piedras Negras. 795 A.D. Late Classic (from Schele and Miller, 1986).

142. Lintel 2 at Piedras Negras. 667 A.D. Late Classic (drawing by D. Stuart, from Schele and Mathews, 1991).

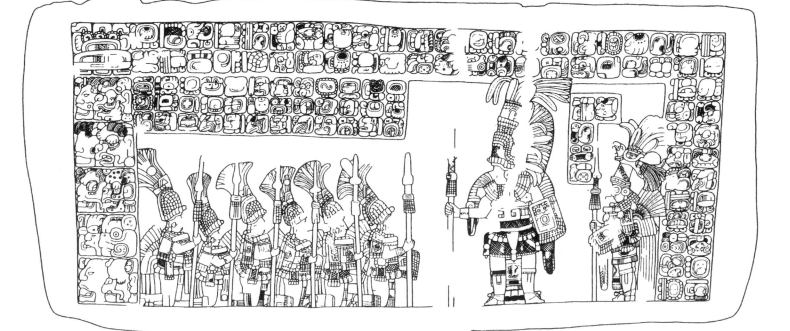

In short, the artists of Yaxchilán distinguish themselves as belonging to the few –among those of Bonampak and Copán– in expressing knowledge of the portrait and the vigor of the human figure.

### Piedras Negras or Petrified Virtuosity

Piedras Negras (Guatemala) had tremendous technical dominion. Steles, lintels, and thrones show a veritable concern for movement (figures 141-144; plates 100-103). The reliefs are masterworks of two perhaps even three-dimensional representations of everyday life and the high-relief is subtly combined with bas-relief.

Scenes also evoke access to power, and its demonstration. Lintel 2 (figure 142) celebrates the victory of the ruler Shelled Jaguar Macaw. Six noblemen are kneeling in profile, one behind the other, portraying themselves as warriors raising their spears before their ruler. He stands and observes. Behind him a nobleman of inferior rank remains standing. The effect of apparent staticity contrasts with the different postures of the characters; the whole scene suggests a certain depth of field.

One of the best works in carved stone can be seen on the back of a throne, which is now preserved at the Amparo Museum in Puebla (Mexico) (plate 100). It represents a fantastic face whose eyes are filled with characters who are staring at each other and at a monster's nose.

But the most revealing monument is Stele 12 (figure 141) (dated in Piedras Negras 795 A.D.) which depicts a scene of military victory. At the highest part of the scene, the ruler, escorted by his two lieutenants, is looking downwards where many prisoners are sitting on the floor. It is surprising because of the vitality of the facial, bodily and gestural expressions of each person, as well as the simultaneity of its planes. This is one of the most realistic images of the Mayan Late Classic known to this day.

### Palenque and Human Sensuality

The human figure played an important role in the aesthetic universe of Palenque (Chiapas). The formal treatment of the human body shows a profound knowledge and

143. Stele 35 at Piedras Negras. Late Clasic (from *Die Welt der Maya*).

144. Lintel 3 at Piedras Negras. 761 A.D. Late Classic (from Schele and Mathews, 1991).

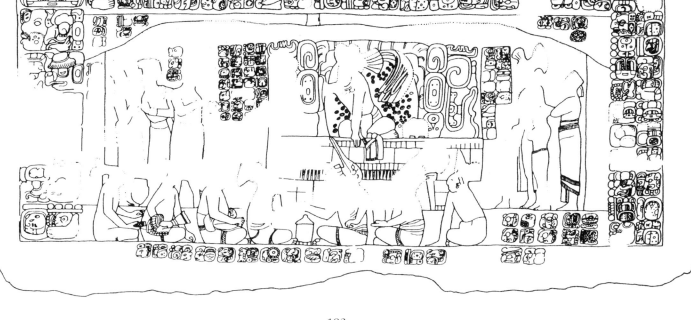

handling of natural proportions and volumes, in a way that they correspond to real-life proportions: six to seven heads per body.

Plaster and limestone are used, due to their malleability or softness and because they could easily depict the voluptuous and natural roundness of the human body.

This is why portraits can be found on all of the elements of architecture: walls, columns, friezes and cresting on the exteriors of buildings, and on slabs and panels at the sanctuaries, as well as in the intimate space of the tombs. The subject is a constant one, and shows the images of the great men in power. In fact, they show the evolution of man throughout his history, his actions, successes, and alliances. Earthly power concentrates on and belongs to, man, but he is also the reflection of a divine will and power.

There are many examples. One of the earliest is the gravestone at the tomb of the Temple of the Inscriptions (684 A.D.) (figure 65). The whole composition evinces the convergence of the main lines of the image on the central character, king Pacal or Shield II. The latter offers an individualized appearance, but through the surrounding features and symbols he is deified and establishes communication among the different cosmic levels: heaven, earth, and the netherworld. He lies half way over the fleshless and monstruous face of the netherworld's image. From the ruler's stomach a cross emerges, the symbol of the Ceiba Tree, the cosmic axis. Generally it can be said that the gravestone reveals a wisely organized vision of the world.

Another work shows the access to power of the second child of Pacal or Shield II: Precious Knot Pécari II. This is the «Palace Panel» (figure 146) (dated 702 A.D.), allowing us to admire the rigor of historical reality and its close link with political rituals. Likewise, the «Slaves' Panel» (figure 147) (730 A.D.) shows a scene of dynastic succession: Red Bat receives his investiture from his parents; the composition is sparse in formal elements but respects the canons of bas-relief and incision.

There are two big works that refer to Palenque's 7th century sculpture, made in jadeite and plaster.

The first is a mortuary mask with the quality of a portrait that helped cover Pacal or Shield II's face upon his death (plate 105). It is made with mosaics put together over a fine plaster covering. It represents the will to make the fisiognomy of the ruler eternal, as is still done today with great personalities.

145. Stucco head, which portrays Pacal II, found in the crypt of the Temple of the Inscriptions at Palenque. Late Classic (from Gendrop, 1972).

146. Detail from the Palace's Panel at Palenque. 702 A.D. Late Classic (from Schele and Miller, 1986).

The second is an extraordinary face in plaster of Pacal or Shield II's first child: Serpent Jaguar II (plate 104). It reproduces a unique figure, where nothing is disguised: one can easily perceive his age, a singular personality, as well as an intense inner concentration. The physical features do not overlook one single element of the character depicted.

## Yucatán Peninsula: The Swan Song

Two main sculptural features differenciate the North Zone from the Central Zone. In one case, there is a lack of human representations. In the other, there is profuse architectonic decoration with geometric stone tiles. In othe words, different sculptural forms appear in direct and intimate association to architecture: this union expresses a tendency –noted by many scholars– to enhance the volume of buildings in such a way that they become monumental sculptures.

This does not mean that the two modes of expression were divorced, since they do coexist, to mention just one case, in the crestings of Petén. But as we have seen, the dominant trend in sculpture were the reliefs.

147. Panel of the Slaves. Palenque. 730 A.D. Late Classic (from Freidel, Schele and Parker, 1993).

In the Yucatán peninsula, these evince an acute sense for tri-dimensionality and rigorous geometrical abstraction. They reflect a peculiar disposition to the cultivation of form characteristic of the northern Lowlands.

The architectural and sculptural developments in Yucatán have their roots in the end of the Early Classic and continue toward the Late Post-Classic. Nevertheless, most of the examples belong to the period between the 8th and 13th centuries A.D. At the same time, throughout the Post-Classic period the introduction of foreign styles in Mayan art created new styles in sculpture.

Sculpture incorporated traditional as well as original forms to architecture, thus conforming three stylistic groups located within three geographical regions: Río Bec, Chenes and Puuc, which have been previously mentioned.

### The Vivid Ceramic of Jaina

Jaina (Campeche), an island separated from land by a narrow canal, is an exceptional case in Mayan sculpture. It would be impossible not to mention the characteristic that places it apart: the ceramic figures made from molds, and painted in varied colors (figure 148; plates 111-114).

Generally speaking, these are small statues for funeral offerings. They symbolize «life» accompanying «death». The subjects are not restricted to human figures though these abound, and their treatment gives them a unique value, since they evoke different types. This rich apparel, headdresses, and jewels of men and women indicate their position in different social classes and activities; they appear, then, invested with earthly powers. Images of various divinities are also incorporated.

Jaina ceramics depict, among a wide variety of human types rulers, dignitaries, court-esans, warriors, ball players, weavers, young and old people, animals, individuals that come out of flowers or are accompanied by different animals; young godesses with older gods in sensual and graceful postures.

They are a unique artistic group and despite their small size, the pieces reflect,

148. Clay figure from Jaina. It represents a young man looking at himself in a mirror (from Gendrop, 1972).

196

through graceful postures and carefully molded forms, the human condition. They express love for life in all its aspects.

## Artificial Nature: Hochob

Hochob (Campeche) may not be a prime manifestation of the Chenes style, but it is an example of human figure in art form.

The «zoomorphic facades» mark out the portals of the buildings, which present huge masks with geometric and fantastic characteristics formed by the juxtaposition of small stones placed face to face. The entrance to the rooms is then transformed into the fauces of a monster, so that the jambs and the lintel simulate its upper dented jaw, at whose sides great eyes with hooked-pupils can be seen. On the floor, in front of the door, different elements suggest, when seen together, the lower jaw, but with teeth and tongue. This composition is sometimes completed with elements such as earrings, vegetal ornaments, and small masks superposed among themselves and at each side of the central one.

The set has been considered the magnified figure of the Earthly Monster; its open mouth is the cave to the mountains which leads into the netherworld. Such is the case of Structure 2. But here the cresting represents various schematized figures of men, rigid, with arms resting on their bodies.

This is one of the characteristics of the sculpture of the Yucatán plains during the Late Classic period.

## Uxmal and Stone Mosaic Harmony

Uxmal, a city in Yucatán, is an outstanding example of the Puuc style. Horizontal structures are predominant in its buildings, and the richness and abundance of its sculptures in mosaic reveal a profound fondness for geometrical harmony that, though repetitive, is not tiresome. Serpents, frets, small columns or drums, flat windows or dentated lacing, huts, characters dressed in luxurious clothes, masks with long and twisted mouths, are some of the sculptural elements added to the walls (plates 64-71). The Quadrangle of the Nuns is one of the noblest groups of buildings in the Puuc style.

Group sculptures with a common theme became part of wall decorations in the site. One of the best known is the «Uxmal Queen» (plate 108). This is a young expressionless face, probably tatooed because its cheek is decorated with a row of points set in frets; her hair is tied with a ribbon formed by discs, and she is issuing forth from the fauces of a serpent.

This type of sculpture is not exclusive of Uxmal. It is found in many cities such as Chichén Itzá (plate 81), Kabah (plates 77-80), Labná (plates 72-74), Oxkintok and Sayil (plates 75, 76).

## The Coarse Features of Kabah and Oxkintok

Various Puuc sites have the same features that can be found in Uxmal, but there are two that incorporate new elements: Kabah and Oxkintok (in Yucatán). To their already well-known sculptures recent archaeological findings have added others, so we can now talk about two characteristic features: carved columns with images of obese beings, on the one hand; and bas-relief steles and jambs, on the other.

The first have been identified as representing human figures that seem detached from the architectural elements. They have fat cheeks with bulging eyes, or very schematized, as with the human figure, whose total height varies from four to seven heads. One example is Column 2 of Oxkintok (figure 149; plate 109), now preserved at the National Museum of Anthropology in Mexico City.

Even when these are high-relief images, sometimes they give us the idea of round bulks. This has been achieved in only a few cases, an example of which is the Codz Pop («Rolled Matting») building, in Kabah. The frieze is decorated with large sized characters (bigger than the original ones), standing and richly dressed, though in keeping with the previously mentioned canons of simplicity and detachment.

Likewise, steles and jambs divide space in one to three levels containing scenes with characters that appear by themselves or accompanied, lacking individuality, and who adopt different postures and attitudes. Relief defines their silhouettes, and, through incisions, different designs, such as faces, dresses, and symbols of political or religious power, are detailed.

In most of the examples with lone figures, figures of women as well as of men can be seen facing forward, but with their faces looking to one side; arms are crossed over the chest, and the feet have their toes separated 180 grades. In the more complex scenes, with two or more divisions, human beings can be seen from one side, sitting on what seem to be thrones. Others are standing, apparently dancing or threatening prisoners of war. It is also possible to find at the top of the sculptures, images of deities or ancestors who are «flying about» above the mortals (figures 150, 151).

Unlike the formal treatment given to the human figure in the southern Lowlands –with the exeption of the obese and round bodies– the sculpted figures are coarse, simplified, and human importance is lost in the midst of the attributes of social, political and sacred status.

149. Column 2 at Oxkintok. Terminal Classic.

## Chichén Itzá and the Dominion of Geometry

Chichén Itzá is well known for its works dated in the Post-Classic period, when the art of the Mayas blended in with the art of the Mexican Plateau.

On other hand, it is well known that the «Old Chichén» sector belongs to the Puuc tradition to which the sculptures are stylistically incorporated.

However, representations called «*Chac Mool*» («red paw») (plate 110) by August Le Plongeon –name that is by no means related with their meaning– are worthy of notice. The oldest have been dated between the 8th and 9th centuries A.D. They are located in front of the access to temples and have been linked to different rituals. They show a strong geometric design, lacking personality. The Chac Mool is the figure of a man lying halfway on his back, with his torso elevated because he is leaning on his elbows, and his head is turned over one of his shoulders. His legs are bent and his ankles are close to his hips. He is holding a disc on his stomach with both hands.

And though these are round bulk sculptures, the treatment evinces a strong hold on geometrical and schematic forms, which are taken to a high degree of development.

## The End of an Era?

Mayan sculpture, with its most used technique –relief– and its favorite subjects –particularly man–, stands out through the centuries as a result of a people's search of a vehicle for representing in concrete objects a particular vision of the cosmos, rich in symbols and objects. Men of the upper social classes dominate the works. They are represented at the height of their political power with terrestrial and divine emblems that justify and validate their actions. They are accompanied by gods and ancestors, or noblemen and prisoners, in ritual activities.

150. Stele 9 at Oxkintok. Classic Terminal (drawing by H.E.D. Pollock, from *Arte Maya. Selva y mar*).

The peak moments of the Classic period express in sculpture a profound love for life whose images move from sensual lines and curves to rigid abstract lines. But as a whole, these are noble works that witness a millenary tradition in sculpture.

## Wall painting

### Cities of Color

The exterior of the Mayan architectural buildings have practically lost all the colors that had been painted over a stucco plaster. Though for as it is difficult to visualize the buildings just as they were kept in the time they were erected, evidence has shown that the buildings were coated with either one or several colors or with painted scenes. Presently, due to the perishable nature of stucco, chromatic layers have been reduced to small fragments.

The use of color was so important that architectural monuments were painted inside and outside. Sculptures were also painted in bright colors, as well as the stone reliefs (steles, lintels and jambs), and the stucco figures of great dimensions, such as the large masks of the Late Pre-Classic period.

Mayan groups handled the language of shapes as an established system in their various artistic expressions. Likewise, chromatism had its own meaning.

Pictorial remains show us that during the Middle Pre-Classic (1000-300 B.C.) pigments were already in use; color samples, mainly red, have been found in platforms and substructures within various sites of the Mayan area.

### Mural Polychromatism

There are different architectural constructions and spaces on which the Mayas represented, from simple monochrome stripes –as a limiting factor of architectural spaces– to colorful and highly symbolic scenes. These pictorial testimonies can be found on gravestones, platforms, staircases, jambs, lintels, cornices, entablatures, friezes and moldings outside temples or palaces. They are also seen on floors, walls, curbs and domes inside the rooms. There was an intrinsic relationship between painting and the architectural space where it was executed.

Likewise, pictorial iconography is diverse, but as a whole it has something to do with the activities of the elite, the gods and their concept of the cosmos and its three levels –heaven, earth and the netherworld–; also represented were rituals of sacrifice and self-sacrifice, scenes of war, dates that record the movements of the stars in time, and events relevant for the nobility, and hence for society.

Images were painted over a layer of plaster (a mixture of lime and sand), which gives a white color. Most of the pigments have a mineral origin. Other hues were formed by the mixture of different pigments, which resulted in a wide array of colors.

Over the architectural surface they put a plaster coating, smoothed out to a uniform layer. Over this, they usually outlined in red the silhouette of the figures that formed part of the scene. Then each was colored in, and finally they repainted the red outlines in black.

Most of the wall remains that have been preserved belong to sites located in Yucatán. There are few from the Central and South Zones. We know about other fragments through references by explorers in 19th and early 20th centuries written accounts. Most fragments have been completely lost or there are only a few traces of them left.

151. Stele 9 at Oxkintok. Terminal Classic. This stele, just like that on the previous figure, has disappeared (drawing by H.E.D. Pollock, from *Arte Maya. Selva y mar*).

199

It is difficult to establish the dates when mural painting arose. It is possible that the wall painting may not have corresponded to the construction of the building and that they could have been done later. Dating of the paintings must take into account information based on architectural, ceramic, archaeological, epigraphical and stylistic studies.

The function of mural painting in exteriors was to express and communicate, through a visual language added to other cultural expressions, cosmological and political concepts as a means to reinforce dynastic power. As to the paintings in interiors, it is possible that they were admired only by noblemen and that the subject-matter was restricted only to them. Therefore, it is also possible that common people were denied access.

## Path to the Netherworld

The murals that have been dated as the oldest in the Mayan area and that correspond to representations in a funerary context belong to the Late Pre-Classic period and to the Petén region.

At Tomb 166 in Tikal, various sitting characters can be seen on one of the walls of a chamber; they were outlined in black and then colored in red (figures 152, 153). They have been identified as deities or ancestors of the individual buried there and who most probably belonged to the ruling class.

Likewise, on the exterior of the temple of building 5D Sub 10-1, over the Tomb 167, there were standing human figures, as well as spirals bordering the paintings, which have now disappeared.

From the Early Classic, glyph texts appear on the impressive tombs 1, 19, 21 and 23 in Río Azul, at the northeastern tip of Guatemala, close to the border with Mexico and Belize.

The paintings from the Tomb 1 are in red over white. They are especially interesting due to their date in Long Count, that corresponds to 417 A.D., date of birth of the individual who is buried there, a ruler from Río Azul. Other god-like figures, serpentine figures, and power symbols, such as *pop* or straw mat can be observed on the walls. Through all these glyphic elements this individual's authority is shown and the netherworld is symbolized. Another date, 457 A.D., was painted on Burial 48 in Tikal.

## Xelhá, the Impressions of a Visitor

The Xelhá site, in Quintana Roo, houses the earliest wall painting that has been discovered in the Yucatán peninsula. It covers both sides of a wall within a substructure. At the southern section a scene of flying birds was represented, framed by wide bands; at the northern side, a swage block and an individual who is facing front reveals elements characteristic of Teotihuacan painting. The archaeological data place it around 450 A.D. Maybe this is one example of the presence or influence in wall painting of groups that travelled there from the Mexican Plateau between 450 and 550 A.D.

## Noblemen and Warriors in Uaxactún

Historical events, one of the features of Mayan iconography, first appeared on painted walls in a scene of an inside wall of Room 7 at building B-XIII in Uaxactún, Guatemala (figure 154). It has been dated between 350-550 A.D. When it was discovered it was separated from the wall and some of its fragments went to the National Museum of Archaeology and Ethnology in Guatemala.

152. Mural paintings in tomb 166 at Tikal. Late Pre-Classic (from Gendrop, 1971).

*previous pages*:
118. Container with polychrome paintings from the Sacred Cenote of Chichén Itzá. Late Classic.

119. Four-legged pot with an anthropomorphous representation. Late Pre-Classic.

120. Plate from the Nakbé region, Guatemala. Late Classic.

121. Vessel with basal rim and lid. Incised decoration. Late Classic.

122. Incense-burner representing the "Old God". Tikal, Early Classic.

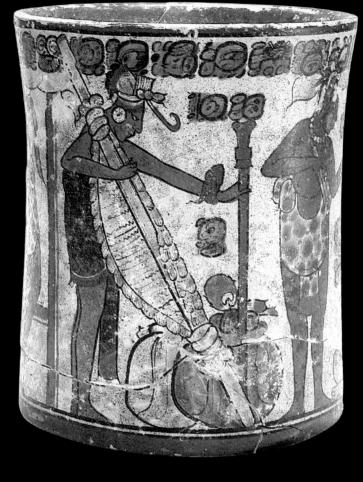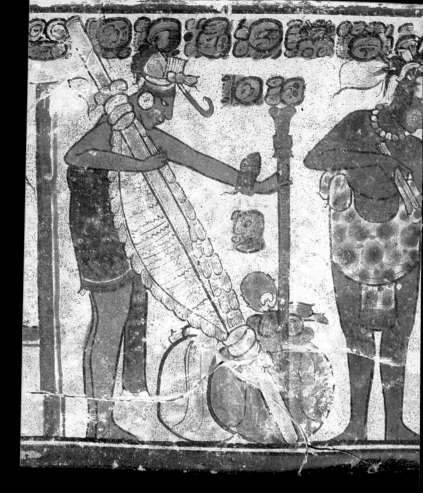

*previous pages*:
123. Cylindrical vessel from the Motul region in San José, Guatemala, Late Classic. The scene represents a nobleman paying tribute to his lord sitting on a straw mat. The text says that the vessel contained a cocoa drink.

124. Scene of a ball game represented on a polychrome cylindrical vessel. Late Classic.

125. Vessel from Tikal. Late Classic. A noblewoman delivers a head (or mask?) to a man.

126. Cylindrical vessel representing a dancer. Late Classic.

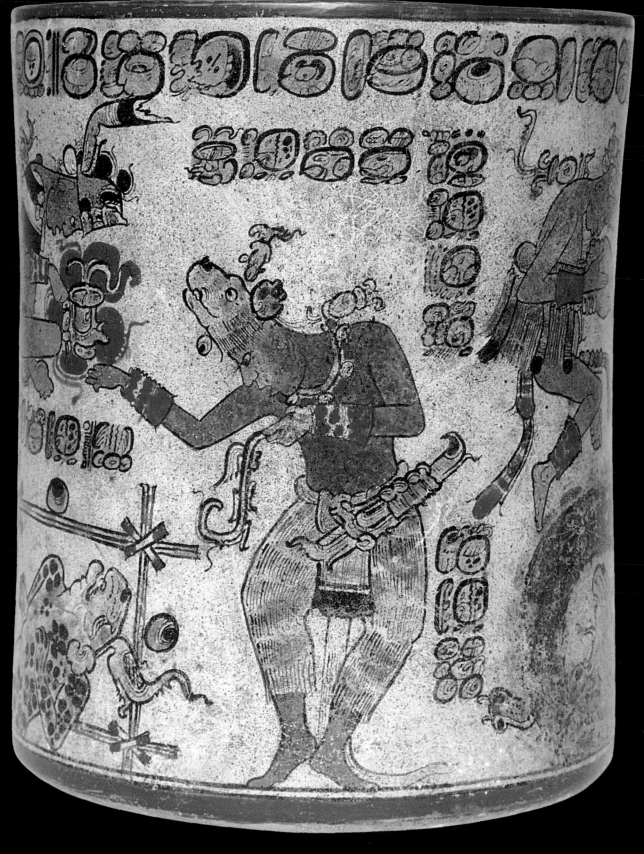

127. Four-legged vessel with lid and a zoomorphic representation.

128. Polychrome vessel with lid and an anthropomorphous representation.

*next pages*:
129. Jade earring from Pomona, Belize. Late Pre-Classic.

130. Jade pectoral found on the chest of a warrior from Nohmul, Belize. Early Classic.

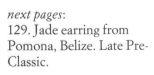

131. Shell pectoral representing a pipe smoker. Late Classic.

132. Shell incised with the image of an *ahau*. Early Classic.

*next page*:
133. Excentric figure in obsidian with four human profiles. Late Classic.

The distribution of figures in horizontal registers would become a constant feature in wall painting. A scene depicting various groups of characters distributed in two registers and accompanied by hieroglyphic inscriptions is an example of this.

There is an architectural construction that captures our attention: in it appear three sitting figures. They might be noblemen because of their clothes. On the left, two people, maybe warriors, one with his body painted in black, seems to be saluting the other figure raising his hand and holding an object.

Bonampak, the Vanity of a King

On the far-western side of the Acropolis stands Structure 1, also known as the Temple of the Paintings. It houses the most elegant and magnificent paintings of Mayan pictorial art. Fifty years after they were discovered, the meaning of the painted scenes that have been preserved thanks to restoration work performed between 1985 and 1987, can now be deciphered.

It has been said that the temple was built between 790 and 792 A.D. because of the glyph dates represented in the walls and lintels.

Most of the interior walls of the chambers are exquisitely painted (plates 116, 117). The images indicate that ritual activities were performed within this temple by ruler Chan Muan II or Harpy Heaven II, and other members of the Bonampak royalty.

On the dome of the temple's Room 1 (figure 156) a group of characters dressed in a white hood are talking. Their posture and hands indicate this. On the far right, a man is holding a child. It is believed that this drawing depicts the presentation of an heir to the throne.

On the other side, the scene is the moment when Chan Muan II, or Harpy Heaven, is being dressed by attendants. Over them, masks and part of a celestial band signify the things that occur in the other levels. On the walls a group of musicians and people disguised as fantastic beings also form part of this scene. Between the dome and the walls is the longest glyph text of these murals.

On three sides of Room 2 (figure 157) there is a body-to-body battle going on, in which the ruler appears as one of the main warriors. On the northern we can see the consequence of these actions: a scene in which the prisoners who are sitting or kneeling down for the sacrifice ritual express their suffering on the staircase of one of the buildings. At the center, Chan Muan II or Harpy Heaven, accompanied by members of the nobility, shows his victory and his power. Close to the dome vaulting and within

153. Further details from the paintings in tomb 166 at Tikal. Late Pre-Classic (from Gendrop, 1971).

154. Mural painting from room 7 in building B-XIII at Uaxactún. Early Classic (from Morley, Sharer, Brainerd, 1983).

medallions there are figures apparently associated with the stars who are watching the events.

In Room 3 (figure 158) various characters are dancing with huge headdresses and rich clothes. On the east side of the dome, over a curb, a self-sacrifice ritual is going on. Women pierce their tongues with a rope and their blood, the sacred liquid, pours over papers in a container. These papers will then be burned and the smoke will put them in contact with the gods, with heaven. On the northern side another group of noblemen in white appears to be conversing. At the top there are other symbolic figures and elements associated with the gods and the stars.

Glyph cartridges are placed alongside some of the characters. These are nominal clauses that carry their names or their royal titles.

The walls in Bonampak are an example of the mastery in technique and composition attained by the Mayas. Scenes are of an extraordinary naturalism: the expressions on their faces, the movements of men in battle. The clothes worn by the characters represented are elegant, with an elaborate series of symbols concealed within the detailed designs on the skirts and capes. The feathered and fantastic animal headdresses cover each of the characters. The colors are a fundamental part of the visual aspect and iconography.

These paintings are the only example of an almost complete picture mural that sheds light on the way the temples of other cities in the Mayan area may have been painted.

It is also important to mention that on the exterior walls of Structure 1 fragments of a band with painted glyphs remain. This sample and others from the north of the peninsula of Yucatán (Structure 2 of Chicanná or the site at Haltunchón, in Campeche) indicate that important events were painted on the facades of these buildings.

The representation of scenes in which glyphic texts appear, as well as members of the ruling class, seems to have become a recurrent theme during this period. The remains of faces and very elaborate headdresses are still preserved in Palenque and Yaxchilán, in Mexico, and in La Pasadita, in Guatemala.

This iconographic and compositional tradition is also present in Petén and in Cobá, 50 kilometers away from the Caribbean coast, in Quintana Roo. The few fragments that remain from the structure known as El Cuartel indicate this.

The Warrior

In the Yucatán peninsula we find other painted testimonies extolling the importance of war, of sacrifice rituals, prisoners, and gods.

*On the following pages:*
Outlines of mural paintings in Structure 1 at Bonampak. 790-792 A.D. Late Classic (from Adams and Aldrich, 1980). 156: Paintings in Room 1.

157. Paintings in Room 2.

158. Paintings in Room 3.

155. Scene of battle depicted on the mural paintings at Mulchic. Late Classic (drawing by L. Staines, based on H. Sánchez Vera).

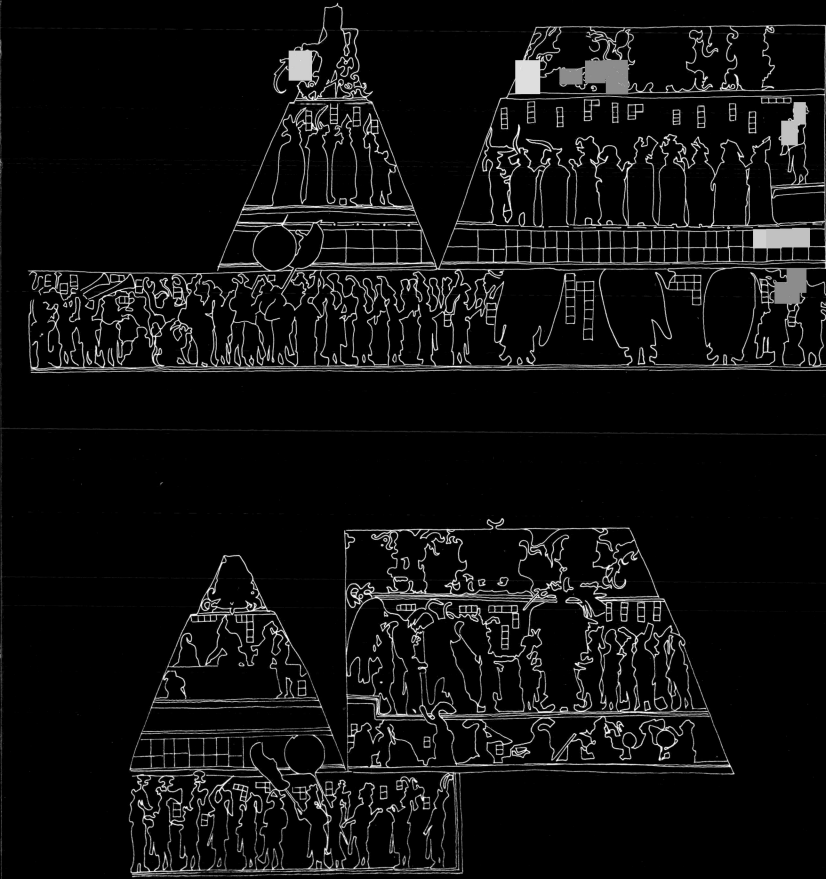

159. Vault covers or capstones at Xnucbec, with paintings representing the god K'awil, Late Classic (picture by B. de la Fuente; drawing by K.H. Mayer).

The Mulchic paintings are distributed along three horizontal registers. On the top one there is a glyph text; in the middle one, which is the broadest, different scenes are taking place. The bottom register depicts figures associated with death and the netherworld.

On one of the walls a battle between two groups is represented (figure 155). The weapons are stones and a body appears to be hanging from a tree. The scene in the back mural, with human figures whose bodies are painted in black, along with skulls and knives, represents prisoners of war who are being presented to the ruler.

At the Ichmac site, also placed on horizontal registers the walls and vaults are covered with paintings of important characters. They represent different events associated with the three levels of the cosmos and with the ritual activities of the members of the nobility.

There are other murals whose iconographic content consists of warriors or war scenes. These can be seen in Sodzil and Chacmultún, in Yucatán. There is a notorious change in composition in the latter: the characters are much smaller in comparison to the murals mentioned above.

## When the Gods Speak

An apparently regional style, in both its subject matter and the space it occupies in the architecture, can be found in numerous sites in Campeche and Yucatán and consists of stone vault carers most of which belong to the Late Classic period.

In the row of stones forming the enclosure of the vault –mainly the central one, which forms an axis with the entrance to the room– there are a series of painted images (figure 159).

The features that define and set these paintings apart are the use of red over white and the fact that the central image is framed on all sides by a fringe of glyphs. They generally measure between 40 and 70 centimeters in high, by 15 to 45 centimeters in width.

The figure that occupies the center is generally a god, most frecquently the god K or *K'awil*, whose fantastic face and a scaled body associates him to a reptile. Sometimes one of his feet is represented as the head of a serpent. This deity is closely related to the members of the lineage in power and among his attributes is his association with abundance and food. Other examples include Dzibilnocac and Xnucbec, where the divinity appears throwing seeds.

## Two Styles at Chichén Itzá

In Chichén Itzá, several paintings on the buildings, such as the Temples of the Nuns, the Jaguars and the Warriors may have belonged to the Terminal Classic or Early Post-Classic periods. Two styles standout: the Classic Mayan and the one from the Mexican Central Plateau.

### The Vessels and their Histories

There is vast information gathered through research on the origins and the technical process of ceramics.

This difficult task has provided valuable information about each of the regions of the Mayan area. A chronology and stages of development have been determined through classification and analysis of the ceramics found.

Likewise, through the materials used and the recognition of specific models in objects, it has been possible to know more about the cultural, commercial and social relations among Mayan peoples and between these and other Mesoamerican tribes or groups.

Materials for making vessels were clay or mud, water, and grease removers; with them, a great variety of objects were created. In order to degrease the object (so it would not break during the baking and cooling processes), they used igneous ash, shell, sand, quartz, and calcite. The type of grease remover, along with the clay mixture, has served to distinguish the different types of ceramics and the regions where they were made.

An example is the ceramic complexes created after a tipology and identified by the nomenclatures of each archaeological site, but the most used for establishing distinctions is the one from Uaxactún, Guatemala.

Ceramic pieces from the Middle Pre-Classic (1000-300 B.C.) and the Late Pre-Classic (300 B.C.-300 A.D.) were found in the *Mamon* and *Chicanel* complexes at Uaxactún (figure 160); *Eb, Tzec, Chuen, Cauac,* at Tikal; as well as in *Nabanche, Komchen* and *Xculul*, at Dzibilchaltún. They show technical expertise and a great variety of forms. Decorations were mostly geometric, abstract, or only clay colored. These features can be seen in pots, vessels, concave dishes, decanters, human or animal shaped glasses, or of complex forms. The most outstanding colors are beige, red and gray, and the globular supports are notewortly.

The development and changes that take place during the first stages of the Early Classic (300-600 A.D.), witnessed mainly through vessels with lids and scenes where human figures are more commonly represented in varied activities and with diverse attributes. Colors are generally the same as those previously mentioned, although blue, white, green, and black are also incorporated, as can be seen in the Tzakol complexes in Uaxactún (figure 162); Cimi and Manik in Tikal; Bizac in Copán, and Blanco, in Cobá.

There are also four-legged vessels, with the legs in the form of animal feet. Their lids also have animal heads, as well as human or animal figures with incised and relief decoration. There is a special emphasis on the representation of whole human or animal figures as censers.

During the Late Classic period, one of the best known complexes is Tepeu, in Uaxactún (figure 162). This was a time of splendor for the fabrication of polychrome vessels with scenes, especially the ritual and funerary ceramics, whose technical perfection and artistic quality are evident. These were objects used by the ruling dynasty and the nobility for ritual purposes, so they are commonly found within the temples, associated with the steles or altars as burial offerings.

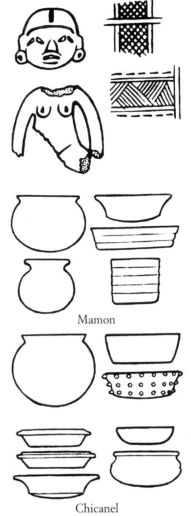

160. Portion of the ceramic sequence from Uaxactún used as basis for the Mayan ceramic sequence. Pre-Classic (R. Smith, from Culbert, 1985).

161. Decoration on a polychrome vessel from Chamá, Guatemala. Late Classic (from Morley, Sharer, Brainerd, 1983).

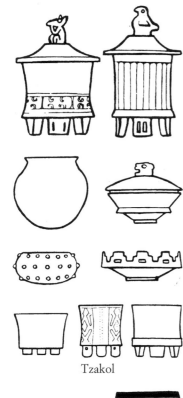

Tzakol

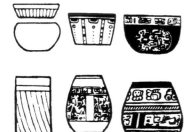

Tepeu

162. Classic stages of the ceramic sequence from Uaxactún (R. Smith, from Culbert, 1985).

163. Two polychrome plates. The one on the left comes from Uaxactún, the one on the right comes from Tikal (from Morley, Sharer, Brainerd, 1983; W. Coe, 1977).

Craftmanslike production must have been intense as is revealed by the great amount of luxurious objects in demand among the ruling elite. It is a fact that the artisans, who probably belonged to a specialized group, acquired great expertise and creativity in the manufacturing of utensils. A great variety of forms in ceramic objects have been found: pots, *apastles*, concave dishes, legless plates or tripods, earthen ware bowls, bowls with divergent walls, jugs, pots with handles, cylindrical glasses with high walls, animal-shaped containers, urns, hearths, and small sculpture in the round (plates 118-128).

Iconography of the painted images varies from symbolic motifs (sleeping mats, swage blocks, water, bands, among others), to one with a historical, religious, and cosmological content (figures 161, 163)

Scenes are often naturalistic and dynamic. Rulers are represented performing the self-sacrifice, sitting on benches while celebrating rituals, or speaking with their ancestors or the deities. Also depicted are warriors, dancers and animals (especially those connected with the netherworld, like birds or jaguars). On the edges of some vessels there are hieroglyphic inscriptions, or enclosed in the scene, and they indicate either dates, or a special celebration.

It is worth mentioning that the numerous containers manufactured for household or practical use, such as dishes, pots, and other vessels, generally were very sparsely ornamented.

### Diverse Materials: Products for the Nobility

Objects are made of different materials in Mayan art work. They were generally made with jade, shell, coral, silex, bone, obsidian, pyrite, and stucco. Objects with animal or human shapes, as well as sculptures in the round have been found; for this type of work the artisans used hard stone, wood, and jade polishers.

The objects that formed part of the ritual, the attire and the ornaments of the ruling class or the nobility had such an iconographic or symbolic importance that they are found in a great number of burial sites, and are also present in stone or stucco, reliefs, in mural pointings, and in polychrome ceramics, as part of the general attire of the individuals there represented.

Jade was one of the hardest stones used by the Mayas; its colors are shades of green, black, blue, and white. It was either carved, used on tiles, or in individual pieces, as in jewels (ear plugs, necklaces, bracelets, anklets, and other ornaments) (plates 129, 130).

For similar uses they were sometimes combined with obsidian, shell, coral and bone. Pyrite was generally used for mirrors.

Designs were engraved on many of these objects. For instance, some pectorals have representations of gods or of the hierarchy of the individual wearing it during a ritual act.

Sea-shells or snail shells (figure 164; plates 131, 132) were not only used as raw material in creating specific objects (human or animal figures, or hieroglyphic inscriptions), but also the original form of the material, on which sometimes designs were etched in with graffito.

Also important are the engravings on bone (figure 165). Simple designs, human figures, deities, or hieroglyphic inscriptions are common.

Other objects are the so called "eccentric" pieces made with obsidian (plate 133) and silex. Among the various forms into which they were made it is comon to find those of deities. On the other hand, it is worth mentioning that feather art must have been another relevant artistic expression, as is evident from the wall paintings in Bonampak, as well as in numerous painted vessels.

We hope this brief journey into Classic Mayan art will foster greater interest in one in the history of the most creative cultures of humanity and whose magnificent creations still preserve unknown secrets.

164. Shell piece with incised decoration. Late Classic (from Schele and Miller, 1986).

Notes

[1] Raw materials for building architectural monuments are diverse. However, limestone was generally used, and stucco (a combination of limestone, lime, and sand) as wall covering.
[2] "Temple" and "palace" do not have any equivalent with regard to the function the Mayas gave to their buildings within their activities.
[3] *Sacbe*, in singular; *sacbeoob*, in plural, whose meaning is "white road", are roadways or roads built of limestone, with a stucco layer, to join architectural complexes at the same site, and to link cities. Their height varies between 1-5 meters, over floor level. They can be up to 5 meters wide. The longest found up to now is the one that joins Cobá (Quintana Roo), with Yaxuná (Yucatán), of some 100 kilometers.
[4] Another stylic region at the western coast, in the Caribbean Sea, in Quintana Roo, which will not be studied now, since it belongs to Post-Classic period.
[5] The Pre-Classic period temples were made of masonry, with wooden posts that held palm-tree ceilings.
[6] Also incorrectly called false arch.

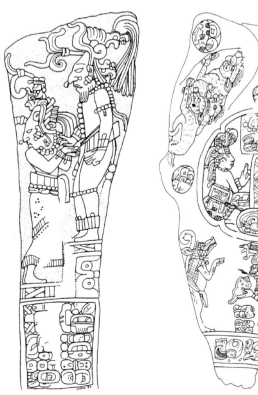

165. Incised bones. Left: jaguar bone with two characters; Late Classic. In the middle: deer's tibia with the image of Lord Yax-Pac and a Lady; from Copán; Late Classic (from Schele and Miller, 1986). Right: peccari skull, from tomb 1 at Copán. 376 A.D. Early Classic (from Fash, 1991).

# Mayan Writing

## *Maricela Ayala Falcón*

When we speak about the Mayas we are speaking of knowledge. Undoubtedly, among the cultures that flourished in the New World the Maya made the greatest progress concerning intellectual development. This does not mean that other cultures did not achieve it, but it was the Mayas who left a record of written evidence.

Modern man is so used to reading and writing, that he seldom stops to think about the origins and evolution of these abilities, or about the fact that present societies depend on communication. This dependence began in the past and it has always required three elements: a transmitter, a means of transmission, and a receptor. If any of these does not exist, there is no message nor its transmission, and consequently no inheritance.

It must have been during prehistoric times when man transformed sounds into «words» or phonemes, but communicating codes had to be characteristic of and recognizable by each group; so the way messages were relayed changed. These resulted in the development of three basic systems: mimical, phonetical, and graphical. The latter has evolved in different ways, none of them alike, but always susceptible of being adopted and adapted.

Before starting our journey into the Mayan writing system it is important to point out that, up to now, there is no definition describing when a graphical system can be recognized as writing. Are rupestrian wall paintings a type of writing? Can the drawings made by North American indians be considered a writing system?

The answer is difficult, for one reason: The experts on the subject, be they philologists, historians, linguists, or anthropologists based the difference between primitive tribes and the civilized or educated ones on whether they had a writing system or not. This concept also gave rise to the now obsolete division between archaeology and history.

The conquerors were interested in dominating and evangelizing the inhabitants of the American continent, and only a few, out of mere curiosity, expressed in their chronicles and accounts what they saw that amazed them. Let us not forget that we are talking about people from 16th century Europe. «There were books that told us everything about them», «they had a way of writing which they used to communicate»,

166. Stele 6 at Izapa. Late Pre-Classic (from Lowe, Lee, and Martínez, 1982).

«they had a sort of receptacle for their books», «they used paper made out of bark» (*ficus* tree), on which they painted their deeds, stories, maps, genealogies, forecasts, etc. They not only had writing, but also a mailing system, and a historic awareness that has given them permanence.

However, and despite the information in the chronicles, scholars denied the existence of American graphical systems. Only recently have anthropologists and philologists, who did not know these chronicles existed and therefore denied American cultures because «they did not have writing systems», reconsidered their position. The best argument against this has been Mayan writing, although there is also the Mixtec, Zapotec and the Mexica writing.

But in order to speak about Mayan writing and culture, it is necessary to look to the past. When man began to leave messages, he used painted or carved symbols. Most of us are unable to understand them, and maybe never will, because we still do not know whether they are historical accounts or prayers. This is what happens with some prehistoric representations: in Altamira, Spain; Lascaux, France; or Izapa, Mexico. They have been called «pictograms», because they realistically represent figures (figure 166).

There is a second stage concerning the evolution of writing that has been referred to as «icons». It is worth mentioning that it is difficult to separate them from the pictograms. In the icons we also find representations of images, but here the object implies an idea. This is, the figure of a «fish» changes its meaning for an idea or a verb: «to fish», «fisherman» (figure 132).

The next step consisted of creating a logographic or phonetical writing, that is, when the symbols could be read either as words or syllables. Among monosyllabic languages, such as Mayan and Sumerian, transition was probably swift, and within the process they resorted to homophonic words which made it possible for them to write concepts which otherwise would have been impossible to be written. Thus, in Sumerian, an arrow, *ti*, was used as *ti* to indicate «life». In Maya, the symbol *kin*, «Sun», could either mean the solar god, the day, and by semantic derivation, the number four (figure 167), although we should add that each meaning can be written in different ways, known as normal ways, head variants and whole body variants.

Graphic symbols evolved in some forms of writing until they became phonemes, like in our alphabet; but the process was long, its history difficult, and, in fact, not all systems reached this stage.

The researchers have considered that only the Egyptian and the cuneiform systems reached phoneticism, that is, when each symbol represents a sound (phoneme). And it is here where one of the problems lies, because there is a previous stage, recognized by many authors, where symbols are read as syllables. This stage is known as syllabical-phonetical, and presents itself mainly in morpho-syllabic words. Specific cases are: Sumerian, Mexican (or Aztec), and Mayan.

### The Process of Decipherment

The problem of the existence of a Mayan writing system is peculiar. When Diego de Landa, bishop of Yucatán, wrote his *Relación de las cosas de Yucatán* (157?), he did not know that document would be ignored for almost three centuries.

We know that Mesoamerica, throughout its history, shared many ideas and products through trading, culture, and war activities. The Mayan area was not an exception, and all those activities, especially the wars, brought as a result that upon the arrival of the Spaniards, their knowledge about writing was almost lost. The priests and some rulers

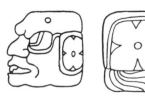

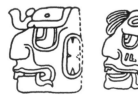

167. Top: Sun glyphs, *k'in*. Bottom: two head variants for number 4, *k'in* (from Marcus, 1992; Thompson, 1978).

were the ones who possessed this knowledge, and «were better praised», as Landa says, because of this.

One of these characters was Gaspar Antoni Chi, who gave Landa all the information about how the calendar, hieroglyphics, or glyphs, corresponding to days, months, and the «Mayan alphabet» (figure 170) worked.

It is important to mention that Mayan languages[1] include sounds, or phonemes, that do not exist in Spanish, which have been referred to as glottal because they are pronounced with a closing of the glottis, and are written in the following fashion:[2] ch', k', p', ts'. There are also long vowels: aa, ee, ii, oo, uu, which some linguists recognize as syllables formed by two vowels with a closing of the glottis between them; and this would result in: a'a, e'e, i'i, o'o, u'u. Besides, in some languages, like the cholanas, there is the sixth vowel Ä. The h sounds much like the j, but much softer; the sounds for d, f, and g, do not exist; while in the Quiché languages [y] is changed for [r].

Communication between Landa and Antoni Chi must have been very interesting, because possibly neither of them realized that they were speaking about two different writing systems. Let us not forget that in Spanish the names of the letters are syllables; thus, for the letter [b] (be), there were two glyphs; the first is a footprint indicating «road», and in Maya it is pronounced be. Letter [h] (ache) was written with two glyphs, a-che, and so on (figure 168).

Landa was not the only one interested in the knowledge of the Mayas. The friars had to learn the languages of the groups they were going to evangelize, and during this process grammar books, dictionaries, calepines, and lexicons, were written and proved helpful either for understanding Mayan culture, or for advancing in the process of decipherment.

Many of these authors, while observing Mayan cities, became interested in finding an explanation about the nature and origins of the symbols they saw in the steles, sculpted monoliths, and buildings. This occurred to the friar Jacinto Garrido, who, while visiting the ruins we now know as Toniná, in Chiapas, would write (ca. 1630-1680) that, in his opinion, the monuments probably told the story about the conquests of other cities, and that the written symbols had to be syllables, because if each of the symbols represented a letter there would not be space enough in the whole monument for one word (figure 169).

Captain Antonio del Río's visit to the Mayan ruins in 1787 and the diary he published about his journey (1822), as well as the visits by Dupaix (1800), and later by John L. Stephens and Frederick Catherwood in 1841, marked the beginning of Mayan archaeology.

But to the information they furnished, we must add another; the publication of the so called *Dresden Codex*.

168. Be, footprint, *bi*, «quincunce» and Landa's *a-che* (from Marcus, 1992).

169. Toniná's altar (from Ayala, 1994).

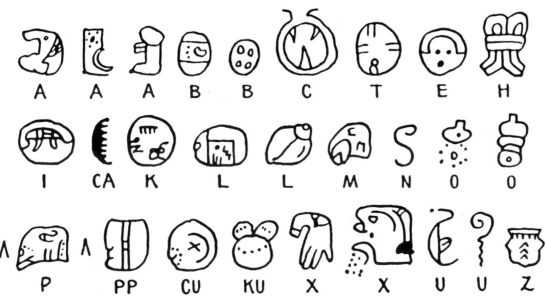

170. Landa's alphabet (from M. Coe, 1992).

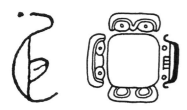

171. Glyph for *u* and glyph T.1 (from Landa; Thompson, 1978).

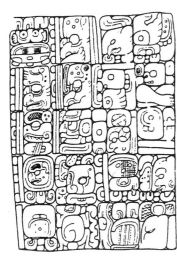

| 1 | 2 | 11 | 12 |
|---|---|----|----|
| 3 | 4 | 13 | 14 |
| 5 | 6 | 15 | 16 |
| 7 | 8 | 17 | 18 |
| 9 | 10 | 19 | 20 |

172. Top: Lintel 29 at Yaxchilán. Bottom: reading sequence (from Graham 1975-86).

chac red    yax green    zac white

ek black    kan yellow

173. Glyphs for colors (from Ayala, 1995).

This manuscript is one of the three Mayan pre-Columbian codices[3] which survived conquest, evangelization, and the religious fervor of the missionaries, when they burned and destroyed all the codices and many monuments considering them things of the devil.

The codex may have been purchased in Vienna, by Johann Christian Götze, director of the Royal Library of Dresden, during a trip around Europe (1739). Upon his return to Dresden he published an inventory in which he mentions the acquisition of «a Mexican Codex». In 1816, Alexander von Humboldt reproduced pages 47-52 of this document. The complete codex was one of those published by Lord Kingsborough (1831-1838) in his *Antiquities of Mexico* (volume 3).

Maybe through these investigations many researchers became interested in the subject, but no one, except for Constantine S. Rafinesque, could understand hieroglyphic scripts. He studied the texts with all the then known inscriptions, publishing his findings in different American magazines and newspapers (1827-1833).

There were also other sporadic treaties. However among the most important was the work of Charles E. Brasseur de Bourbourg, who established Mayan epigraphy among modern disciplines. Brasseur found the copy of Diego de Landa's manuscript, which he published in 1864. He also identified another Mayan codex in Madrid, the Troano, which he published and read (1866), with the aid of Landa's alphabet.

It is worth mentioning that he was the one who recovered and published in French the translation made by the priest Francisco Ximénez of the *Popol Vuh*, from Quiché to Spanish. This book has been essential for the understanding of Mayan myth. He also rescued the *Rabinal Achí* drama, the only evidence of Mayan theater still extant.

It is true that Brasseur's phonetic reading of the *Troano Codex* was incorrect, because, misreading it, he thought that each symbol represented a phoneme, as Landa estimated. Of all his readings, only one was right: the one according to which the glyph represented the *u* morpheme, which in Yucatán Mayan belonged to the pronoun of the third person singular (figure 171).

Despite his mistakes, undoubtedly Brasseur was the one who set in motion the sistematic approach to Mayan epigraphy.

The next 130 years include many researchers who were interested in this problem, even when at first only a few of them were able to devote themselves full time to solving it.

On the process of decipherment, many books have been written recently; none of them include all the trends nor all the works, as this would be almost impossible due to so many articles and books on the subject.

There is a great list, so we will limit ourselves to the most important. These works were divided into two groups: the ones dealing with the symbols, in an effort to read them phonetically, and the ones that focused on the calendar, mathematics, and astronomy. And as the latter was the group that obtained more palpable results, it was the one that concluded that the glyphs were ideograms.

In this trend there are many important authors, such as Ernst Förstemann, also director of the Dresden Library, who published the Dresden Codex in a yet unsurmountable version (1892). Förstemann identified the symbols for the numbers: the dot standing for number 1, the bar indicating number 5; the «zero» symbol as well as the positional value of each number. He also discovered that the mathematical system was vigesimal. He also identified the so called «Venus» and «Eclipses» charts in the *Dresden Codex*.

His work was primal for the correct interpretation of the inscriptions. Thanks to his findings regarding the calendar, another researcher, Léon de Rosny (France, 1873), discovered the order for reading the Mayan texts. These are read by double columns, from left to right, and from the top to the bottom (figure 172). De Rosny also identified the symbols for colors (figure 173), and made a catalogue of Mayan glyphs.

During this period there were other researchers, such as Paul Schellhas, who studied the relationships between text and figures in the codex, identifying the hieroglyphic names of the gods and animals represented in it. As he could not name them, he assigned to each of them an alphabetic nomenclature which, after being later corrected by Günter Zimmermann and Eric Thompson, is still in use.

Meanwhile, the phonetic trend slowly developed, though it often failed. Cyrus Thomas, from the United States, using Landa's alphabet, and based on the relationship between figure and text, tried to read the hieroglyphs of the codices.

In 1893, Thomas proposed a number of arguments in support of the phonetic reading, such as: *a)* one glyph could both have a phonetic and a symbolic (or logographic) value; *b)* in these different kinds of writing, many symbols, though different, could have the same sound. Thus, he was able to read the cartridges[4] for «trap» and «to catch», in the *Matritensis Codex* (figure 174), which he read as *u le*, and corrected Rosny's reading for «turkey», *kutz* (figure 175); «house», *otoch*; and «macaw», *moo*.

Unfortunately for the history of the decipherment, he lost sight of his principles and concluded a series of unsustainable readings, after which his work lost relevancy.

The beginning of the 20th century was critical for Mexico; president Porfirio Díaz had finally assigned a place for the National Museum of Anthropology; and the school of anthropology was founded. Excavations began using an archaeological method, in downtown Mexico City, Teotihuacan, and Monte Albán, Oaxaca.

But the Mayan area rebelled, as it has always done through history, and after this attempt of the central government to look for the Mexican roots, the Mayan area was relegated, leaving foreign institutions in charge of its study, recognition, and exploitation.

At the end of the 19th century, United Fruit had arrived in Yucatán. Among the group was Alfred Percival Maudslay, author of *Biologia Centrali-Americana* (1889-1902), a work in twelve volumes. The first five books describe the Mayan pre-Hispanic cities the author had seen during his journey, as well as the monuments he had taken pictures of.

Based on his photographs, Annie Hunter drew the monuments together with the inscriptions, and they had such quality that only a few corrections have been made. The sixth book was written by J. T. Goodman (1897). From this author's contributions, it is worth highlighting the correlation he established between the Mayan and the Christian calendars, which was first corrected by Juan Martínez Hernández (1928), and then by Eric Thompson (1936), and is the one currently used by the epigraphers.[5]

At the beginning of the 20th century two more researchers, Franz Blom and Sylvanus G. Morley, entered the field of Mayan archaeology. Exploring the area, they came upon new sites and monuments.

Morley, representing Carnegie Institution of Washington, and Blom, of Tulane University, opened the area to archaeological, anthropologic, ethnographic, and epigraphic research.

Morley found various important sites, such as Uaxactún, «8 year/stone», as he called it because that was the place where he found the first stele dated 8 *baktun*.[6] He also deciphered calendar texts with multiple inscriptions, which he published in two important works: *The Inscriptions of Copán* (1920), and *The Inscriptions of Petén* (1937-1938).

In a pioneering work, *An Introduction to Mayan Hieroglyphic Writing* (1915), he dared to advance an hypothesis previously entertained by Herbert H. Spinden (1913) about the historic content of Mayan writing.

His argument was supported on the fact that the Mayas built steles each 5 *tunes* (360 days year), and that there were no astronomical events with such periodicity. Neither his nor Spinden's opinion had any echo.

For the first half of the century, the decipherment of Mayan writing was solidly established in calendars, astronomy, and consequently in astrology.

e   l   e   lé

174. Glyphs for «trap» and «to catch» *u-le* (Matritensis Codex and phonetic reading: *e-l-e-lé* (from Landa).

 Landa's cu

 cu-iz (u) cutz-turkey

 cu-ch (u) cuch-to carry

175. *Kutz*, «turkey».

Landa's L

tzul (u)
tzul-dog

(bu)-lu-c-(u)
buluc-eleven

176. Glyph for *Ku*) in Landa, and in the words *tzul* (dog), and *buluc* (eleven) in the *Dresden Codex*. Down, the number 11 in the bar and dot system, and glyph head variants (from Ayala and Mathews; Thompson 1978).

The ideographic-calendaric school was blooming. Researchers went so far as to create numerical hypotheses in order to give an astronomical meaning to all time reckonings. Such evidence, due to the partial decipherment of Mayan texts, lead researchers to consider the Mayas as an ethnic group devoted to the observation of the transition of stars, and thus, only concerned about the passing of time. The only important things were dates and gods.

This is how the Mayan people became the epitome of Indian noblemen.

The Carnegie Institution was the one that worked in this region, and among its contributions was the establishment of the periodicity of the ceramic sequence of Uaxactún, carried out by Robert Smith (1950), and derived from the relationship between ceramics and the dated monuments of the site. Eric Thompson was responsible for dating them.

Undoubtedly, Thompson was the last «Maya scholar». Even though he was an archaeologist, he had gained expertise in many other fields. He possessed vast knowledge about Indian, Spanish, and other colonial documents. He was the first to postulate that hieroglyphic texts may have been written in one of the Cholan tongues. He realized the importance of commerce throughout the region and was very interested in the religion and ethnography of the region and its relationship with the rest of Mesoamerica. Thompson revised the Maya-Christian correlation and published a catalogue of Mayan hieroglyphics (1962), still in use among all epigraphers.

However, his concept about Mayan philosophy about time, and the image of the Indian nobleman, restrained him from recognizing the evidence that was beginning to come to light with respect to Mayan writing. He said that the collapse of the Mayas and the culture's gradual decline was due to the «attack of uncivilized tribes from remote northern latitudes».[7]

In 1933, the American linguist Benjamin Lee Whorf returned to the old problem of phonetics in Mayan writing. His arguments had nothing to do with decipherment, but rather with the structuralist school that was beginning to take shape at the time.

Whorf began by analyzing the different Mayan tongues, and concluded that Mayan writing had to have been syllabic. Under these plots, he read the cartridge for the Mac (figure 177) month, but apparently his work went unnoticed, except for the Russian historian Yuri Knorozov.

In 1950, Knorozov presented before the Mayan Researchers International Congress his readings of the Mayan codices, which unlike the former were based on a syllabic or morphemic rendering of the symbols. His ideas were opposed by Eric Thompson and Thomas Barthel from Germany.

Thompson criticized Knorozov for assigning different values to the same symbol, according to his personal interests. Barthel, on the other hand, proved that, except for the number 11 (*bu-lu-k*) (figure 176), the rest of the readings had already been postulated.

Mac

177. Glyphs for the month *Mac* (Thompson, 1978).

Contering all of these objections, in 1963 Knorozov published his first and greatest work: *Pis'menost' Indeitsev Maya*, in which he included his hieroglyphic catalogue with the previous readings for each symbol, as well as his new interpretations.

But these readings, together with the works of a group of Soviet mathematicians –Ebreinov, Kozarev, and Ustinov–, who tried to read the Mayan codices with computers (1962), were widely criticized by the connoisseurs of the Yucatán Mayan tongue.

However, Knorozov postulated something very important. He was the first one to talk about a hieroglyphic grammar, and was also the discoverer of a grammatical syntax in hieroglyphic texts.

Knorozov, in his work on codices, noted that every time the gods do the same thing, the first cartridge of each sentence is the same. He also noted that the objects the gods hold are sometimes reproduced in the texts. Based on this, he started speculating on subjects, verbs, and objects.

Thanks to this grammatical explanation, it was possible to recognize something that Thompson had already mentioned: Mayan written language had to be Cholan, and the codices and northern inscriptions had to be from Yucatán.

But it was many years and vicissitudes before scholars arrived at this conclusion.

In 1958, a German archaeologist living in Mexico, Heinrich Berlin, recognized several very interesting cartridges.

Berlin, working on Thompson's book, *Mayan Hieroglyphic Writing, An Introduction* (1952), realized that the so called «aquatic group»[8] (figure 178) was always associated with the *ben-ich* prefix, and both served to frame a main symbol,[9] which changed from one city to another (figures 179, 31). For this reason, and for their use in inscriptions, he called them «emblem glyphs», and stated the possibility that their function consisted in identifying the cities, even when he did not know if they belonged to the name of a site, a deity, or the site's lineage.

In 1959, analyzing the hieroglyphic texts from the Temple of the Inscriptions, at Palenque, he recognized various associated cartridges he had identified as the emblem glyph of the site. The cartridges appeared in three places: at the base of the sarcophagus, in relation with the characters which were represented there; at the edge of the tombstone; and in the texts of the panels (figure 180). From here he deduced that they were the same characters, and that these were people who had lived in that place; that is, they were historical characters.

The far-reaching effects of these findings did not take long being felt, and the immediate response was the work of a Russian-American researcher, Tatiana Proskouriakoff.

Tania, as her friends called her, was an excellent sketch artist and scholar of Mayan iconography. At the end of the fifties, Proskouriakoff was studying the «serpent/dragon» from the inscriptions at Piedras Negras, Guatemala, when she noted that the hieroglyphic texts of this place presented an interesting association.

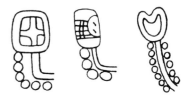

178. Aquatic group (from Marcus, 1992).

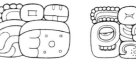

179. Some emblem glyphs. From left to right and from top to bottom: Naranjo, Machaquilá, Piedras Negras and Seibal (from Thompson, 1978).

180. Nominal glyphs on the sarcophagus from Palenque (from Berlin, 1958).

181. Stele 11 at Piedras Negras. 731 A.D. Late Classic (from Schele and Miller, 1986).

Inscriptions were related to the buildings, and each group presented a pattern that was meaningful with respect to Berlin's findings. That is, the logged dates for each group corresponded to a human life cycle.

But that was not all. With the earliest date of each group there was always one and the same cartridge, which Tania called «first event». The same occurred with the later dates. She also identified another cartridge, which she considered might refer to «death» of the people mentioned in the texts (figure 182).

Delving deeper into this hypothesis, she continued studying the relationship between the dates and the individuals mentioned in the prayers, and she found that something happened to people between the ages of 6 and 13. Returning to Landa's data, she related this event with the appointment of an heir.

What came next was to identify the glyph for «enthronement». It is worth mentioning that among the steles at Piedras Negras there are some which go beyond the standards. They have a niche at the front, inside which there is a character sitting with his legs crossed in the «lotus» position (figure 181). Underneath there are footprints, which are ascending towards this character. Their dates varied, but the associated cartridge was the same, and the author identified it as the ruler's «enthronement».

Her hypothesis about the historical content of the inscriptions was ratified in her research on the inscriptions at Yaxchilán, Chiapas (1963-1964). Here she found the same combinations, although of course there were different characters. This marked the beginning of the new Mayan epigraphy.

The stones began to recover their voices, and the written history about pre-Hispanic Mayas began to reveal itself.

To the glyphs for «birth», «enthronement» and «death», the «capture», «capturing», and «sacrifice» glyphs were added (figure 182). And the image of the Mayas as a culture devoted to star gazing and to the measurement of time began to change; but not all the authors agreed with this.

One of them, the American archaeologist David Kelley, who had been studying inscriptions under Knorozov's approach, used Tatiana's arguments at Quiriguá, Honduras. With these techniques, and using historical information, Kelley identified and read, for the first time in modern history (1968) the name of a ruler from Chichén Itzá: *Kakupakal* (figure 183).

The Commission for Research on Mayan Writing, lead by an American linguist living in Mexico, Mauricio Swadesh, was founded in 1963. The original project attempted to uncode Mayan writing with the aid of computers, but using a different method than the

182. From left to right, top row: three glyphs for the vierb «to be born», and two expressions for «to die». Middle row: several glyphs for «enthronement». Down row: glyph for «capture», glyph for «the one who catches», and three glyphs for «sacrifice» (from Proskouriakoff and Schele).

Soviets. Swadesh found the glyph constants in the codices. Unfortunately he died and his students were unable to follow his research guidelines because they knew too little about his project. Research in Mexico was diverted towards the study of the origins and evolvement of Mayan writing. Years later, when a method for decipher was developed, it was obvious that Swadesh was attempting to develop a structural analysis method with the aid of computers.

183. The name *Ka-ku-pa-ka-l*, lintel at Chichén Itzá.

In 1974, a group of epigraphers met at Dumbarton Oaks, among them David Kelley, the linguist Floyd Lounsbury, Linda Schele, and Peter Mathews. This group identified the Palenque dynasty (figure 204) as well as the favourite construction of inscriptions consisting of temporal marker/verb/subject. Lounsbury, Sapper's disciple, had a background in comparative and structural methodology, which proved to be the key for uncoding Mayan hieroglyphic writing. Once the text structure had been established they began to identify subjects, verbs, and objects, based on their position, even when they did not know what they meant. Another great breakthrough was identifying glyph substitutions. This could be noted when analyzing and comparing all Mayan texts, thus they could find out that there were sentences or similar clauses, where a glyph was substituted for another (figure 184).

The success of his teamwork led them to continue working together, proving that cooperation among archaeologists, epigraphers, linguists, and historians is necessary. One of the immediate results was the series of conferences by epigraphers and interested researchers known as the Palenque Round Tables, organized by Merle Greene R. and the Maya Workshops in Texas, with Linda Schele as chairman. These meetings became periodic. Knowledge about writing began to spread and more epigraphers arose.

During that first stage the process continued as it had been planned: dating of inscriptions; research on and identification of known cartridges; recognition of new glyphs with the same functions through comparative analysis. It was through this process that they discovered dynasties in various cities, the names of their rulers, their life periods, and the actions they were interested in recording. The list of emblem glyphs became bigger, and their presence in other cities allowed researchers to establish existing relationships, even if at the beginning they had no knowledge as to their nature. When they began to identify the kinship connections, a task which was initiated by the archaeologist Christopher Jones (1977) in the late monuments at Tikal, texts began to furnish further details on the Mayan system of inheritance, as well as on the links between cities. Marriage alliances began between a woman from a certain place with the ruler of another area. With time, it has been discovered that there were other types of

184. Examples of glyphic substitution. Temple of the Inscriptions at Palenque.

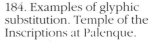

185. Title and name of *Mah k'ina Pakal*, from Palenque, identified by Lounsbury.

alliances; that rulers were imposed by the lord of a more important place; that there were wars between allied cities and their common enemies; in short, that the emblem glyph became a key element in the new findings.

The works of the last twenty years have been published, and are not of an anecdotal nature anymore. They are news and as such they must be taken cautiously until they are proven. When the book *The Blood of Kings*, written by Mary Miller and Linda Schele, was published in 1986, the Mayas acquired a new perspective. Mayan inscriptions written on steles, altars, lintels, thrones, buildings, ceramics, and ornaments, began to disclose their message: a message akin to those about other rulers in the world. The texts referred to their lives and main acts of government, which means that it was a manipulated history.

When *A Forest of Kings* (Schele and Freidel, 1990) was published, the message was more obvious. Rulers spoke about their victories, the rituals they had to perform to maintain order, not only within their societies, but also in the cosmos itself.

The rulers identified themselves with the gods. They were in charge of feeding the deities, who in turn would provide humans with their favors, and thus, the cosmic order would not be altered. The philosophic concept is very interesting; it is a mutual relationship between gods and men, where one cannot live without the other.

As the *Popol Vuh* says, the gods did not rest until they were able to create beings in charge of remembering and worshipping them. But their main duty was to be fed by them.

And thus they began to identify these actions. Of course the Mayan people are not mentioned. Messages are regularly short, and it has been necessary, in order to obtain a clearer idea of the facts, to refer to related disciplines: archaeology, history, ethnography, linguistics; in short, anything that could help to complete the message.

With all this information it has been possible to start rewriting pre-Hispanic Mayan history, not only with the data collected by archaeologists, or the deductions by historians or anthropologists through colonial documents, but with what the Mayas themselves said and how they said it. This history will never be complete, and is not completely true.

Let us not forget that many texts have been lost forever. Others have been and are still being stolen, so most of the vital information has been lost. There must be many monuments that have not been rescued yet, and, above all, we are speaking about personal lives told the way their writers wanted them to appear.

That is why comparative analyses of Mayan texts is basic. What one ruler may not have said, another one will, especially regarding casualties and the taking of prisoners during wars.

Mayan epigraphy has turned into a discipline, and is adjusting its findings. Each year there are new identifications, and now there are new readings. But this stage is very recent.

186. Examples of phonetic readings proposed by Stuart; glyph T17 and «eye» symbol for the *yi* sound. *Yi-la-h(i)*, «he or she sees him», *yi-ta-h(i)* «accompanied by», *yi-tzi-n* «younger brother» (the two glyphs at the bottom).

In 1973, Lounsbury had read one of the prefixes that goes with the emblem glyphs, the one called *ben-ich*, which Thomas Bartel (1968) had recognized as a «rank prefix». Lounsbury proved that it could be read *Ah-pop, Ajpo*,[10] identified in some Cackchiquel documents written during the colonial period as a title used to designate their superiors as «Lord of the Sleeping Mat» or throne.

In order to carry out his readings, he corrected Knorozov's and Whorf's proposals dealing with the syllabic nature of glyphs. Lounsbury proved that when someone wanted to phonetically write a word in the consonant-vowel-consonant structure (cvc, a predominant pattern of Mayan words), the final consonant was represented with a syllabic symbol whose vowel harmonized with the vowel of the previous syllable. For example, the verb «to carry», *cuch*, was written *cu~chu*. Using his knowledge on Mayan tongues,

Lounsbury perfected the reading system and read the title *Mah k'ina*, «great Sun Lord», formed by the glyphs for *ma k-'in-(n)a*, and the name of a ruler from Palenque, *Pakal*, «Shield», written *pa-k(a)-l(a)*, a reading suggested by Kelley (figure 185).

The system for testing glyph readings was developed by David Stuart, a young American archaeologist who in 1987 had been able to read ten glyphs, syllabically, in different combinations which proved the accuracy of his proposals (figure 185).

Readings have proliferated, and now there is a «spelling-book», besides many new findings concerning the message and content of the texts.

In a book recently written by Stuart and Stephen Houston, *Classic Maya Place Names* (1994), both authors concentrated efforts in identifying not only the «when», and the «who», but also the «where» of the events referred to in the texts.

Toponyms also began to appear. Currently some names of cities have been read, as well as of geographic sites, such as mountains and lakes, besides those built by man: temples, plazas, altars and thrones (figures 187, 188).

A particular emblem glyph inspired these findings. This glyph also served to identify the social and political relationships between the different Mayan cities and their evolution.

Such relationships may have been established either through marriage or through alliances, but there were also wars, which seem to have been more frequent than it was thought. Inheritance systems were sometimes affected by the death or the capture of a ruler, or of his successor; thus social order was also affected.

Among the latest findings, not yet totally proven, is the alleged presence of two big capital cities: Calakmul, and Tikal, which, according to Nicolai Grube and Simon Martin, tried to dominate over the rest of the region by alliances or wars among the cities which were part of their circle of influence.

As can be seen, the message of Mayan texts has been changing as their content is better understood. Beginning with calendaric and astronomical texts, the messages later revealed information about the private lives of the rulers. Then it moved from anecdote to history and uncovered a religion that was practically unknown, to one that was much more real because it was told by the Mayas themselves. Later the message started covering knowledge areas that need the participation of epigraphers, as well as researchers in other fields.

The problem of war, the systems of lineage and inheritance, the forms of government within the cities and in relation to the larger centers of power, partially comprise the paths to be cleared in the reading of monuments.

But the great test is yet to come: the reading of the Mayan codices, written during the Post-Classic period in the language of Yucatán. As far as it is known, they contain forecasts, prayers, astronomical information, and events in which their deities participated. This material is of religious content. The great advantage of the texts in the codices is that, as far is now known, the cartridges are mainly phonetic. This implies that as there is progress in the syllabic reading of the monuments, the codices will be clearer; but, due to its fundamentally cryptic character, once they have been read, there will be another important stage: trying to understand their meaning.

### Mayan writing: the Calendar

In Mesoamerica, writing has always been linked to mathematics because the texts that survived the conquest are related to the calendar, and the mathematics we know from this region and period are just that: calendaric accounts.

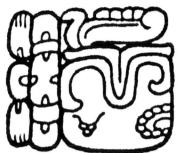

187. Names of Aguateca city, *K'inich wits*, «Sun mountain» (from Stuart and Houston).

188. Geographical place names. From top to bottom, *Witz*, the mountain, «the black hole enclosing water»; the square by the river at Yaxchilán; *yotot*, house (from Ayala, 1995).

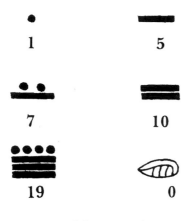

| | |
|:---:|:---:|
| • | ▬ |
| **1** | **5** |
| •• | ▬▬ |
| **7** | **10** |
| •••• | ⬬ |
| **19** | **0** |

189. Bar and dot numerals, as well as the zero.

The only Mesoamerica document that contains numerical notes not used merely for registering dates is the *Tribute List*, of Mexica origin, but its date remains uncertain. Some authors, like Martínez Marín (1974:232), have placed it during the time of the Mexicas' decline, «...during the siege of their city, or when smoke had already dissipated». That is, when the conquest began. It is believed that it might have been a conqueror's demand to receive the tribute which was given to the Mexica rulers.

It is a document that records, using Mexica numbers and glyphs, the tributes received by the empire. The document has been transcribed into Nahuatl, but with a Latin alphabet, which allowed researchers to know its meaning. This is the only text in which the numerical system[11] was used for things which were not temporary, in other words, for logs and dates.

The Mayan numerical system does not belong to the Mayan culture. The earliest logs come from Monte Albán, Oaxaca, and belong to Steles 12 and 13 (González Licón, 1990: figure 26). There, the numbers are recorded with dots, which stand for number 1, while the bar stands for number 5. Mesoamerican pleople based their numerical system on number «20», which makes it a vigesimal system.

Everything indicates that the Mesoamerican calendar, as it was originally created, failed to record the solar year, which was also agricultural, social, and religious, and it was necessary to correct it. The rest of Mesoamerica decided to stop recording it. The Mayas created a calendar which is unique in the world. It is so efficient that no dates will be repeated before millions of years. To do this, they needed to create a concept equivalent to zero. They even created a positional mathematic system, which is the basis of our own calendar.

But, in order to understand this, we have to go to the calendar.

Based on the information we currently have, it was the people from Monte Albán who created the first calendar. This is formed by two cycles: one records days, and the other records «months», or groups of twenties.

Each day and each score are accompanied by a numeral; days: 13; months: 20.

The system works as follows: there cannot be more than four dots, because number five is a bar, and there could not be more than three bars. The highest number that could be written in this system was 19, with three bars and four dots (figure 189). But the question arises: What happened with the number 20? According to Alfonso Caso, a specialist in Zapotec culture, number 20 was glyph «W» upside down. But this has not been proven yet. The important thing is that such a calendar system was the basis for all Mesoamerica, including the Mayan area. Each day had its own glyph (figure 191), and although the way of writing it varies for each region, the days are the same. Scores also had their own glyphs (figure 191). As it has already been mentioned, numbers were written with dots and bars, whose total amount never exceeded 20.

The cycle of days was the basis of the Mesoamerican calendar; it was formed by 20 sign-days associated with 13 numerals, written with bars and dots. So that a day, any day, could return to the same number, 260 days had to elapse (20x13=260). The name of this cycle in Nahuatl was Tonalpohualli. In Mayan it has been given different names, because it is still not known what its original name was. The one most used is *Tzolk'in*, or the «Count of Days», but this was an invention. Thompson called it Sacred Almanac due to its use in codices.

Twenty days made a «month»; each day of the month had its own associated numeral, from 1-20, or from 0-19. But how can one write 20 in a numerical system that does not use more than four dots, and not more than three bars (15)? Here, the highest number that could be written was 19. What happens with the 20?

That was the great step in Mayan mathematics, and it was taken not only because of the need to record days accurately, but to manipulate science as well.

The Mesoamerican calendar was based on a 260 day-cycle, because it was the one that ruled each day, and all life and activity depended on it. Every time something happened –a birth, a marriage, an enthronement, even death–, the Mayas looked for a propitious date. The basis was the combination of the numeral and the day. If the forecast was ominous, it was changed. For the Mayas, numbers and days were gods who exerted influence over society as a whole.[12]

The 260 day-cycle was combined, as has been said, with the solar year, formed by 20 scores (20 days each), plus the 5 «spare», «ominous» or «sleeping» days, as they have been called in different translations. The solar cycle then is formed as follows:

18 x 20 = 360 + 5 = 365. This was the Mesoamerican solar-agricultural year.

But the solar year is longer than 365 days, and the Mesoamericans may have had problems because after 500 years the rainy months did not correspond to the rainy season.

And worst of all, the 260, and 365 day-cycles are repeated every 18980 days (260x73=18980, 365x52=18980), and for Mesoamericans it was very important to know time recurrence beforehand. Why? Because the gods would be joined together and the events that had already happened would repeat themselves. And this certainly did not happen (especially when months were shifting), and this resulted in a loss of credibility for sages, rulers and priests.

Something like this must have been the reason that lead the Mayas to observe the heavens and the movement of the stars, the Sun, the Moon, Venus, and the other planets, which gave them an accurate knowledge of the duration of the solar year and the movement of the stars.

Hence the creation of a calendar log that, even if based on the solar year, was so complex that its dates could never be repeated. Due to the fact that numbers did not have more than 20 logs, they created the numerical-positional system, in which the numbers increase their value depending on their position. But this was from bottom (units with value=1) to top, and as the basis was the solar year, the basic position was the third, that is, the *tun* (360 day year=18 twenty-day cycles). The numbers, according to their position, have the following values:

5th position
144 000 =7 200 x 20
4th position
7 200 = 360 x 20
3rd position
360 = 18 x 20
2nd position
20 = 1 x 20
1st position
1

Of course, no position has a limit; thus it is possible to write any quantity by using only three symbols: dots, bars, and the «zero». With this system, number 18 980 is written as follows:

4th position
7 200 x 2 = 14400
3rd position
360 x 12 = 4 320
2nd position
20 x 13 = 260
1st position
1 x 0 = 0
Total 18 980

190. Stele 2 at Chiapa de Corzo (from Marcus, 1992).

*On the following pages:*
191. Left: glyphs for the days.
Right: glyphs for the months (from Thompson, 1978).

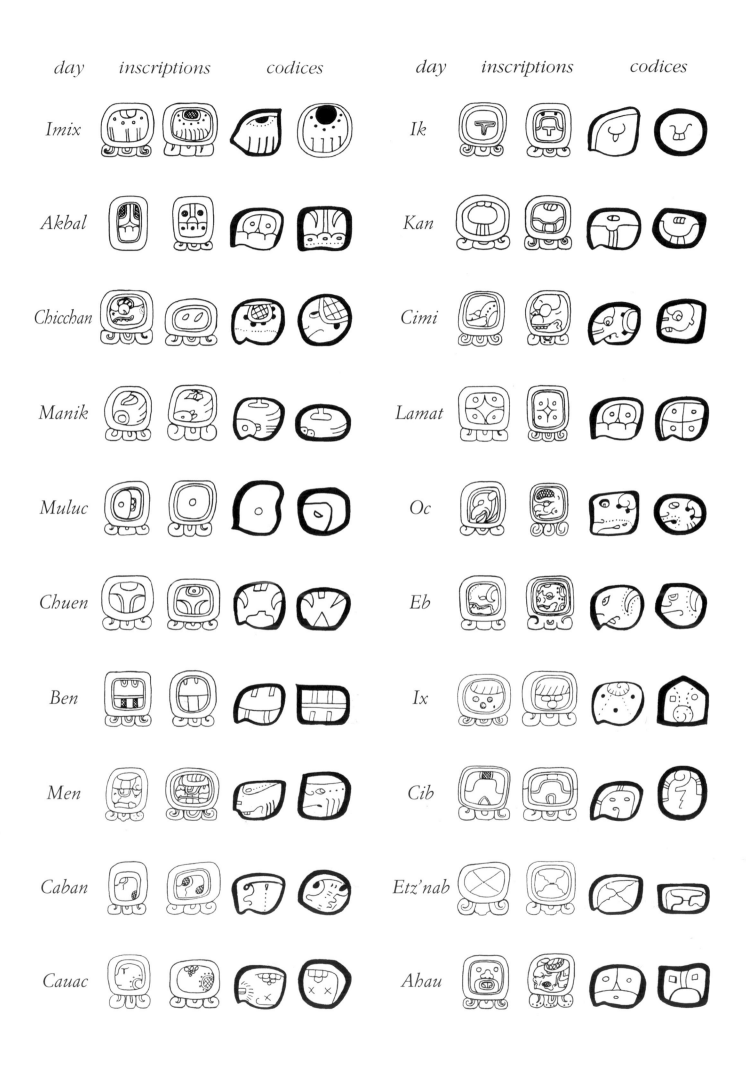

| day | inscriptions | codices | day | inscriptions | codices |
|---|---|---|---|---|---|
| Imix | | | Ik | | |
| Akbal | | | Kan | | |
| Chicchan | | | Cimi | | |
| Manik | | | Lamat | | |
| Muluc | | | Oc | | |
| Chuen | | | Eb | | |
| Ben | | | Ix | | |
| Men | | | Cib | | |
| Caban | | | Etz'nab | | |
| Cauac | | | Ahau | | |

| month | inscriptions | codices | month | inscriptions | codices |
|---|---|---|---|---|---|
| Pop | | | Uo | | |
| Zip | | | Zotz' | | |
| Zec | | | Xul | | |
| Yaxkin | | | Mol | | |
| Chèn | | | Yax | | |
| Zac | | | Ceh | | |
| Mac | | | Kankin | | |
| Muan | | | Pax | | |
| Kayab | | | Cumku | | |
| | | | Uayeb | | |

The earliest inscription with this system is Stele E.2[13] at Chiapa de Corzo, which is a fragment of an inscription written in numerals. The date recorded is: 7.16.3.12.13,5 Ben (Lowe, 1962:194) (figure 190).

We will explain this system based on Stele E.29 of Tikal (figures 10, 11), which is the earliest known from the Mayan region, because it shows the characteristics of these inscriptions, in other words it shows a Mayan ruler, and the text written at the rear of the monument; it has a date with the corresponding glyphs of the cycles. It is the first text with Mayan writing.

The basis of the calendar is a mythic date, invented by the system's creator or creators. This goes as far as August 13, 3114 B.C. (Correlation G-M-T), and in Mayan it reads: 13.0.0.0.04 ahaw 8 kumk'u.

This inscription begins with the Introductory Glyph of the Initial Series (IGIS), and from top to bottom it can be read that: 8 *baktunes*,[14] 12 *katunes*, 14 *tunes*, 8 *winales*, and 15 *k'ines* had elapsed since the era date; the corresponding day was (13) Men, and the month (3 zip).[15] Thus we have that the date recorded on the Stele 29 tells us the time elapsed:

5th 8 cycles
8 x 144 000
4th 14 *katunes*
14 x 7 200
3rd 12 *tunes*
12 x 360

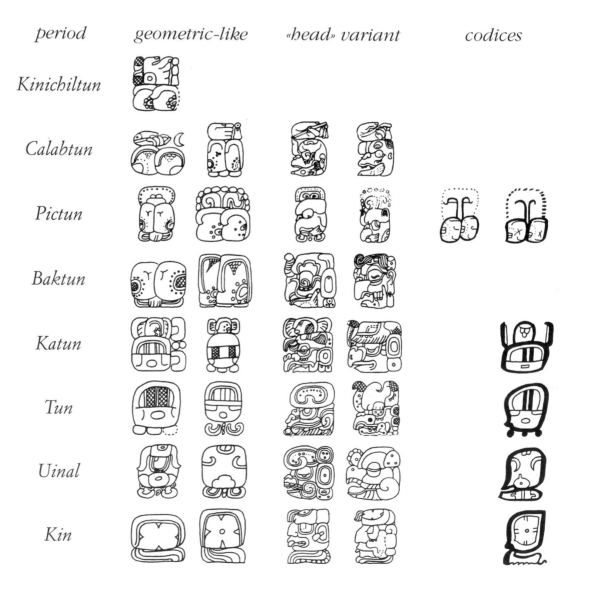

| period | geometric-like | | «head» variant | | codices | |
|---|---|---|---|---|---|---|
| Kinichiltun | | | | | | |
| Calabtun | | | | | | |
| Pictun | | | | | | |
| Baktun | | | | | | |
| Katun | | | | | | |
| Tun | | | | | | |
| Uinal | | | | | | |
| Kin | | | | | | |

192. «Geometric»-like and head variant glyphs for periods or cycles (from Thompson, 1978).

2nd 2 *uinales*
8 x 20
1st 16 *k'ines*
16 x 1

As can be seen in the inscription each numeral goes with the glyph that corresponds to the periods written with the so called Head Variants (figure 192). Up to this point, the inscription is in one column, but on the left bottom edge a numeral 1 (dot) can be seen, which implies that the rest of the inscription was in two columns.

The Mayas found different, less elaborate ways, for recording dates. The most common are Distance Numbers (DN), which mark the time elapsed between two events. This was the type of log that lead Maya researchers to think the Mayas were obsessed with time. Now we know they are establishing different events in the lives of the rulers who always tried to link their actions with the so called Final Period Dates, those ending in «zero». The reason is very simple. They tried to imitate the actions of the gods, and as the present world was created in 13.0.0.0.0, the final period dates indicated a rupture, and it was their responsibility to reinitiate time. This was done through sacrifices. Their gods had to be fed so that they could keep doing what they had to.

To give an example of their dating system, the reading order, and the structural features of Mayan writing, we will refer to another early text: the Leyden Plate (figure 193), an object carved in jade which might have been part of a ruler's belt, as the ruler's image can be seen carved at the front of the plate.

The text, which begins with the IGIS, records the date 8.14.3.1.12, the day of the *Tzolk'in* was 1 Eb, and the *Tun* day was 0 Yaxkín (September 17, 320 A.D.), occupying the first ten cartridges. The first seven are in a column; starting from the eighth, the cartridges read from left to right,[16] in double columns. This is the basic form for reading Mayan glyphs, even when variations can be found. The last five belong to the text and begin by «enthronement»; then comes the name of the subject, «zero buzzard/*way-chak*/*kan*», and ends with the emblem glyph of the site (Tikal) over which the subject ruled.

Observing glyphs 8 and 9 of column B, we see they are the same one. The one that is on B8 is the «numeral» of the month, written with a logogram: verb *chum* «to sit». As it has been said, for the Mayas the cycles, days, and numbers, were gods. When they finished their journey, they came back, as it says in *Chumayel's Chilam Balam*, «to the place of their peace», that is they «sat», and this is what the ruler did on that day: *chumahy* «he had sat», that is, he was enthroned.

In this small text we have seen three features of Mayan writing: repetition of symbols; substitution, and basic grammar structure; tense marker, verb, subject, and predicate (in this case it is a toponym). The problem in this script is precisely knowing what each symbol means. For this reason other symbols were created which indicate when the reading is to be understood as *a)* a logogram (word), or *b)* a morpheme (phonetic-syllabic). These symbols are known as: *a)* determinative, whose function consists in indicating the sense or value of the main symbol, and *b)* phonetic predicates, which indicate how the main symbol must be read.

193. Leyden's plate. Obverse (top) and reverse (bottom) (from Schele and Miller, 1986).

*How Mayan Writing Works*

Today most epigraphers agree that Mayan writing is a phonetic system composed of glyphs which represent complete words, logograms, and other which indicate syllables (CV).

1. *Logograms* represent either the sound or meaning of a whole word. Pictograms correspond to this type of symbols; they are iconograms that reproduce objects, and

194. Top: geometric-like and head variant glyph for *ahaw* day (from Thompson).

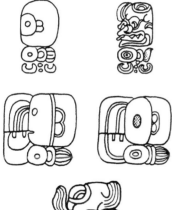

195. Event markers. Before, *ywal* and after, *uti*, with the glyph *ta/ti*.

196. Cartridge glyph for «enthronement».

there are plenty of them, mainly of animals, even when there are many representations of objects that refer to the environment.

2. The so called *rebus* symbols, or *charade writing*, represent the sound of a word with another that sounds alike, with homonyms, and are used for writing concepts. They are rare in Mayan writing. Schele refers that there is only one, which was identified by John Justeson. It is a symbol for «east» written with a *lak* dish, meaning «next». The problem with such symbols is that due to their polyvalence, they could cause difficulties. In this type of writing symbols only have one reading, but the meanings can be many; or conversely, symbols can have one meaning, but readings can be many. For example, the glyph for «shield» can be read *chimal* or *pakal*. To avoid the possible ambiguities Mayas created two more types of symbols:

3. *Semantic-determinative*, which tell the reader the precise value of the symbol. Take, for instance, the *ahaw* day; when it is written to signify day, it is «framed». But the word *ahaw* also means «lord» (sovereign, or king),[17] and has that phonetic value, even when it could also be written with the representation of a diadem, or triangular shawl, on an individual's head (figure 194), indicating that it is referring to a «sovereign».

4. *Phonetic predicates*. These are glyphs that indicate the particular phonetic value of the main symbol, when this can have various sounds. Let us take, for example, the *ahaw* glyph. This day, it also means «flower», *nik*, so when you want to specify that it is about this reading, you add a phonetic predicate that has the *ki* value. Thus, the complete cartridge would read *ni-(i)k*.

The clearest case of all these variables is the sign for «buzzard», or «vulture». There are many Mayan words that refer to this animal: *k'uch*, *ch'om*, *xulem*, and *ta'hol*. Besides using the pictogram referring to this animal, this is also used for establishing the locative *ti* on the Markers of Previous and Subsequent Events, as well as on one of the enthronement cartridges (figure 195).

The reason for doing this seems to be based on the animal's name in Chol tongue, *ta'hol* (*ta'* «excrement», *hol* «head»), maintaining the first syllable for the locative *ti*, *ta*, *ta* (according to the tongue) «in, toward». To emphasize the correct reading, you add a small symbol *ti* to the animal's head. This is the phonetic complement.

The first identified expression for the word «ascension» or «enthronement» was the «toothache» glyph, as Thompson called it, whose main symbol is in glyphs T644 and T648[18] (figure 196). It is always accompanied by a prepositional phrase formed by the *ti/ta* prefix, written with the buzzard's head, or by the corresponding prefix, a title, and the phonetic symbol *le*.

The title usually is prefix T168, *ahpop*, or *ahaw*, «Lord of the Sleeping Mat», or lord, which sometimes is substituted by the *ahaw* glyph, or by the buzzard's head. In order to differentiate the buzzard's use in each case, the *ti* prefix, or a small *ahaw* symbol, or the triangular shawl, are added, in order to establish that it referred to a member of the sovereignty. In this case, the triangular shawl is a semantic determinative (figure 197).

The previous cases are good examples of glyph substitution. As mentioned previously, it was the basic principle of the new epigraphy, and was based on structural analysis allowing context identification, where different symbols are substituted on the same position. We suppose that there are different ways to say the same thing. The latest findings have proven that such substitution is usually phonetic, considerably enlarging the Mayan spelling-book, which was originated with the identification of the glyphs present in Landa's alphabet.

Although we have already spoken about grammar structure and its principles, let us look at an example: the best can be found in the codices due to symbol repetition and its relationship with figures. Let us not forget that the reading order is from left to right, two by two, and from top to bottom (figure 172). On the text that goes from D.5b to 6b[19] (figure 199) we can see that the four figures are drilling something. All of them are doing the same thing, and the first cartridge of every sentence is the same, although the last one is written differently the verb is *ho-ch'* «to drill, to bore». The second cartridge is the same one in each case, and it is the object that is being drilled. The third one is the name of the deity (subject), and they end with the marker, either positive or negative, of each omen.

Every time the gods carry out the same action, the same cartridge, the verb, repeats itself.

When actions vary, verbs vary too. This was the pattern found by Proskouriakoff in her research and which helped her identify several actions or verbes.

The order, then, especially in monuments, is usually verb-subject-object, but this does not mean it is the only one, as in the codices the order may vary. There are some cases in which the first cartridge refers to the object. For example, in the section on women of the *Dresden Codex* (D.16b-17b) we can see the goddess I, Young Moon, carrying gods and birds on her back. In each sentence the first cartridge refers to the object held; the second is the verb *u ku-ch(u)* «her load»; the third is the name of the goddes, and the fourth is the type of omen.

The identification of verbs and subjects has led to other important identifications, like the markers for people, or pronouns. One feature of Mayan writing is that, for all we know up to now, it is written in third person singular. It is worth mentioning that Mayan tongues belong to the so called «ergative» tongues, which are characterized by having two series of pronouns whose function depends on the transitivity of the verbs. The A Series is used as the subject of the transitive verbs, and is the one accompanied by possessive pronouns («his, her, its»). The B Series, or Absolute series, is used as a suffix of verbs, and as the subject of intransitive verbs, and object of transitive verbs (Schele, 1996:31, 33). In Yucatán and Cholan tongues (the one represented in texts), the A series is in front of the verb, while the pronouns of the B series are added at the end of the verb verb root.

The first pronoun that was identified is a *U* pronoun (identified by Brasseur), which corresponds to the third person singular of the A series («his, her, its»), which can be

197. Titles *ah po* and *ahaw*, turkey buzzard, *ahaw* and phonetic (from Schele and Miller, 1986).

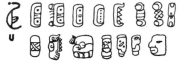

198. Variants of sign *u*, pronominal for the third person of the singular (from Schele).

199. Dresden 5b-6b. Scenes of gods drilling; god of the Earth, god of the death, Itzamná and God Q (from Villacorta and Villacorta).

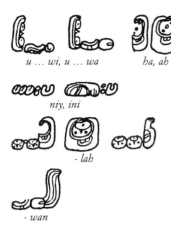

*u ... wi, u ... wa*          *ha, ah*

*niy, ini*

*- lah*

*- wan*

200. Tense markers: transitive, passive, intransitive, completive, positional (from Schele).

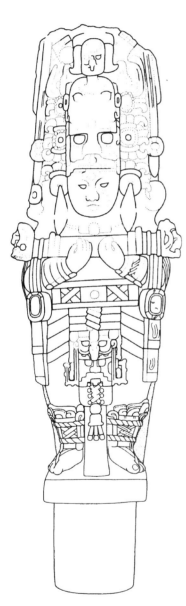

201. Stele 26 from Toniná, front view. National Museum of Anthropology (drawing by Mathews).

found prefixed to names at the expected position for a possessive pronoun. Obviously, any other sign that has this position should have the same use and meaning, which has made possible the identification of different variations of the same sign (figure 198). Up to now no personal pronouns for the first and second persons, or the series B pronouns, have been found, and this is logical in a basically historical narrative. It is possible that in another type of texts these could be present.

In order to finish this section about glyphic grammar[20] we will refer to tense markers, which are a series of affixes which are linked to verbs, which makes their identification possible. These usually mark inflections and derivations, and are phonetically written. That is, they do not have semantic value. We are talking about syllables such as *-ah* (T181), which indicate past tense, that can be linked with an affix *-vl* (l-vowel) (T124); derivational affix to give names and characteristics, as well as inflectional ending for verb roots (figure 200).

Among the latest findings are the markers *ut*, *utix*, *ywal ut* and *utom* (figure 202), which are fundamental to understand the sense of glyphic texts, and a good example of how new epigraphy works.

The *Ut* glyph composition, «happened», comes from the identification made by Eric Thompson of the so called «Previous and Subsequent Events Marker». Thompson realized that, associated with *Distance Numbers*, there were always two cartridges formed by three glyphs, two of them constant and one variable (figure 195). The constant ones were: the main glyph and the *ti* affix. The variable established if the date went «forward» or «backward».

In 1985, David Stuart, analyzing these cartridges, and possibly, with the idea of element substitution, began to note there was a pattern that explained substitutions, not only in the markers, but most important of all, in how variable affixes functioned in writing. Stuart observed that the main glyph, *xok* for Thompson,[21] could be substituted with the *muluk* day glyph, which at the same time, in other contexts, was used to indicate *u* pronoun, marker of the third person singular (T1) (cfr. figure 198).

Stuart deduced that the two constant glyphs should be read *u-ti(i)*, a term which is translated «happens». Two years before, John Justeson and Will Norman had found that the marker prefix of a previous event T126, and the postfix T679, the subsequent event marker, were in different clauses linked to verbs. And in those cases they worked like the Distance Numbers. That is, based on Distance Numbers, they detected that affixes T679 and T126 were linked with previous or subsequent events depending on the case. Both authors proved that the cartridge with the prefix T679 occupied the same place as in the Mayan Colonial sources, and it belonged to *yuual* «...a conjunction which introduces a subordinate sentence: then, when, so» (Smailus, 1975:179); in other words, the reading of the cartridge would be «then happens...», which in colloquial language would correspond to «and then» (figure 202).

The other cartridge that includes postfix T128, was explained by Kathryn Josserand and Nicholas Hopkins, both scholars of modern Chol. They observed that there is a specific suffix that comes at the end of verbal roots when they are in the pluperfect tense. This is suffix *-y(i)'/y(a)* (figure 202), which in the previous marker of Distance Numbers is understood as «since», and in the verb forms, joined with *ut* forms *ut-y*, «had been».

The last verb tense is also the work of various authors. Schele was the first to identify it, and Terrence Kaufman explained its function. It is a future marker *u-to-m* (figure 202). This is usually linked with dates that will take place, something the rulers wrote when they were interested in associating their actions at the end of a period «which would take place».

202. Tense indicators utix «had -ed», *ywal ut* «and then», *utom* «it will be».

Throughout this work, we have explained that Mayan texts written on the monuments are mainly historical, but it is a story where gods and human beings act together; it is a Sacred History. It has been this information that has allowed us to recover Mayan thought. Most of the texts are short, and they are written on steles, altars, lintels, thrones, ceramics, and ornaments, although there are wider texts such as the Palenque panels.

A great amount of the new information comes, not only from what the texts say, but also from the way in which they say it. Glyph substitutions have been an element in the decipherment in order to get to deeper levels in our knowledge.

It is obvious that each ruler told his history, and each one also told what he thought was the most important event in his life. It has been estimated that there are about ten thousand monuments, and that these refer to particular stories about rulers. And, as occurs with every writer, each one finds his own style. This is how Mayan literature was born. Even when most of the texts we know from the past are historical, the *Gilgamesh Chronicle*, the *Dead Sea Scrolls*, or the *Bible* are totally different from each other. The same thing happens with Mayan texts. This is why we are going to choose the life of a ruler, which will serve as a guide, so if we compare it with the other *Ah tzib* «scribes», we will know what the main concerns of these authors were.

What goes next is the life of a ruler, a specific one, who will serve us as a guide in order to understand the historical message of Mayan texts.

Evidently, the lives of the rulers are not the same; there cannot be a life that is identical to another. However, all of them were born, became rulers, and died. In this road, there were particular activities but, as we cannot give everything in detail, we will refer to the most popular, and well known.

We will take one of the best known of all cases, Hanab Pacal (II) of Palenque. He is known for his architectural inventions, the magnificence of his tomb (the first to be found within a pyramid), and the difference between the age that was determined by his bones and what he wrote. He recorded his history in different texts which were found in two buildings: the Temple of the Inscriptions, and the Palace.

There are very important differences between Palenque and other cities. At Palenque, history was first written during the Pacal's era. Unlike other cities such as Tikal, Uaxactún, or Copán, whose inscriptions started during the 8 Cycle (early Classic), at Palenque there is no evidence of early texts, mainly because they have not been found yet, or maybe, and this is a personal opinion, because the previous texts were «erased». There are other cities, such as Toniná, and Tortuguero, where writing started later. The difference between them and Palenque is that their writings are more contemporary, while at Palenque history can be traced back to 993 B.C.

Another difference between Palenque and the other Mayan cities is that here there are no steles or altars. There is only one stele that goes beyond the standards because it is not a quadrangular monolith sculpted on one or all of its sides. It is similar to the ones they made at Toniná. Here steles are human sculptures in the round (figures 201, 203) with the inscription on their backs. The Palenque stele is so eroded that it has not been possible to see if it had text, which would have explained its presence in this city. Palenque's texts are on the Panels, to which the name of the building where they were found has been added.

The earliest are the ones located in the Temple of the Inscriptions (TI), which have been called TIe (east), TIc (central), TIw (west), the longest text (except for the codices) in the Mayan area. These panels, the Inscriptions of the Sarcophagus (in the same building), and the Panel of the Cross, written by Pacal's first son, permitted the reconstruction of the site's history.

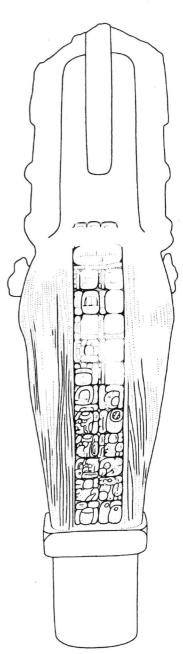

203. Stele 26 from Toniná. Rear view (drawing by Mathews).

247

*K'uk' Balam*

*"Casper"*

*Manik*

*Akul-Ah Nab I*

*K'an-Hok'-Ch'itam I*

*Akul-Ah Nab II*

*Kan Balam I*

*Señora Ol-Nal*

*Newal*

*Señora Sek-K'uk'*

*Hanab Pakal*

The panels in the Temple of Inscriptions comprise the periods from 9.4.0.0.0. to 9.1.12.0.0.0. The first researcher who identified the formula used in these texts was Floyd Lounsbury (1975). He realized that the formula consisted of linking, through DN (distance numbers), the dates of the rulers' enthronement with the End of Period. They gave preference to the *K'atunes* (20 *tunes*) or any of their subdivisions; 5 *tunes* (*hotun*), 10 *tunes* (*lahutun*), or 13 *tunes* (*oxlahuntun*). The rulers who were recorded in the text are: Akul-Ah Nab I; K'an-Hok'-Chi'itam I; Akul-Ah Nab II; Kan-Balam I, Lady Ol-Naval, Newal; Lady Sak-K'uk', and Pacal II (Schele and Mathews, 1993:93) (figure 204).

Palenque's dynastic history, as it has been recorded in the Panel of the Cross (PC) goes as far back as March 11, 431 B.C. It began with the founder of the lineage, called K'uk'-Balam, «Quetzal-Jaguar» (figure 204), although there were two previous rulers. The first one was the Mother Goddess, and the second was U-K'ix-Chan, the «Olmec», as Schele calls him. The glyph name of the goddess is interesting because it is formed by a glyph meaning «white», *sak*, and a variation of the head of the city's emblem glyph (figure 205). Americans have identified it as a quetzal, but if this glyph is compared with the names of Pacal's mother and the founder's name (figure 204), which are quetzals, they are different from those of the goddess. Her glyph and the emblem glyph of Palenque and its head variant are alike, whereas his is substituted by a skull, or a bone, *bak*, which means «bone», and «heron». Thus, the Mother Goddess should be named *sak bak*, and Palenque is *Bak*.

Between the founder and Pacal (II) there were ten rulers, two of which were women. One of them was Sak-K'uk', Pacal's mother. There are no dates of the births of the rulers because they did not record their births nor their kinship, according to their beliefs. For example, we do not know the birthday of Shield-Jaguar «the Great», or Yaxchilán's Itzam Balam, because none of the texts he wrote has this log.

For our own purpose, when speaking of Pacal's life, we have his date of birth in many places. We are interested in the Hieroglyphic Stairway of the House C in the Palace (figure 206). Its inscription begins with the date log 9.8.9.13.0.8 Ahaw 13 Pop (March 26,603 A.D.). It has been said this type of log does not repeat itself, so there is no doubt about this date, and it can also be found at the Calendar's Wheel (day numeral, month numeral) on the gravestone of its Sarcophagus, and on the TIw (figure 206).

The text on the Hieroglyphic Stairway continues to say: *hul-ah-y mah-k'in-naha-nabpa-ka-lah-po-k'ul-bak*; «great Sun was born, shield lilly, Lord of the sacred blood of Heron/Bone (Palenque)». Then there was a Distance Number; 12.9.8, that takes us back to the date (9.9.2.4.8) 5 Lamat 1 Mol (July 29, 615), which is also in the Temple of the Inscriptions (TIw, E1-E9) (figure 206). And although the verb is written differently, both record Hanab Pacal's enthronement when he was 12 years old, when his mother gave up the trone to her son. Before Pacal, there was another ruler, «Casper»,[22] who was also enthroned when he was 13 years old (figure 204).

American epigraphers consider that having received power from their mother must have been a problem to them because the Mayan system tended to be patriarchal. Decipherment has gone further and proven that women could also be rulers. Another similar case can be found at Naranjo, Guatemala, where a woman, Lady Wak Chaanil, appointed her son as a ruler of the site when he was 13 years old.

The events that took place to appoint heirs can be seen, among other places, on the mural paintings at Bonampak (figure 156), on Lintel 2 at Yaxchilán (figure 69), and in the construction of Temple 55 at Yaxchilán. It was built by Bird-Jaguar, or Yaxun Balam, in order to recall the End of a Period, linking this with his son's appointment, Chel Te (lintel 52), as a heir to the Yaxchilán throne.

Pacal married a lady called Tz'ak Ahaw on 9.9.13.0.17 7 Kaban 15 Pop (March 22,

626). His first son, Kan Balam II, was born on 9.10.8.9.3. 9 Ak'bal 6 Xul (June 17, 641); his second son, Kan Hok'Chitam II, was born on 9.10.11.17.0.11 Ahaw 8 Mak (November 5, 644). Kan Balam was appointed heir when he was six years old, and he left this log on his monuments, the Panels of the Crosses.

Pacal's mother survived 25 years after her son's enthronement. We do not have much information about what happened during this period. However, thanks to new readings, and in accordance with the text of the Hieroglyphic Stairway of the House C (figure 206), the following date has been identified, which corresponds to 9.8.5.13.8. (April 21, 599). This text refers that at the time there was a *ch'akah* «cut» or "to sever" at Lakam Ha, capital city of the Palenque kingdom. The attacked was called Kal?-Kaan, from Calakmul, one of two great powers that wanted to dominate the entire land. The other power was Tikal.

The result of this war was that the Palenque gods were «thrown», *yaleh*, and this could mean they were destroyed. In the Temple of the Inscriptions, there is another attack from Calakmul against Palenque, recorded on 9.8.17.15.14.4 Ix 7 Pop (April 4, 611) (figure 206). Perhaps these wars caused Lady Sak K'uk to be enthroned.

There is sufficient evidence in the texts of other cities like Bonampak, (*Ake*), Pomona (*Pia*), Yaxchilán (*Sian Chan*), Toniná (*Poo*), and Tortuguero in Mexico; and Piedras Negras (*Yocib*), Dos Pilas, and Naranjo in Guatemala, to name a few. They refer to a series of wars carried out during different dates, between the two factions: Calakmul? (*Chan*), and its allies, against the people from Tikal (*Mut?*). These wars and their participants are mentioned in their monuments.

The aforementioned text of the Hieroglyphic Stairway serves as an introduction to the following events related by Pacal, which talk about his involvement in various wars and captures.

The text of the scale continues to refer to the celebration of a moon eclipse (figure 207) (9.11.6.16.11 7 Chuen 4 Chen, August 7, 659). Present at the celebration were the ruler from Tikal, Nu Balam Lakam Chak (cfr. Lintel 3, from Temple 1 at Tikal), and Shield Jaguar from Yaxchilán, who was at the time eleven years old and was not yet a ruler. The clause concludes with the capture of the ruler from Tikal. The reasons why he arrived in Palenque and was captured and later died is still unknown. The text that can explain this

205. Glyphic name of the Mother Goddess and emblem glyphs of Palenque.

*Previous page:*
204. Palenque's genealogy: Palenque's rulers list from the founder, *K'uk Balam*, to *Hanab Pakal* the Great.

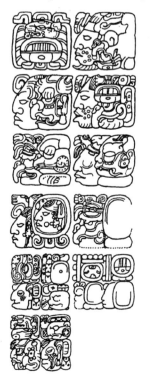

206. Left: the log for Pakal's birthdate on the Hieroglyphic Stairway in the house C of the Palace. Center, top: that same date as recorded on Pakal's sarcophagus. Center, down: the same date on the east panel of the Temple of the Inscriptions. Right, top: attack on Palenque by a character from Calakmul, as recorded on the stairway of the house C of the Palace (Schele). Right, down: Second attack on Palenque from Calakmul at the date 4 Ix 7 Pop. Temple of the Inscriptions (Schele).

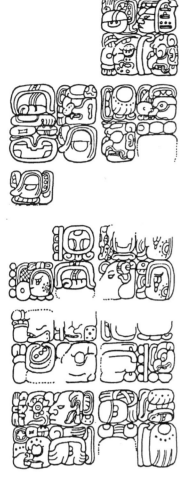

is found on the Hieroglyphic Stairway 2 at Dos Pilas. According to the readings of epigraphers like Schele, Martin, and Grube, the problem were the wars that occurred between Calakmul and Tikal, and their respective allies.

Despite the defeat of the ruler from Tikal, an ally of Palenque, Pacal started more wars and he was always triumphant. Evidence of this is the text on the Hieroglyphic Stairway (figure 207), and the place where it was located.

This text started with the date, on Calendar Wheel 7, Chuen 4 Chen (same as the eclipse), followed bt *yitah* «(in), (with, by)». The companions mentioned are four of the six prisoners represented on the gravestones of the panels at the Palace's patio. Such captures must have ensured Pacal his right to be enthroned, because they are associated with the building's dedication.

The history of events linked to the wars and political activities has not yet been deciphered. We know that Nu Balam Lakam Chak arrived in Palenque as a refugee, and then he was captured and killed.

Despite this, Pacal could reaffirm his rule, his right to the throne, and he appointed his heirs. The first one was Kan Balam II, who inherited a firmly established state that could enable him to devote most of his time to observe the gods that ruled the cosmos, and thus prove that his right to the throne came from the Mother Goddess.

His history, in icons, begins where his father's history ended; with the Cosmic Tree, the Milky Way, bearing witness to Pacal's death and Kan Balam's ascension to the throne (figures 65, 64). His texts speak of the buildings he had constructed, called the Group of the Crosses. Perhaps because his kingdom was so firm the main event during his government was an astronomical occurrence, which has been recorded sculpted on the three Panels. It was the conjunction of planets that took place during his reign. At the time, 2 Cib 14 Mol (July 23, 690), Jupiter and Saturn were at a stable point, and Mars and the Moon were at a very close position.

Kan Balam II did not have heirs. His brother, Kan Hok Chitam II, inherited Palenque's kingdom. Wars continued, and Baknal Chak, ruler of Toniná, captured him (figure 208).

But this was not the end of a story. It is only the beginning.

207. Hieroglyphic Stairway in the house C. Top: commemoration of a moon eclipse watched by Nu Balam Chak, from Tikal, and Shield-Jaguar from Yaxchilán, as well as the capture of the first named. Bottom: Date commemorating the moon eclipse with four prisoners taking part.

208. Monument 102 at Toniná. Commemoration of the capture of Kan Hok Chitam II from Palenque. Late Classic (from Schele and Miller, 1986).

It is the beginning of a story that has already begun: the history of the American cultures. It is true that much is yet to be discovered, and even understood. It is a new story, the history of the New World.

## Notes

[1] Linguists have been able to identify 35 Mayan tongues for the Pre-Columbian period. Twenty eight are still extant.

[2] This group of phonemes has been written in different ways through time. Friars used special symbols, or the same repeated letter for establishing strong or glottized consonants. Modern linguists have preferred the (') sign, which was (?) before.

[3] There are three Mayan codices of the Pre-Columbian period. There are no doubts about them: *Dresden Codex*, *Matritensis Codex* (or *Tro-Cortesian*), *Paris Codex* (*Peresian Codex*). There is a fourth codex, *Grolier Codex*, whose authenticity has not been completely proved.

[4] Hieroglyphs or glyphs are the minimum writing unity. The union of two or more glyphs is what is called a cartridge, that generally forms a word.

[5] This correlation is known as G-M-T. or Goodman-Martínez-Thompson. Due to Thompson's corrections there are two correlations: 524283, and 524285.

[6] A Baktun is a Mayan calendar cycle which comprises 14,000 days. Practically, all the Mayan Classic period fell within the 9 Baktun.

[7] Thompson, 1984: 360.

[8] Eric Thompson was the one who designated this group of preffixes as "aquatic group", because they always have a series of circles he identified as "liquid".

[9] Hieroglyphs are divided, according to their function and size, in affixes (smaller ones), and main symbols.

[10] Spelling of Mayan words varies, depending on each author, or the document taken as a reference. Substituting (h) by (j) is common.

[11] It is worth mentioning that the numbers used on inscriptions are not dot and bar, but a new system that was developed by the Mexicas, which allowed writing amounts higher than 20, even when the vigesimal system was maintained.

[12] 260 days cycle was so important that it was the only thing that prevailed in all Mesoamerica as a stable calendar standard. That is, days were the same in the whole cultural area. Besides, it is still being used in many regions. All connoiseurs still use it with divinatory-medical purposes.

[13] In Mayan epigraphy they use symbols. From now on, the term and symbol will be written in parenthesis. This symbol will be used throughout this work, for example, Stele E.

[14] The names of the first four cycles are known throughout Colonial texts. Mayan terms used for calling top immediate superior cycles are names that were invented by epigraphers, and are formed by a numeral plus the word *tun*, "360 day-calendar", "stone".

[15] When Mayan dates are eroded, or are implied, they are written in parenthesis. As it is a mathematical system, most of the time the missing dates can be obtained through the logs.

[16] Epigraphers agreed on left-right designation, which is mentioned with respect to the reader.

[17] American epigraphers translate *ahaw* as king, which in English implies a kinship; but "king" in Spanish does not have the same sense. So we will use ruler, or sovereign, to mean "lord" in the same sense as dictionaries and sources.

[18] Letter T refers to the Thompson Catalogue (1962), and the number is the code that corresponds to it in that work.

[19] D.M.P. are used to designate the Dresden, Madrid, and Paris codices. The numbers which follow are page references, and the section letter: a, is the superior, b, next inferior, and so on.

[20] To anyone interested in this subject we suggest two books: Victoria Bricker's *A Grammar of Mayan Hieroglyphs* (1986), and Linda Schele's *Maya Glyphs, the Verb* (1982).

[21] Thompson identified the head variant in this group of cartridges, as the shark's head, *xoc*, that is a homonym for "counting".

[22] The name of this ruler was given by Floyd Lounsbury, but as it has not been deciphered, or read, this name has not been changed.

# Bibliography

## The Mayas of the Classic Period

Adams, Richard E.W. (comp.), *Los orígenes de la civilización maya*, Mexico, FCE, 1989.

_____ and R.C. Jones, «Spatial Patterns and Regional Growth among Classic Maya Cities», in *American Antiquity*, vol. 46, no. 2, 1981, pp. 301-322.

Alcina Franch, José, «Las ruinas de Palenque a la luz de los viajes de Guillermo Dupaix», in *Anuario de Estudios Americanos*, tome XXVII, Sevilla.

*Arqueología Mexicana*, «Palenque. El mundo fascinante de los mayas», vol. I, no. 2, Mexico, INAH-Raíces, June-July 1993.

_____, «Arquitectura del mundo maya», vol. II, no. 11, Mexico, INAH-Raíces, January-February 1995.

_____, «Quintana Roo. Nuevos descubrimientos en la zona maya», vol. III, no. 14, Mexico, INAH-Raíces, July-August 1995.

*Arqueología. Memoria e Identidad*, Mexico, CNCA-INAH, 1993.

Baudez, Claude and Sydney Picasso, *Lost Cities of the Maya*, London, Thames and Hudson, 1992.

Benavides Castillo, Antonio, «El norte de la zona maya en el Clásico», in *Historia Antigua de Mexico* (Linda Manzanilla y Leonardo López Luján, coords.), vol. II: *El horizonte Clásico*, Mexico, 1995 (b), pp. 101-137.

_____, «El sur y el centro de la zona maya en el Clásico», in *Historia Antigua de Mexico* (Linda Manzanilla y Leonardo López Luján, coords.), vol. II: *El horizonte Clásico*, Mexico, 1995 (a), pp. 65-99.

Berlin, Heinrich, «El glifo 'emblema' en las inscripciones mayas», in *Journal de la Société des Américanistes*, vol. 47, 1958, pp. 111-119.

Bernal, Ignacio, *The Olmec World*, University of California Press, 1969.

Brunhouse, Robert L., *En Busca de los Mayas. Los primeros arqueólogos*, Mexico, FCE, 1989.

Cardós, Amalia, *El comercio de los antiguos mayas*, Mexico, INAH, Acta Antropológica, segunda época, vol. II, 1959.

Carrasco, R. y S. Boucher, «Calakmul», in *Arqueología Mexicana*, vol. II, no. 10, pp. 32-38, Mexico, INAH-Raíces, October-November 1994.

Coe, Michael D., *The Maya*, London, Thames & Hudson, 4th edition, 1987, 5th ed., 1994.

Coe, William R., *Tikal, guía de las antiguas ruinas mayas*, Philadelphia, Guatemala, The University Museum, University of Pennsylvania-Editorial Piedra Santa, 1977.

*Colha e i maya dei bassipiani*, Erizzo, Venice, 1982.

Cortés, Hernán, *Cartas de Relación*, no. 7, Mexico, Porrúa, 1988 (Colección «Sepan Cuantos...»).

Covarrubias, Miguel, *Indian Art from Mexico and Central America*, New York, A. Knopf, 1957.

Culbert, Patrick T. (ed.), *The Classic Maya Collapse*, Albuquerque, University of New Mexico Press, 1973.

_____, *Classic Maya Political History. Hieroglyphic and Archaeological Evidence*, School of American Research Advanced Seminar Series, Cambridge, Cambridge University Press, 1991.

Demarest, Arthur A., «The violent saga of a Maya Kingdom», in *National Geographic*, vol. 183, no. 2, pp. 94-111, February 1993.

Díaz del Castillo, Bernal, *Historia verdadera de la conquista de la Nueva España*, no. 5, Mexico, Porrúa, 1988 (Colección «Sepan Cuantos...»).

Fash, William L., *Scribes, Warriors and Kings. The City of Copan and the Ancient Maya*, London, Thames and Hudson, 1991.

Fernández Tejedo, Isabel, «Intercambio sin mercados entre los mayas de las tierras bajas», in *Temas Mesoamericanos* (Sonia Lombardo y Enrique Nalda, eds.), Mexico, CNCA-INAH, 1996, pp. 111-133.

Freidel David, Schele Linda and Joy Parker, *Maya Cosmos. Three Thousand Years on the Shaman's Path*, New York, Quill William Morrow, 1993.

García Bárcena, Joaquín, «Proyectos Especiales», in *Arqueología Mexicana*, Mexico, INAH-Raíces, vol. II, no. 10, October-November 1994, pp. 6-11.

González, Arnoldo, «Palenque», in *Arqueología Mexicana*, vol. II, no. 10, Mexico, INAH-Raíces, October-November 1994, pp. 39-45.

Graham Ian, *Descubriendo el mundo maya, Siglo XIX*, Mexico, Celanese Mexicana, 1987.

Hammond, N. and G.R. Willey (eds.), *Maya archaeology and ethnohistory*, Austin, University of Texas Press, 1979.

Justeson N., Terence Kaufman, «A Decipherment of Epi-Olmec Hieroglyphic Writing», in *Science*, vol. 259, pp. 1703-1711.

Kubler, George, *The Art and Architecture of Ancient America, The Pelican History of Art*, Penguin Books, 1984.

Landa, Fray Diego de, *Relación de las cosas de Yucatán*, Mexico, Porrúa, 1966.

López Austin, Alfredo and Leonardo López Luján, *El Pasado Indígena*, Mexico, El Colegio de Mexico-FCE, 1996.

Lowe, Gareth, Lee, Thomas Jr., Martínez Espinosa Eduardo, *Izapa: An Introduction to the Ruins and Monuments*, Provo, Utah, Papers of the New World Archaeological Foundation, no. 31, 1982.

Maldonado, Rubén, «Dzibilchaltún», in *Arqueología Mexicana*, Mexico, INAH-Raíces, vol. II, no. 10, October-November 1994, pp. 26-31.

Manzanilla, Linda and Leonardo López Luján (coords.), *Atlas Histórico de Mesoamérica*, Mexico, Larousse, 1989.

Marcus, Joyce, «Lowland Maya Archaeology at the Crossroads», in *American Antiquity*, vol. 48, no. 5, 1983, pp. 454-488.

_____, *Mesoamerican Writing Systems. Propaganda, Myth, and History in Four Ancient Civilizations*, Princeton University Press, 1992.

_____, «Ancient Maya Political Organization», in *Lowland Maya Civilization in the Eighth Century A.D.* (Jeremy A. Sabloff y John S. Henderson, eds.), Washington, D.C., Dumbarton Oaks Research Library and Collection, Trustees for Harvard University, 1993, pp. 111-183.

_____, «Where is Lowland Maya Archaeology Headed?», in *Journal of Archaeological Research*, vol. 3, no. 1, 1995, pp. 3-53.

Martin, Simon and Nikolai Grube, «Maya Superstates», in *Archaeology*, Archaeological Institute of America, November-December 1995, pp. 41-46.

Matheny, Ray T., «El Mirador. An Early Maya Metropolis Uncovered», in *National Geographic*, vol. 172, no. 3, September 1987, pp. 316-339.

Mathews, Peter, «Maya Early Classic Monuments and Inscriptions», in *A Consideration of the Early Classic Period in the Maya Lowlands* (Gordon R. Willey and Peter Mathews, eds.), Albany, State University of New York-Institute for Mesoamerican Studies, no. 10, 1985, pp. 5-54.

_____, «Classic Maya Emblem Glyphs», in P. Culbert (ed.), *Classic Maya political history: hieroglyphic and archaeological evidence*, Cambridge, Cambridge University Press, 1991, pp. 19-29.

Miller, Mary and Karl Taube, *The Gods and Symbols of Ancient Mexico and the Maya. An Illustrated Dictionary of Mesoamerican Religion*, London, Thames and Hudson Ltd, 1993.

Morley, Sylvanus G., *La Civilización Maya*, Mexico, FCE, 1972.

_____, Brainerd, George W., Sharer, Robert J., *The Ancient Maya*, 4th edition, Board of Trustees of the Leland Stanford Junior University, 1983.

Nalda, E., L. E. Campaña and J. L. Camacho, «Sur de Quintana Roo», in *Arqueología Mexicana*, Mexico, INAH-Raíces, vol. II, no. 10, October-November 1994, pp. 14-19.

*Palenque. Esplendor del arte maya*, Mexico, Editora del Sureste, 1980.

Perlman, Marc S., «Drought and the Maya Demise», in *Archaeology*, Archaeological Institute of America, November-December 1995, p. 19.

Proskouriakoff, Tatiana, «Historical Implications of a Pattern of Dates at Piedras Negras, Guatemala», in *American Antiquity*, vol. 25, no. 4, 1960, pp. 454-475.

*Proyectos Especiales de Arqueología*, Mexico, CNCA-INAH-Fondo Nacional Arqueológico, 1993.

Ruz Lhuillier, Alberto, *El pueblo maya*, Mexico, Salvat Mexicana de Ediciones, 1982.

Sabloff, Jeremy A., *The New Archaeology and the Ancient Maya*, New York, Scientific American Library, 1994.

_____, *Las Ciudades del Mexico Antiguo*, Mexico, Diana, 1995.

_____ and John S. Henderson (eds.), *Lowland Maya Civilization in the Eighth Century A.D.*, Washington D.C., Dumbarton Oaks Research Library and Collection, Trustees for Harvard University, 1993.

Sanders, William T., «The cultural ecology of the lowland Maya: A reevaluation», in P. Culbert (ed.), *The Classic Maya Collapse*, Albuquerque, New Mexico, University of New Mexico Press, 1973, pp. 325-365.

_____ and Barbara J. Price, *Mesoamerica. The Evolution of a Civilization*, New York, Random House, 1968.

Schele, Linda, David Freidel, *A Forest of Kings. The Untold Story of the Ancient Maya*, New York, William Morrow and Company, 1990.

_____ and Mathews, Peter, «Royal visits and other intersite relationships among the Classic Maya», in P. Culbert (ed.), *Classic Maya political history: hieroglyphic and archaeological evidence*, Cambridge University Press, 1991, pp. 226-252.

_____, Mary E, Miller, *The Blood of Kings. Dynasty and ritual in Maya art*, Forth Worth, N.Y., George Braziller-Kimbell Art Museum, 1986.

Schmidt, Peter, «Chichén Itzá», in *Arqueología Mexicana*, Mexico, INAH-Raíces, vol. II, no. 10, October-November 1994, pp. 20-25.

Schobinger, Juan, *I primi americani*, Milan, Jaca Book, 1994.

Stephens, John L., *Incidents of Travel in Central America, Chiapas and Yucatan*, 2 vols., reprint, New York, Dover, 1962.

*The Art of Maya Hieroglyphic Writing*, New York, 1971.

Thompson, J. Eric S., *Grandeza y Decadencia de los Mayas*, Mexico, FCE, 1964.

Weaver, Muriel Porter, *The Aztecs, Maya and their Predecessors. Archaeology of Mesoamerica*, 3rd ed., New York, Academic Press, 1993.

Willey, Gordon, *An Introduction to American Archaeology*, vol. 1, *North and Middle America*, Prentice Hall, 1966.

Willey, G.R., and W.R. Bullard, Jr., «Prehistoric settlement patterns in the Maya lowlands», in *Handbook of Middle American Indians* (R. Wauchope, ed.), vol. 2, Austin, University of Texas Press, 1965, pp. 360-377.

Yadéun, Juan, «Toniná», in *Arqueología Mexicana*, Mexico, INAH-Raíces, October-November 1994, vol. II, no. 10, pp. 46-48.

## THE SACRED FORCES OF THE MAYAN UNIVERSE

Adams, Richard E.W., «Río Azul», in *National Geographic Magazine*, Washington, D.C., vol. 169, no. 4, April, 1986.

Aveni, Anthony, *Skywatchers of Ancient Mexico*, Austin, University of Texas Press, 1980.

Barrera Vázquez, Alfredo *et al.*, *Diccionario Maya Cordemex*, Mérida, Ediciones Encuentro, 1980.

Baudez, Claude F., «La casa de los cuatro reyes de Balamkú», in *Arqueología Mexicana*, Mexico, INAH-Raíces, vol. III, no. 18, March-April 1996.

Campaña, V., Luz Evelia, «La tumba del Templo del Búho, Dzibanché», in *Arqueología Mexicana*, Mexico, INAH-Raíces, vol. III, no. 14, July-August 1995.

Carlson, John B., «Astronomical Investigations and Site Orientation Influences at Palenque», in *Segunda Mesa Redonda de Palenque*, Pebble Beach, California, Pre-Columbian Art Research, The Robert Louis Stevenson School, 1976.

Carrasco, Ramón, Silvianne Boucher, «Calakmul, espacios sagrados y objetos de poder», in *Arqueología Mexicana*, Mexico, INAH-Raíces, vol. II, no. 10, October-November 1994.

Champeaux, Gerard de, Dom Sebastien Sterckx, *Introducción a los símbolos*, Madrid, Ediciones Encuentro, 1989.

Coggins, Clemency, «The Manikin Scepter: Emblem of Lineage», in *Estudios de Cultura Maya*, Mexico, UNAM-IIF/CEM, 1988, pp. 123-157.

Cohodas, Marvin, «The Iconography of the Panels of the Sun, Cross and Foliated Cross at Palenque», part II, in *Primera Mesa Redonda de Palenque*, Pebble Beach, California, Pre-Columbian Art Research, The Robert Louis Stevenson School, 1974.

_____, «The Iconography of the Panels of the Sun, Cross and Foliated Cross at Palenque», part III, in *Primera Mesa Redonda de Palenque*, Pebble Beach, California, Pre-Columbian Art Research, The Robert Louis Stevenson School, 1976.

Fash, William L., Scribes, *Warriors and Kings. The City of Copán and the Ancient Maya*, London, Thames & Hudson, 1991.

Freidel David, Schele Linda and Joy Parker, *Maya Cosmos. Three Thousand Years on the Shaman's Path*, New York, Quill William Morrow, 1993.

Garza, Mercedes De la, *La conciencia histórica de los antiguos mayas*, Mexico, UNAM-IIF/CEM, 1975.

_____, *El hombre en el pensamiento religioso náhuatl y maya*, Mexico, UNAM-IIF/CEM, 1978.

_____, *Literatura maya*, Compilación y prólogo, Biblioteca Ayacucho, Venezuela, Barcelona, Edit. Galaxis, 1980.

_____, *El universo sagrado de la serpiente entre los mayas*, Mexico, UNAM-IIF/CEM, 1984.

_____, «Los mayas. Antiguas y nuevas palabras sobre el origen», in *Mitos cosmogónicos del Mexico Indígena*, Mexico, INAH, 1987.

_____, *Sueño y alucinación en el mundo náhuatl y maya*, Mexico, UNAM-IIF/CEM, 1990.

_____, *Palenque*, Mexico, Miguel Ángel Porrúa-Gobierno del Estado de Chiapas, 1992.

_____ and Ana Luisa Izquierdo, «El juego de los dioses y el juego de los hombres. Simbolismo y carácter ritual del juego de pelota entre los mayas», in *El juego de pelota en Mesoamérica, raíces y supervivencias*, Mexico, S. XXI, 1992.

_____, «Sacbeoob, caminos sagrados de los mayas», in *Revista Universidad de Mexico*, vol. 48, December 1993.

_____, «Espacio-tiempo en la antigüedad maya y náhuatl», in *Mexico-India, similitudes y contactos a través de la historia*, Mexico, FCE-India: Indian Council for Cultural Relations, in press.

Gendrop, Paul, *El Mexico antiguo-Ancient Mexico*, México, Trillas, 1972.

González, Federico, *Los símbolos precolombinos*, Barcelona, Obelisco, 1989.

Graham Ian *et al.*, *Corpus of maya hieroglyphic inscriptions*, Cambridge, Harvard University, Peabody Museum of Archaeology and Ethnology, vol. 3, part 1, 1982.

Hartung, Horst, «Entre concepto y evolución. Apuntes sobre lo creativo en la arquitectura maya precolombina», in *Cuadernos de arquitectura mesoamericana*, Mexico, UNAM-Facultad de Arquitectura-División de Estudios de Posgrado, no. 9, January 1987.

Hellmuth, Nicholas M., *Monster und Menschen in der Maya-Kunst. Eine Ikonographie der alter Religionen Mexikos und Guatemalas*, Akademische Druck-und Verlagsanstalt, Graz, 1987a.

_____, *Ballgame Iconography and Playing Gear*, Foundation for Latin American Anthropological Research, 1987b.

Henderson, John S., *The World of the Ancient Maya*, London, Orbis Publishing, 1981.

Holland, William, *Medicina maya en los altos de Chiapas, un estudio del cambio socio-cultural*, Mexico, INI, 1978.

Landa, Fray Diego de, *Relación de las cosas de Yucatán*, Mexico, Porrúa, 1996 (Biblioteca Porrúa, 13).

León-Portilla, Miguel, *Tiempo y realidad en el pensamiento maya*, 2nd ed., Mexico, UNAM, 1994.

*Libro del Chilam Balam de Chumayel* (trans. Antonio Médiz Bolio), Mexico, SEP, 1985 (Cien de México).

Lowe, Gareth, Lee, Thomas. Jr., Martínez Espinosa Eduardo, *Izapa: An Introduction to the Ruins and Monuments*, Provo, Utah, Brigham Young University, Papers of the New World Archaeological Foundation, no. 31, 1982.

Maudslay Alfred P., *Biología Centrali-Americana, Contributions to the Knowledge of the Fauna and Flora of Mexico and Central America*, 2 vols. London, 1889-1902. Facsimilar edition by Francis Robicsek, New York, Melipatron Publishing Corporation, 1974.

*Memorial de Sololá, Anales de los cakchiqueles* (trans. Adrián Recinos), in M. de la Garza, *Literatura Maya*, 1980.

Morley, Sylvanus G., Brainerd, George W., Sharer, Robert J., *The Ancient Maya*, 4th edition, Board of Trustees of the Leland Stanford Junior University, 1983.

Nájera, Martha Ili, *El don de la sangre en el equilibrio cósmico*, Mexico, UNAM-IIF/CEM, 1987.

Nalda, Enrique, Luz Evelia Campaña, Javier López Camacho, «Sur de Quintana Roo, Dzibanché y Kinichná», in *Arqueología Mexicana*, Mexico, INAH-Raíces, vol. II, no. 10, October-November 1994.

Norman, V. Garth, *Izapa Sculpture*, Provo, Utah, Brigham Young University, New World Archaeological Foundation, Papers of the New World Archaeology Foundation, no. 30, 1973.

Ortega Chávez, Germán, «Teoría de las ciudades mesoamericanas», in *Cuadernos de arquitectura mesoamericana*, Mexico, UNAM-División Estudios de Posgrado, no. 16, 1992.

Pollock, Harry E.D., *The Puuc. An Architectural survey of the Hill Country of Yucatán and Northern Campeche, México*, Cambridge, Harvard University, Peabody Museum of Archaeology and Ethnology, (Memoirs of the Peabody Museum, volume 19), 1980.

*Popol Vuh, Las antiguas historias del Quiché*, 9th ed. (trans. Adrián Recinos), Mexico, FCE, 1968 (Col. Popular, 11).

Reents-Budet, Dorie, *Painting the Maya Universe: Royal Ceramics of the Classic Period*, Durham and London, Duke University Press, 1994.

Robicsek, Francis, *Copán Home of the Mayan Gods*, New York, The Museum of the American Indian, 1972.

_____, «The Mythological Identity of God K», in *Tercera Mesa Redonda de Palenque*, vol. IV, Monterey, Cal., Herald Printers, 1978.

Romero, E. Ma. Eugenia, Juan H. Riqué Flores, «Explorando un nuevo sitio: Chacchoben, Quintana Roo», in *Arqueología Mexicana*, Mexico, INAH-Raíces, vol. III, no. 15, September-October 1995.

Ruz Lhuillier, Alberto, *Costumbres funerarias de los antiguos mayas*, Mexico, UNAM-Facultad de Filosofía y Letras, 1968.

_____, *El templo de las Inscripciones, Palenque*, Mexico, SEP.

Schele, Linda, David Freidel, *A Forest of Kings. The Untold Story of the Ancient Maya*, New York, Quill William Morrow, 1990.

_____ and Mary E. Miller, *The Blood of Kings. Dynasty and ritual in Maya art*, Forth Worth, N.Y., George Braziller-Kimbell Art Museum, 1986

Schellas, Paul, *Representation of Deities of the Maya Manuscripts*, Cambridge Mass., Harvard University, Papers of the Peabody Museum of American Archaeology and Ethnology, 1904.

Sosa, John, «Astronomía sin telescopios. Conceptos mayas del orden astronómico», in *Estudios de Cultura Maya*, México, UNAM-IIF/CEM, vol. XV, 1984.

Sotelo Santos, Laura Elena, *Yaxchilán*, Mexico, Gobierno del Estado de Chiapas-Espejo de Obsidiana, 1992.

Spinden, Herbert J., *A Study of Maya Art. Its subjects matter and historical development*, New York, Dover Publications, 1975.

Thompson, J. Eric S., *Maya Hieroglyphic writing. An Introduction*, Norman, Oklahoma, University of Oklahoma Press, 1950 and 1978.

_____, *A Catalog of Maya Hieroglyphs*, Norman, Oklahoma, University of Oklahoma Press, 1962 (The Civilization of the American Indian Series).

_____, *Maya History and Religion*, Norman, Oklahoma, University of Oklahoma Press, 1970.

Villa Rojas, Alfonso, «Los conceptos de espacio y tiempo entre los grupos mayances contemporáneos», Apéndice I, in Miguel León-Portilla, *Tiempo y realidad en el pensamiento maya*, 1994.

Yadeum, Juan, *Toniná, el laberinto del inframundo*, Mexico, Gobierno del Estado de Chiapas-Espejo de Obsidiana, 1993.

_____, «Toniná, espacio sagrado de la guerra celeste», in *Arqueología Mexicana*, México, INAH-Raíces, vol. II, no. 8, June-July 1994.

## ART. SENTRIES OF ETERNITY

Adams, Richard E.W., Aldrich Robert C., «A Reevaluation of the Bonampak murals: A Preliminary Statement on the Paintings and Texts», in M. Greene Robertson (ed.), Austin, University of Texas Press, *Third Palenque Round Table*, part 2, 1980, pp. 45-59.

Álvarez Aguilar, L. Fernando, M. Guadalupe Landa and J. Luis Romero Rivera, *Los ladrillos de Comalcalco*, Mexico, Instituto de Cultura de Tabasco y Gobierno del Estado, 1990 (Serie Arqueología).

Andrews, George, *Maya Cities: Placemaking and Urbanization*, Norman, Oklahoma, University of Oklahoma Press, 1975.

_____, «Chenes-Puuc Architecture: Chronology and Cultural Interaction», in *Arquitectura y Arqueología, metodologías en la cronología de Yucatán*, Mexico, Centre d'Études Mexicaines et Centroaméricaines, Études mésoaméricaines, série 11-8, 1985.

_____, *Los estilos arquitectónicos del puuc, una nueva apreciación*, Mexico, INAH-SEP, 1986 (Colección Científica).

_____, «Arquitectura maya», in *Arqueología Mexicana*, México, INAH-Raíces, vol. II, no. 11, January-February 1995, pp. 4-15.

Arellano Hernández, Alfonso, «Voces del más allá: Río Azul», in press.

*Arte Maya. Selva y mar*, Mexico, Editora del Sureste, 1981.

Barrera Rubio, Alfredo, «Mural paintings of the Puuc Region in Yucatan», in *The Palenque Round Table*, 1978, Series, vol. 5, Third Palenque Round Table, part 2, Austin and London, University of Texas Press, 1980.

Baudez, Claude F., Becquelin, Pierre, *Les Mayas*, Paris, Gallimard, 1984.

Benson, Elizabeth P., *The Maya world*, New York, Thomas Cromwell, 1977.

Berlin, Heinrich, «Arte maya», in *Historia del arte mexicano*, Madrid, Editorial La Muralla, vol. 2, 1982.

Coe, Michael, *The Maya*, New York, Thames and Hudson, 1984.

Coe, William R., *Tikal. A Handbook of the Ancient Maya Ruins*, Philadelphia, The University Museum of Pennsylvania, 1967.

*Colha e i maya dei bassipiani*, Erizzo, Venice, 1982.

Culbert, Patrick, «Maya Ceramics» in *Maya Treasures of an Ancient Civilization*, New York, Abrams, 1985.

De la Fuente, Beatriz, *La escultura de Palenque*, Mexico, UNAM-IIE, 1965 (Estudios y Fuentes del Arte en México, XX).

_____, «La escultura maya clásica», in Ciudad Ruiz, Andrés *et al.*, *Los mayas. Esplendor de una civilización*, Madrid, Sociedad Estatal Quinto Centenario-Turner Libros, 1990, pp. 73-84 (Colección Encuentro, Serie Catálogos).

*Die Welt der Maya*, Mainz am Rhein, Von Zabern, 1992.

Fash, L. William, *Scribes, Warriors and Kings. The City of Copán and the Ancient Maya*, London, Thames and Hudson, 1989.

Freidel A. David, «Late Preclassic Monumental Maya Mask at Cerros, Northern Belice», in *Journal of Field Archaeology*, 4 (4), 1977.

_____, Schele Linda and Joy Parker, *Maya Cosmos. Three Thousand Years on the Shaman's Path*, New York, Quill William Morrow, 1993.

Gendrop, Paul, *El México antiguo-Ancient Mexico*, Mexico, Trillas, 1972.

_____, *Los estilos Río Bec, Chenes y Puuc en la arquitectura maya*, Mexico, UNAM-Facultad de Arquitectura-División de Estudios de Posgrado, 1983.

_____ and Doris Heyden, «Arquitectura Mesoamericana», in *Historia Universal de la Arquitectura*, Pier Luigi Nervi (coord.), Madrid, Aguilar, 1975, pp. 92-221.

Greene R., Merle *et al.*, *Maya sculpture*, Berkeley, Lederer, Street and Zeus, 1972.

Greene R., Merle, *The sculpture of Palenque*, 4 vols., New Jersey, Princeton University Press, 1991.

Hammond, Norman, *Ancient maya civilization*, New Brunswick, N.J., Rutgers University Press, 1982.

Kubler, George, *Studies in Classic Maya Iconography*, New Haven, Academy of Art and Sciences, 1969 (Memoirs of the Connecticut Academy of Art and Sciences, 18).

_____, *The Art and Architecture of Ancient America*, The Pelican History of Art, Penguin Books, 1984.

Márquez López, José María, *Guía de Tikal*, Guatemala, Artemis & Edinter, 1992.

Marquina, Ignacio, *Arquitectura prehispánica*, Mexico, INAH-SEP, 2 vols., 1981.

Matheny, Ray, T., «El Mirador, An Early Maya Metropolis Uncovered», in *National Geographic Society*, Washington, D.C., September 1987.

*Maya Treasures of an Ancient Civilization*, New York, Abrams, 1985.

Mayer, Herbert Karl, «Gewölbedecksteine mit Dekor der Maya-Kultur», in *Archiv für Völkerkunde*, Herausgegeben von Verein, Freuden der Völkerkunde, 1014, Vienna, Museum für Völkerkunde im Selbstverag, Sonderdruck, 1983.

_____, «Maya-Wandmalereien in der Puuc-Region (Mexiko)», in *Antike Welt*, Zeitschrift fur Archäologie und Kulturgeschichte, Sonderdruck, 21 Jahrgang, 1990, p. 26-44.

Michel, Genevieve, *The Rulers of Tikal. Historical Reconstruction and Field Guide to the Stelae*, Guatemala, Publicaciones Vista, 1989.

Miller, Mary E., *The Art of Mesoamerica*, London, Thames & Hudson, 1986.

Morley, Sylvanus G., Brainerd, George W., Sharer, Robert J., *The Ancient Maya*, 4th edition, Board of Trustees of the Leland Stanford Junior University, 1983.

Nájera Coronado, Marta Ilia, *Bonampak*, Mexico, Espejo de Obsidiana Ediciones-Gobierno del Estado de Chiapas, 1991.

Pollock, H.E.D., «Architecture of the Maya Lowlands», in *Handbook of Middle American Indians*, pp. 378-440, 1970a.

_____, «Architectural Notes on Some Chenes Ruins», in *Monographs and Papers in Maya Archaeology*, Cambridge Mass., Harvard University, Papers of the Peabody Museum of Archaeology and Ethnology, Harvard University Papers 61, Published by the Peabody Museum, 1970b.

_____, *The Puuc. An Architectural Survey of the Hill Country of Yucatan and Northern Campeche, Mexico*, Cambridge Mass., Harvard University, Memoirs of the Peabody Museum, vol. 19, Peabody Museum of Archaeology and Ethnology, 1980.

Potter F., David, «Maya Architecture of the Central Yucatan peninsula, Mexico», in *National Geographic Society-Tulane University Program of Research in Campeche*, New Orleans, Tulane University, Publication 44, Middle American Research Institute, 1977.

Proskouriakoff, Tatiana, *A study of Classic Maya Sculpture*, Washington, D.C., Carnegie Institution of Washington (Publication, 593), 1950.

Schele, Linda and David Freidel, *A Forest of Kings. The Untold Story of the Ancient Maya*, New York, William Morrow and Company, 1990.

_____ and Mathews, Peter, «Royal visits and other intersite relationships among the Classic Maya», in P. Culbert (ed.), *Classic Maya political history: hieroglyphic and archaeological evidence*, Cambridge University Press, 1991, pp. 226-252.

_____ and Mary Ellen Miller, *The blood of kings. Dynasty and ritual in the Maya art*, Forth Worth, N.Y., George Brazillier-Kimbell Art Museum, 1986.

Staines Cicero, Leticia, «Propuestas para el estudio iconográfico de la pintura maya del área norte», in *Universidad de México, Revista de la Universidad Nacional Autónoma de México*, UNAM-Coordinación de Humanidades, January-February, nn. 528-529, 1995, pp. 26-30.

Tate, Caroline E., *Yaxchilán: The design of the Maya ceremonial city*, Austin, University of Texas Press, 1992.

Valdés, Juan Antonio *et al.*, *Obras Maestras del Museo de Tikal*, Guatemala, Parque Nacional Tikal-Instituto de Antropología e Historia de Guatemala-Ministerio de Cultura y Deportes, 1994.

Willey, Gordon, *An Introduction to American Archaeology*, vol. 1, *North and Middle America*, Prentice Hall, 1966.

## MAYAN WRITING

Ayala F., Maricela, *El fonetismo en la escritura maya*, Mexico, UNAM-IIF/CEM, 1985.

_____, «La escritura jeroglífica maya», in *Los Mayas su tiempo antiguo*, México, UNAM-IIF/CEM, 1995, pp. 147-197.

Berlin, Heinrich, «El glifo emblema en las inscripciones mayas», in *Journal de la Société des Américanistes*, Paris, 1958, N.S. 47: 111–119.

_____, «Glifos nominales en el sarcófago de Palenque», in *Humanidades*, Guatemala, Universidad de San Carlos, 1959, 2 (10): 1-8.

Coe, Michael D., *Breaking the maya code*, London, Thames and Hudson, 1992.

Graham, Ian *et al.*, *Corpus of Maya Hieroglyphic Inscriptions*, Harvard University, Cambridge Mass., Peabody Museum of Archaeology and Ethnology, 1975–1986.

Harris, John F. and Stephen K. Stearns, *Understanding Maya Inscriptions. A Hieroglyph Handbook*, University of Pennsylvania, The University Museum of Archaeology and Anthropology, 1992.

Kelley, David, «Kakupacal and the Itzás», in *Estudios de Cultura Maya*, Mexico, UNAM-Seminario de Cultura Maya, 1968, vol. VII: 255-268.

Lowe, Gareth, Lee, Thomas Jr., Martínez Espinosa Eduardo, *Izapa: An Introduction to the Ruins and Monuments*, Provo, Utah, Brigham Young University, Papers of the New World Archaeological Foundation, no. 31, 1982.

Marcus, J., *Mesoamerican Writing Systems. Propaganda, Myth and History in Four Ancient Civilizations*, Princeton University Press, 1992.

Maudslay, Alfred P., *Biología Centrali-Americana*, 4 vols., London, Dulau and Co., Reprint Edition, 1974, Millparton Publishing Corp, 1889-1902.

Norman, V. Garth, *Izapa Sculpture*, Provo, Utah, Brigham Young University, Papers of the New World Archaeological Foundation, vol. 30, 1976.

Proskouriakoff, Tatiana, «Historical Implications of a Pattern of dates at Piedras Negras, Guatemala», in *American Antiquity* 25: 454-475, 1960.

_____, «Historical data in the inscriptions of Yaxchilán», parts I y II, in *Estudios de Cultura Maya*, vols, III: 149-167 y IV: 177-201, Mexico, UNAM-Seminario de Cultura Maya, 1963-1964.

Schele, Linda, *Notebooks for the Maya Hieroglyphic Workshop at Texas*, The University of Texas at Austin, 1979-1987.

_____, «The wars of Hanab Pakal», MS, Preliminary Paper prepared for the 1995 Mesa Redonda de Palenque, 1995.

_____ and David Freidel, *A Forest of Kings. The Untold Story of the Ancient Maya*, New York, William Morrow, 1990.

_____ and Peter Mathews, *Notebook for the XVIIth Maya Hieroglyphic Workshop at Texas*, The University of Texas at Austin, 1993.

_____ and Mary E. Miller, *The Blood of Kings. Dynasty and ritual in Maya art*, Forth Worth, N.Y., George Braziller-Kimbell Art Museum, 1986.

Stephens, John and Frederick Catherwood, *Incidents of Travels in Central America, Chiapas, and Yucatan*, New York, Harper and Brothers, 1841.

Stuart, David, *Ten Phonetic Syllables*, Washington D.C., Center for Maya Research, Research Reports on Ancient Maya Writing, 14, 1987.

_____ and Stephen Houston, *Classic Maya Place Names*, Washington. D.C., Dumbarton Oaks Research Library and Collection, Trustees for Harvard University, 1994.

Thompson, J. Eric S., *Maya Hieroglyphic Writing. An Introduction*, Norman, Oklahoma, University of Oklahoma Press, 1950 and 1978.

_____, *A Catalog of Maya Hieroglyphs*, Norman, Oklahoma, University of Oklahoma Press, 1962.